PERFORMER TRAINING

Contemporary Theatre Studies
A series of books edited by Franc Chamberlain, University College
Northampton, UK

Please see the back of this book for other titles in the Contemporary Theatre
Studies series

PERFORMER TRAINING

Developments Across Cultures

Edited by

Ian Watson

Rutgers University – Newark, USA

harwood academic publishers
Australia • Canada • France • Germany • India
Japan • Luxembourg • Malaysia • The Netherlands
Russia • Singapore • Switzerland

Amsteldijk 166
1st Floor
1079 LH Amsterdam
The Netherlands

British Library Cataloguing in Publication Data
Performer Training: developments across cultures.
  (Contemporary theatre studies; v. 38)
  1. Actors – Training of   2. Actors – Training of – philosophy
  3. Actors – Training of – social aspects
  I. Watson, Ian, 1947–
  792'.028

  ISBN 90-5755-151-9

Cover illustration: Iben Nagel Rasmussen training with small sticks.
Photo: Odin Teatret.

*To Susana and the children
who continue to grow:
Violeta, Gaspar, Carmen
and my very own David*

CONTENTS

Part III: Some Recent Trends

INTRODUCTION TO THE SERIES

Contemporary Theatre Studies is a book series of special interest to everyone involved in theatre. It consists of monographs on influential figures, studies of movements and ideas in theatre, as well as primary material consisting of theatre-related documents, performing editions of plays in English, and English translations of plays from various vital theatre traditions worldwide.

Franc Chamberlain

LIST OF PLATES

ACKNOWLEDGMENTS

This collection of essays owes a debt to a number of people. My initial debt is to those who helped formulate my interest in performer training. The first of these was my Australian acting teacher, the late Bryon Syron, who introduced me to the possibilities of performer training and generated my fascination with the acting process. Secondly, Richard Schechner, the professor at graduate school in the United States who shaped my curiosity into a serious concern with the way in which performances are made in different cultures around the world. And lastly, the Italian/Danish founder of the Odin Teatret and the International School of Theatre Anthropology (ISTA), Eugenio Barba, whose productions and research I have followed off and on since the mid-1980s. Barba guided me to an understanding of what it means to talk about performer training across cultures.

Formulations aside, my most direct impetus in gathering these essays was a casual conversation at an ISTA conference I attended in Brazil in 1994. Nicola Savarese, an Italian scholar who has worked closely with Barba for many years and is his co-editor of the *Dictionary of Theatre Anthropology*, invited me to write about training in the United States for an issue of the Italian theatre journal *Teatro e Storia* that he was about to edit. The initial version of my contribution to this collection subsequently appeared in Italian in the Savarese issue of *Teatro e Storia* (1995, volume 17).

My research for the *Teatro e Storia* piece made me curious to discover more about the training histories of other countries and about experiments in the acting process in general. Luckily, I was directed to Franc Chamberlain, the editor of this series and of *Contemporary Theatre Review*. Franc was equally enthusiastic about what preoccupied me and suggested that I approach other theatre people with similar interests to see if they would be willing to contribute articles about their research or creative work to a special issue of *Contemporary Theatre Review*. Subsequent events led to the collection being issued as part of Harwood's Contemporary Theatre Studies series rather than as a journal but, nevertheless, I owe Franc a double debt of thanks, for his early encouragement and for his astute guidance during the editing phase of the volume. What you are about to read has benefited greatly from his input.

Lastly, I must mention those who have given most to this volume, the writers. All of those I approached, following a lengthy correspondence via email, fax and the good old-fashioned postal service, agreed to contribute. As you will see, it is their efforts that I need to acknowledge most.

INTRODUCTION

What does it mean to train for the theatre? Why do we generally say that an actor "trains" rather than "studies" theatre? To study infers a quality of contemplation, of cognition favored over action. But training implies the physical, a learning process in which the body as much as the mind is involved. Training, much like its more sedentary cousin studying, is predicated upon the notion that there is something to be learned, a body of knowledge which the student must engage, it is how this knowledge is engaged that distinguishes an actor's training from the philosopher's studies. Acting may well be an art, as many have suggested; there is no question that it is a craft. And, just as every apprentice artisan must learn the secrets of their profession by working with the material and tools of the trade, performers must steep themselves in the lore and practice of their chosen form if they are to one day fill Peter Brook's "empty stage" with their presence.

Training is a generic term that means different things to different people. In the United States it might well mean studying one of the many variations on the Stanislavsky system taught at a prestigious university or in a private studio in New York; in France it could conjure up images of neophyte actors learning how to tackle the classical repertory at the Conservatoire or of young performers from many parts of the world studying mask and physical theatre at the Lecoq school; in Kerala, India one could find young men undergoing body distorting massages coupled with exhausting physical exercises while they learn dances, roles, and the repertory of traditional Kathakali from master performers.

Regardless of differences, the ultimate goal of all actor training is to prepare its students to perform. It develops various skills such as corporal acuity, vocal flexibility and control, as well as the ability to project emotional intensity. It provides students with a means of preparing a performance, be that preparation a lengthy rehearsal process, as is common in the West, or nothing more than a discussion with the musicians and chorus members who will perform the traditional Noh play that they have studied together for years during their training. And, in combination with experience, prepares the actor to face his or her greatest challenge, the audience.

There are basically two approaches to training, indirect and direct. Indirect training is most common in the West. Actors in this tradition learn a basic grammar of performance and apply that grammar to creating performances. Among other things, actors trained in this approach usually study movement, voice, psycho-emotional techniques, improvisation, how to create a character, and ways in which to analyze a text so that they can transform literature into a corporal reality. The learning of a craft that can be applied to creating the next production is at the heart of this form of training.

Direct training is mostly found in the traditional performance cultures of Asia. In performance forms such as Noh, Beijing Opera, Kathakali, and the various forms of Balinese dance drama students are taught roles from the traditional repertory directly. They often learn skills in addition to the roles; in Beijing Opera, for example, students learn martial arts and acrobatics, separate from work on repertory, which will eventually be incorporated into certain plays, and Kathakali students are exposed to an intense regimen of physical training, quite apart from their study of prescribed plays and roles, that are designed to strengthen their bodies and provide greater physical precision during performance. The focus of training in most traditional performance cultures is, however, on the transmission of performance texts from an established repertory. In this approach to training, most of the physical, vocal, and psycho-emotive skills learned by the young actors are a byproduct of the work on the repertory rather than the focus of the training. Mastering a fixed repertory of roles and plays is the cornerstone of this type of training.

Roots

Performer training is an ancient vocation. India's treatise on theatre, the *Natyasastra*, which was reputedly compiled over a four hundred year period between the second centuries B.C., and A.D., has its roots in the even older Sanskrit drama. Despite its age, a large part of the *Natyasastra* is devoted to prescriptions about performance. Quite apart from its discussion of performance esthetics and guidelines for playwrights, the *Natyasastra* provides detailed descriptions concerning body positions, the use of gestures, voice, and the role of music in performance. These prescriptions imply an ideal that performers had to learn and aspire to.

The Western counterpart of the *Natyasastra*, Aristotle's *Poetics*, privileges the art of the playwright over that of the performer. In doing so, Aristotle offers little to the actor who has to breathe life into the playwright's scribblings. But Aristotle is not the classical world's final word on the stage for, as one might expect of a people enamored of oratory, contemporary accounts suggests that by Roman times actors did receive training in gesture, movement, and vocal technique.

With the chaos, barbarity, and demise of the city state (not to mention the critical attitude of the church) during the Dark and Early Middle Ages, theatre and the training that supported it went into a demise. Evidence suggests that the family apprenticeship model, in which skills were passed from one generation of actors to the next, prevailed among the itinerant players that constituted the professional theatre of the day. Family members or the odd outsider who had caught the acting bug and attached himself (dare one say herself at the time?) to a family of performers learned their craft from their more experienced elders.

The family apprenticeship model appears to have survived the High and Late Middle Ages and even made its presence felt in Shakespeare's England. Shakespearean scholars believe that a number of the boy apprentices who were attached to companies such as the King's Men remained with the troupes that had trained them beyond their years of playing young female roles to become full members of the company; while families of actors, such as the Burbages who headed Shakespeare's troupe, passed their leadership from one generation of the family to the next.

This generational model of performer training, though usurped down through the ages by more formal institutional academies, has continued to be a factor even into this century. The Italian actress and playwright, Franca Rame, who frequently performs and writes with her husband, the Nobel Prize winner Dario Fo, is the product of a theatre family rather than a conventional training, as was Sammie Davis Jr., whose roots are in his family's life on the vaudeville circuit in the United States.

Asia shares a similar heritage of the family apprenticeship model of performer training. Noh theatre, as we know it today, for example, was formulated during the latter part of the fourteenth and early fifteenth centuries in Japan. This formulation was realized through what is surely one of the great theatre families, the renown Noh performer Kan'ami and his son Zeami. Zeami, who, besides being a great Noh actor who almost certainly learned his art from his father, wrote numerous plays that remain as part of the Noh repertory and articulated the theoretical principles upon which contemporary Noh is based.

The preoccupation with what some have called vertical transmission, that is, performance knowledge being passed from one generation to the next, remains a potent force in Asia, even though most of the major traditional performance forms have well established training schools. This notion of vertical transmission is probably nowhere more obvious or celebrated than in Japanese Kabuki where, when he retires, a great actor passes his name onto a younger actor who he has helped train to take his place. In keeping with this tradition, several of the most famous names, such as Nakamura, Kanzaburo, and Ichimura Uzaemon, are being used by seventeenth and eighteenth generations of actors.

The Restoration saw England's first acknowledgment that something more than familial training was needed to train actors for the theatre. William Davenant and Thomas Killigrew, leading figures in the patent theatres of Restoration England, established that country's first training company. By the early eighteenth century, young actors at the Drury Lane Theatre were required to attend training sessions three times a week to learn singing and dancing, while the more experienced members of the company were sometimes paid to teach beginners. And even the great David Garrick instructed young actors himself after 1750.

England was hardly alone in recognizing the need to establish some kind of formal training for actors. At much the same time as Garrick was teaching, Konrad Ekhof, a leading actor and theorist of the German stage, established a school to train actors in Schwerin. It, like other similar efforts on the European Continent at the time, failed, but Ekhof's vision was in keeping with the times.

Seventeen eighty-six saw the culmination of Europe's move towards the institutionalization of performer training with the establishment of the Royal Dramatic School in Paris. The school was an adjunct to the Comédie Française, France's national theatre in all but name, and was Europe's first drama school formed by a major theatre company under royal patronage. It was also the forerunner of the present Conservatoire, arguably still France's leading traditional actor training academy.

Asia also saw changes during this period. The generational apprenticeship model of training has always been important in Eastern traditional performance because of the emphasis on a fixed repertory and the preference for the direct transmission of performance knowledge. Nevertheless, training academies have come to play an ever increasing role in performer training, most especially during this century.

The Noh theatre was one of the first Asian forms to establish training schools. These schools, some of which not only train actors but musicians and chorus members also, have their origins even earlier than their counterparts in Europe. Some, such as the Komparu and Kanze schools, continue to thrive today and teach a broad range of afficianados from amateurs to those with serious professional aspirations.

Kathakali, which had always relied on a familial form of training from its inception around the time of Shakespeare through to the early part of this century, was a dying artform until the poet Mahakavi Vallathol Narayana Menon had the vision to establish a training academy, the Kerela Kalamandalam, in the 1930s. The Kalamandalam, which has revitalized the genre, developed its training methods by adapting the traditional familial model to its current institutional setting.

Similarly, in Bali one can now study at the National Institute of Arts in the capital, Denpasar, whereas in the past traditional genres could only be learned in the villages from master performers and their families. And Beijing Opera, which shares much of the intermingling of the apprenticeship model with the institutional that is common in classical Asian forms, boasts fine academics, such as the Fu-Hsing Dramatic Arts Academy in Taiwan, that trains performers both for its own professional troupe and for other companies throughout the island.

Despite the gradual institutionalization of training in Europe during the eighteenth century, most actors continued to learn their craft on the job and by imitating their teachers who were the company's seasoned performers. This changed in the second half of the nineteenth century with the first successful attempt to develop a systematized approach to acting by the Frenchman François Delsarte. Reflecting the temper of the times, with its emphasis on science and scientific methods – even in the arts, Delsarte made an exhaustive study of how human emotions and attitudes are reflected in the body. He then translated these observations into an elaborate prescription of how one's feet, legs arms, torso, head etc., communicate these various emotions and attitudes. These prescriptions became the basis of a rhetorical method that Delsarte taught both public speakers and actors.

Even though Delsarte's ideas eventually failed because they were judged to be over mechanistic, his contribution to the development of actor training in the Europe and America is difficult to overestimate. His approach suggested a codification of acting for the first time, a method that could be learned, transmitted, and applied to stage performance. And, even though he had erred on the side of science, he was the first to imply that acting did not have to be slave to the inexactitudes of inspiration, that it could be a craft rooted in the mastering of a system. He was the forerunner of Constantine Stanislavsky and all that has followed the Russian genius.

As is taken up in greater detail in my article in this collection, Delsarte had an even more direct influence on the development of training in the United States. It was a former American pupil of his, Steele MacKaye, who, in his attempts to introduce Delsarte's methods to North America, established what eventually became the continent's first acting schools. MacKaye laid the foundations for conservatory training in 1884 when he founded an acting program at New York's Lyceum Theatre which in subsequent years became the American Academy of Dramatic Art. He was also a factor in establishing actor training at universities since two of his pupils, Charles W. Emerson and Samuel S. Curry both founded schools of oratory in Boston that also taught actors and which became liberal arts colleges in the late thirties and forties. They, in conjunction with Carnegie Mellon Tech, which was the first academic institution to offer a degree in theatre in the United States (in 1914), helped legitimize what is an accepted tradition in North America today, performer training in the academy. However, as invaluable as MacKaye's contribution was in the United States, the country, like its European counterpart, would have to await the emergence of Stanislavsky before actor training would be established as a growth industry.

Stanislavsky is ubiquitous in the West (and in much of the East), he is all but synonymous with actor training in many parts of the world. His system or any one of its myriad adaptations still form a large part of many acting programs, even though it was originally formulated in the early part of this century. The success of his system lies in the way in which it combines a balance between the psycho-emotive inner world of a character with the physical and vocal means of expression of the actor. This balance addressed much of the criticism about over mechanization leveled at Delsarte. Much like Delsarte before him, Stanislavsky offered a systematic approach to acting that could be learned, transmitted and applied in performance in front of an audience. Unlike Delsarte, however, Stanislavsky not only suggested a training process that catered to both the inner and outer needs of the actor, but he also developed a way for the actor to analyze a literary text and transform it into performance.

Regardless of his success, as anyone interested enough in training to read this introduction knows, Stanislavsky is not without his critics. Much of this criticism centers on his work with emotions and owes a debt to Stanislavsky's contemporary, Meyerhold. Meyerhold rejected Stanislavsky's concern with emotions primarily on the grounds that they cannot be controlled effectively by the actor nor read with any degree of precision by an audience. His reaction to Stanislavsky was to develop an alternative training strategy, Biomechanics, which favors the physical over the psycho-emotional. Meyerhold's Biomechanics is essentially a series of physical etudes and exercises that actors master in conjunction with vocal training in order to be able to portray characters and situations on stage through a precise technical control of the voice and body. Meyerhold was so committed to performer training that, even though he was primarily a director, he established several acting schools that offered a range of training but with the emphasis always on the actor's physical and vocal means of expression. These schools and Meyerhold's theories have done much to encourage avant-garde theatre, particularly from the 1960s onward; Stanislavsky, meanwhile, claimed much of the conventional training directed to preparing actors for the writer's theatre that dominates Western stages, television, and the mainstream film industry.

Through his success as a director and guiding light of the actor training program at the Moscow Arts Theatre (MAT), Stanislavsky transformed the notion of actor training. The legendary quality of the acting at the MAT, which was witnessed first hand by many more than could travel to Russia when the company toured in Europe and the United States, Stanislavsky's writings on acting, and the legacy of fine actors who, after having worked with Stanislavsky at the MAT, turned to teaching

(Boleslavsky and Ouspenskaya in the United States, for instance, or Michael Chekhov in Britain and North America) internationalized the Stanislavsky System. In doing so, it also confirmed what was very much in the air with France's Conservatoire already firmly established and the formation by Beerbohm Tree in 1904 of the theatre school in England that was to become one of the most prestigious acting conservatories in the English speaking world, the Royal Academy of Dramatic Art. Acting was being recognized as more than a collection of good advice to be passed down from one generation to the next. It was acknowledged as a complex craft that called for extensive training and the best place to do that was in a conservatory-type setting.

Some Contemporary Shifts

The twentieth century has witnessed an explosion of opportunities for actors to train in the West. There are a plethora of conservatories, universities, and private studios in most major theatre centers in Europe and the Americas where would be actors can (if they are accepted) study acting. Young performers can choose to study experimental techniques or a more conventional approach to training. They can take up the Method, a training rooted in the performance of the classics, the Suzuki Technique, Brechtian acting, voice work influenced by the likes of Cicely Berry or Kristin Linklater, a variety of different movement techniques, or musical theatre. Equally, those training young actors have, in addition to their experience as teachers and performers themselves, been shaped by a variety of influences. There has been an increased interest in the body techniques of Eastern performance and martial arts, for instance, and a number of seminal figures, such as Copeau, Saint-Denis, Strasberg, Adler, Grotowski, Barba, Chaikin and Benedetti have developed training philosophies and programs that have informed their teaching as well as their own professional work on stage, screen, and television.

Ironically, this expansion of interest in training has led to a shift in concern that in some ways rejects the very notion of systematized training and the teacher/pupil model that it is predicated upon. Experimentalists like Grotowski and Barba especially, who have been deeply concerned with acting and the acting process, have moved away from the idea of developing a system of training consisting of skill development and perfected techniques. Their concerns are with the individual actor, with providing a means for each actor to explore his or her own creative potential and extend his or her psycho-physical limitations as a performer rather than with developing a universal training model that can be transmitted from teacher to actor. Their heritage may have its roots in Stanislavsky, Meyerhold, and Copeau, but their influences also include the ideas of Osterwa, Artaud,

Zeami, and Mei Lan-Fang, as well as Kathakali training and indigenous ritual techniques from several different cultures.

The eclectic nature of these influences hint at another contemporary trend, the internationalization of performing training. The success of the Stanislavsky System laid the foundation for this shift. He developed his system in Russia with Russian actors, but by the 1950s his approach to acting and/or variations on it were in wide use in many parts of the world. If a Russian can provide a model for work, why not an Asian, a Latin American, or an Israeli? Many of those seriously concerned with acting have expanded their horizons beyond their national or immediate cultural borders. As touched on earlier, Grotowski and Barba followed Meyerhold's lead and looked beyond the confines of Europe in their examination of the actor's process, for instance. Bejing Opera, Kathakali, the writings of Zeami, Noh, Kabuki and Balinese dance drama were but some of the areas they explored in the formulation of their approaches to acting. And, as I write this in New York in the late 1990s, an actor can study any number of techniques and approaches to theatre in the city ranging from homegrown variations on Stanislavsky to the Suzuki Method, from Balinese dance drama to Lecoq-based mask work, from classical British vocal technique to Roy Hart's experiments with the voice, or from Tai-Chi to Feldenkreis' take on movement. As Barba rightly argued in a manifesto he gave participants at the 1987 International Gathering of Group Theatres in Bahía Blanca, Argentina, we live in an age in which actors can (and should, Barba maintains) distinguish between national and professional identity. The geographical underpinnings of a national identity have little to do with the contemporary actor. He or she can study any number of different techniques with teachers from a range of countries and performance genres. Professional identity is formed by those with whom one studies, not by the country in which one lives or by the ethnic group to which one belongs.

The Collection

Most of the essays in this collection speak to the globalization of performer training. Even the first selection of articles, which focuses on institutional training that by definition tends to the conservative, bear the hallmarks of influences that ignore national boundaries. Kazimierz Braun's "Theatre Training in Poland" is a history of theatre training in his homeland from its beginnings at the Warsaw National Theatre's Drama School, established in the early nineteenth century, through to the post-communist present day. Yet, even Poland, with its fierce nationalism fed by the constant threat of extinction from its powerful neighbors, Germany and Russia, has drawn some of its inspiration from outside its borders. According to Braun, influences have included the likes of Stanislavsky, Vakhtangov, Meyerhold, Reinhardt, Piscator, and Brecht.

Stephen Earnest's "The Hochschule für Schauspielkunst 'Ernst Busch' Berlin – Theatre Training in Post-GDR Berlin" describes the teaching methods in one of Germany's leading theatre conservatories. As one might expect of a school that has its origins with Max Reinhardt and was for many years an integral part of East Germany's state supported theatre system, its training methods are rooted in Reinhardt's and Brecht's theories of acting. But even when it was an East German institution, the school recognized Stanislavsky as one of the major influences on its program.

Barry O'Connor's "Mapping Training/Mapping Performance: Current Trends in Australian Actor Training" which, as its title indicates, examines training in Australia, identifies influences ranging from the Method to Lecoq, Laban, and the American Eric Morris technique.

My own contribution, "Actor Training in the United States: Past, Present, and Future(?)," which follows the major developments in training in the United States from the nineteenth century onward, cites a plethora of influences on those developments from outside of the Americas, included among others, the ideas of Delsarte, Stanislavsky, Decroux, Laban, Linklater, Grotowski, and Suzuki.

The following two sections of the book, "The East and Experiments" and "Some Recent Trends," all but ignore national boundaries in their discussion of the sources and formulation of training and/or dramaturgical methodologies stemming from the training. There are two exceptions, "Invisible Training in Balinese Performance" by Ron Jenkins and I Nyoman Catra and Roxane Rix's "Alba Emoting: A Revolution in Emotion for the Actor." The former focuses on traditional Balinese performance as it traces the training sources of the intangible linguistic, philosophical, religious, historical, and topical elements evident in Balinese dance drama. The latter describes a method for generating emotional states on stage through physical patterning techniques developed by two Chilean neuroscientists, Susana Bloch and Guy Santibañez-H. The reason why this training method owes little if anything to theatrical influences is because, as Rix's paper details, it has its origins in scientific research into the physiological links between emotion and corporal expression rather than in theatre.

Janne Risum's "A Study in Motley: The Odin Actors" examines the evolution in training at the Odin Teatret, the company directed by Eugenio Barba, an ardent interculturalist who founded the International School of Theatre Anthropology (ISTA) in order to investigate the connections between performance forms from different cultures.

Jerzy Grotowski's intercultural preoccupations, through his interest in ritual techniques and performative paradigms across cultures, are as well, if not better, known than those of his former pupil Barba. But, as Lisa Wolford points out in "Ambivalent Positions: Grotowski's Art as vehicle and the Paradox of Categorization", even though this interest has moved him far from the theatre he left in the seventies, his latest research suggests a return of sorts to performance and even possibly conventional theatre production.

Rounding out the second section of the collection is Jonah Salz's "Beckett in Kyogen Style: Lessons in Intercultural Translation" which describes and analyzes Salz's experiments in combining traditional Japanese Kyogen acting techniques and dramaturgy with Samuel Beckett's *Act Without Words I*.

In addition to Rix's piece, the final section of the book includes three articles which report on some current developments in performer training. The first, "Workshops for the World: The International Workshop Festival" by Clive Barker and Dick McCaw, details the history and future plans of the International Workshop Festival. The Festival, which began in 1988, arranges workshops, both in London and regional centers around the United Kingdom, which are led by physical artists, directors, and choreographers representing a variety of national and international performance traditions. Eelke Lampe, meanwhile, provides a comparative description and discussion of the links between the training methods developed by Anne Bogart and Tadashi Suzuki in "SITI – A Site of Stillness and Surprise: Anne Bogart's Viewpoints Training Meets Tadashi Suzuki's Method of Actor Training." And "Entering the Political Discussion by Artistic Means: ELIA Masterclasses in Acting 1994" is a summary of the report on the Masterclass on Actor Training organized by the European League of Institutes of Arts by one of the facilitators of the masterclass, Jacqueline Martin. The masterclass, which actually consisted of two extended workshops, was broken into a number of studio sessions taught by several teachers from different countries, all of them with very different formations and influences in their teaching.

PART I

INSTITUTIONAL TRAINING

1

THEATER TRAINING IN POLAND

Kazimierz Braun

Historical Perspective on Theater Training in Poland

The origins of professional acting instruction in Poland

The origins of systematic, methodical, professional acting instruction in Poland are connected with the creation of the National Theater in Warsaw, an institutional, public, state-supported theater opened in 1765. Wojciech Boguslawski, considered "the Father of Polish National Theater," headed the Warsaw institution beginning in 1783, and organized its Dramatic School in 1811, with the objective of preparing actors for the National. Boguslawski himself taught acting and wrote an acting manual. The Dramatic School had a three-year program. There were six teachers and twelve students (an enviable ratio according to contemporary standards), who lived together in a dormitory. Practical instruction was given in acting, singing, dance, manners, and playing musical instruments. General education subjects included the history of Poland, the history of Polish literature, and foreign languages: French, Italian, and German. The program was modeled on the various curricula of professional (for example agricultural) and military schools, which on the one hand taught the practical skills of a given profession, and on the other provided a general education, suitable for the higher social classes. Boguslawski, a member of the so called "petty nobility" himself, treated and envisaged the profession of acting as proper for a nobleman or woman (a "gentleman" or a "lady"). Thus from the very beginning of the history of professional theater education in Poland, actors and actresses enjoyed a high social status while acting was viewed as a serious profession, a civil service, which not only entertained the public, but also concerned itself with national causes. An acting career did not have to be mere self-fulfillment; it could be a vocation unselfishly contributing to the well being of one's fellow citizens, and the nation as a whole. Actors began to enjoy public esteem and were regarded as valued members of the nation's community.

The Dramatic School in Warsaw was headed, after Boguslawski's retirement, by a leading National Theater actor, Bonawentura Kudlicz. In

1835, a second specially was added to the acting stream, a dance division, and in 1837 a third one, singing. Consequently, the School had three departments and prepared scores of actors, singers, and dancers for the National Theater, which had two separate companies, one for drama (straight theater), and the other for opera and ballet. Some of the school's students ventured into other theaters in other cities or joined traveling companies. Following the uprising in 1863-1865, the School was closed in 1868, by the Russian authorities, a victim of anti-Polish repression. The Warsaw Dramatic School laid a solid and diversified foundation for professional theater training in Poland for years to come. It produced many excellent professionals — actors, dancers, and singers.

From 1868 until 1889, in Warsaw, and in some other cities, various actors offered private acting classes, while many provincial entrepreneurs conducted their own private acting instruction. More complex and formal acting and voice training was instituted by Warsaw's Music Society in 1889, which developed into the Warsaw School of Drama in 1916, subsidized by the municipality. About forty students, men and women, participated in a two-year program, encompassing acting, singing, declamation, dance, gymnastics, and fencing; they also took classes on the history of theater and drama, the history of Poland, the history of Polish and world literature and poetry, and, finally, in foreign languages; full-scale student productions crowned the program. Warsaw's star actors taught along with Warsaw University professors.

Creation of The National Theater Institute (State School of Drama)

In 1932, a governmental decree transformed the Warsaw School of Drama into a state subsidized academy, the National Institute of Theater Arts. The Institute consisted of four departments: acting, directing, film, and theater history and theory. The acting department opened in 1932, and the directing department followed in 1933; it was the first department of directing on the academic level in the world. The film and theater history and theory departments did not materialize before World War II.

Instruction in both the acting and directing departments in the Institute lasted three years, and graduates received the professional certificate, the right to join the Actors' Union (ZASP-Zwiazek Artystów Scen Polskich — the Union of Artists of Polish Stages), and to work in professional theaters. The ZASP (which also had a directing division) restricted employment of actors and directors in the professional theaters to their membership; therefore, the Institute certificate was a necessary step to enter the theater. An additional avenue was opened when ZASP instituted an exam (or audition) for "externs," that is, amateurs actors and directors, who prepared for the exam in different private studios or by working in either amateur theaters or as "apprentices" (also licensed by ZASP) in professional theaters. The "external exam" was difficult and not many people entered the profession by passing it. The Institute offered a more secure avenue for young people seeking careers in the theater.

The acting department in the Institute was led by an outstanding actor and master-teacher, Aleksander Zelwerowicz. The directing department was headed by Leon Schiller, a director considered to be *the* leading "theater artist" (as Gordon Craig used to say) in Poland in those days. The faculty included the "crème de la crème" of Warsaw's stages — acting stars and directing masters. The candidates for both acting and directing had to have a high school certificate; the directing students usually were professions actors. The admission exam (audition) was very competitive.

The acting program was divided into two blocks of classes, "practice" and "theory." A 50%–50% balance between them was sought," but in reality "practice" occupied about two thirds of the schedule. "Practice" classes included: acting (on three different levels), improvisation, movement, dance, pantomime, voice training, declamation/diction, singing, fencing, and make-up. The three-year acting training was divided as follows: first year — general corporal, vocal, and psychological preparation, second year — building a role; and third year — playing a role in a production. The "theory" classes encompassed history of theater, history of literature, history of culture, history of costume, phonetics, and foreign languages. After the three-year program the students faced a final exam, which included a written thesis, an oral exam, the presentation of an audition piece, and, finally, acting a role in a school production.

The directing program was also broken into two parts, "practical" and "theoretical." The "theory" was especially emphasized, in order to provide future directors with a good general liberal arts education, matching a university's. In fact, university professors taught the "theoretical" classes which included history of theater, history of drama, history of literature, theory of drama, theory of poetry, history of music, history of opera, history of ballet, history of culture, history of stage design, aesthetics, philosophy, sociology, and psychology. The "practical" classes were divided into two groups: first, directing seminars, led by professors who were masters in the field; students participated in directing seminars through all three years of the program; and second, "technical subjects:" stage movement, choreography, acting exercises for directors, music appreciation, voice technique, and set and costume design. During the first year, students focused on theory and took some preparatory technical subjects. In the second year, they worked as assistants to the professors/directors in actual Warsaw theater productions. In the third year, the students, while still attending school, were expected to direct a production under a professor's supervision that served as the "diploma production" and was presented as a part of the final exam, which also included a written thesis and an oral exam.

The Theater Arts Institute suspended classes during the siege of Warsaw at the beginning of World War II and was formally closed by the Germans after Warsaw fell.

The "Reduta Institute" (The Reduta Acting School)

Besides the succession of institutional and public schools of drama, there was also a strong tradition of acting studios. They were either run by individual actors, or operated in various theaters. In 1919, Juliusz Osterwa, a great actor, director and pedagogue, created the Reduta Theater in Warsaw, a laboratory-stage at the National Theater, and in 1922 he opened an acting school at the Reduta, called the Reduta Institute. The student-apprentices, carefully selected in lengthy auditions, had a very demanding training program: acting classes with various professors; movement, dance, voice, and diction; the history of drama and theater, theater ethics, and other humanistic subjects. The students also appeared in small parts in Reduta Theater productions. Osterwa believed that the work of both students and actors requires constant training. He connected the class training with rehearsals and performances. In his training methods he emphasized the psychological aspect of acting, but equally strongly stressed physical training, offering in his school classes of movement, gymnastics, corporal expression, dance, fencing, and horse riding. Above all, Osterwa sought to form an actor as a conscious and productive member of society. He tried to imprint in the minds and souls of his students the attitudes of cooperation within a creative group, reverence for selfless work, devotion to theater, and service to the nation, as well as to endow them with human virtues and an almost religious spirituality. All the students of the Institute lived as a community, sharing the same lodgings, having a common kitchen, and even communal money.

In the *Outline of the Reduta Program* (1922) Osterwa presented and discussed his approach to theater in general and acting in particular. The main points of the *Program* could be summarized as follows:

First, truth is the main objective of theater work and of acting. Truth has a theatrical aspect, but most of all, truth has a moral dimension. The ethics of the actor, and his/her moral influence upon the public, are of primary importance. The activities of all people involved in theater have moral and social functions.

Second, the truth of an actor should be his/her own, personal truth, based on his/her own morality. The personal, individual morality of each actor is the foundation for the moral impact of the theater, of an acting company, and of every performance. Thus, moral values are the core of theatrical creation.

Third, the actor is a sacrificer; he/she does not only play/perform, he/she commits an act of sacrifice, or an act of redemption for the spectators, who are the witnesses of his/her sacrifice. The being of theater should not be "a play for the public," but "a sacerdotal sacrifice for the congregation," offered by actors for and with the congregation. The theatrical act executed on the stage during the performance, is not merely an artistic act, it is a sacred act as well.

Fourth, theater is a deeply human art, as well as an interpersonal process of communication. Theater is an artistic communion between the actor-priests and the congregation of spectators.

In his Institute and in all his theater works Osterwa endeavored to implement these principles in practice. And, even though never fully successful, he was able to produce scores of fine and dedicated actors, directors, and teachers of acting who have carried on his ideals.

During the interwar years, Warsaw, with the Theater Arts Institute, the Reduta Institute, and several private acting studios, was the national center of both theater and theater education. Drama schools or acting studios were active in eight other major cities (Cracow, Lwów, Wilno, Poznan, Lódz, Bydgoszcz, Torun, and Katowice); they functioned on a permanent or temporary basis.

The majority of teachers used a variety of psychological methods. Stanislawa Wysocka, a great actress, associated with Stanislavsky in the teens of the century, taught her own version of the Russian master's method in her studios. Other towering stage personalities taught the students their own techniques; teachers of lesser stature followed the masters. Together, they made acting instruction in prewar Poland flourish.

Acting instruction during World War II

In 1939 two totalitarian states, the Third Reich and the Soviet Union, attacked, divided, and occupied Poland; one third of the country was immediately incorporated into Germany, the other into the Soviet Union, while another part fell under German occupation. In the part incorporated into Germany, Polish theater was prohibited outright and made virtually impossible. In the occupied territories, public drama & opera were closed (if they had not already been destroyed during the fighting) and professional, artistic Polish theater was prohibited. With rare exceptions, only low, entertainment-oriented genres, such as cabarets, reviews, and vulgar comedies were permitted and had to serve Nazi propaganda purposes. Drama schools and acting studios were closed, sharing their fate with the whole education system, which was abolished. The aim of Nazi policy was to degrade Polish culture and to deprive the Poles of education; no schooling above the fourth grade was allowed!

The Polish theater milieu formally (yet clandestinely, of course) declared a boycott on the German-controlled theaters, and, at the same time, developed an underground (illegal) theater life, which included productions, playwrighting, criticism, and theater scholarship. Acting training was also resumed clandestinely, which meant that classes were held in professors' private homes or apartments, and productions were prepared in living rooms, using the simplest means. The public was invited by word of mouth, and both actors and spectators observed strict precautions. Of course, these classes and productions, like all other underground activities, were prohibited; the penalties were imprisonment, deportation to a concentration camp, or death.

Although the campaign of 1939 dispersed both Theater Arts Institute's faculty and students, many of them were able to return to Warsaw and the classes were continued underground, with new students accepted each year. Clandestine acting studios also operated in Cracow. Additionally, some theater groups created underground studios which conducted their own acting training.

The situation of theater was different in the Polish territories occupied in 1939 by the Soviets and incorporated into the Soviet Union soon thereafter. Polish theaters on these lands remained open and provided a safe haven for many artists. But they were subject to Soviet control, as well as political and ideological indoctrination and manipulation. During the year and half of Soviet rule (from September 1939, until the German attack on the Soviet Union in June 1941), Polish theater people put up a gradually weakening resistance and tried to defend their old ideals, but they were forced to dance as their new masters demanded: to neglect their best national dramas, to produce unwelcome and inferior Soviet plays, and to follow the tenets of social realism (so called "socrealism"). The prewar acting studios in Lwów and Wilno, two major cities incorporated into the Soviet Union, were shut down by the fighting and did not reopen under Soviet rule. A clandestine acting studio was established in Wilno in the Fall of 1941 (under German occupation) with a very fine group of faculty, consisting of both theater artists and university professors. Immediately after the German retreat in August 1944, a public production of scenes worked on by the studio's students was presented.

Reconstruction and expansion of acting and directing education after the War

In 1945, after World War II, a communist totalitarian regime was installed by the Soviets in Poland and lasted until 1989, when it was peacefully overthrown by the rising tide of Solidarity.

In spite of the country's captivity, the theater milieu energetically threw itself into rebuilding theatrical life, joining the whole nation's effort at reconstruction. The shortage of professional, well-trained actors was one of the most important problems facing theater after the war, a situation created by the death and emigration of hundreds of artists, along with the post-war increase in the number of professional theaters with permanent companies.

This deficiency was remedied by establishing professional schools of drama with experienced teams of educators, first in Lódz and Cracow, and later in Warsaw, where the Theater Arts Institute was recreated under the name of the State Higher School of Theater (Panstwowa Wyzsza Szkola Teatralna; we are going to call it the School of Drama for simplicity's sake).

Second, acting studios at several provincial theaters were opened, with local actors as instructors. The best known studios were led by the Galls, Iwo and Halina, a theater artist couple: a director/designer and an actress/pedagogue in Cracow and then in Gdynia, and Tadeusz and Irena Byrski in Kielce, a couple who were both actors and directors.

When the initial postwar shortage of actors was remedied, the acting studios run by theaters, were gradually closed, and only the state, professional schools of drama remained open; though the Kielce studio was an exception to the rule, it was established in 1952 and functioned until 1958. In later years, special acting training was offered by the experimental theaters for their company members and temporary residents, as in the Laboratory Theater of Jerzy Grotowski, the STU Theater in Cracow led by Krzysztof Jasinski, the Akademia Ruchu company in Warsaw headed by Wojciech Krukowski, and the Gardzienice Association Theater of Wlodzimierz Staniewski.

Third, the postwar lack of actors was dealt with by organizing exams (auditions) for amateurs who wanted to become professional actors. The first such test, modeled on the prewar format, was arranged by the Actors' Union in 1945 and had high standards and strict criteria; the next tests were supervised by the Ministry of Culture, which lowered the standards.

Some of the candidates entering the acting schools and studios or appearing at the auditions had received solid training during the war in underground acting classes. They enriched the theater companies that they joined. But others came without any training at all. They were accepted into the schools or studios and passed the external exams based on their membership in the Communist Party or the Communist Youth Organization. Their social background also mattered, since candidates from workers' or peasants' families were given preference. In some provincial studios, they did not receive adequate instruction. When they became professionals, they lowered the standards of acting and brought with them a parvenu mentality.

They broke the traditional code of ethics of the Polish theater. Some of those actors made political careers, becoming secretaries of thc Communist Party cells in the theaters and advancing to managerial positions.

Acting and directing instruction was not immune to the political, ideological, and propaganda pressure imposed on the whole nation by the regime. Marxist philosophy, Russian language, and a narrowly interpreted Stanislavsky method were introduced as obligatory subjects in all schools of drama and acting studios. Students' productions had to include so-called "socrealistic plays, " and the Communist Party and Communist Youth Organization activists put their noses into all school matters. But as far the professional training was concerned, be it acting or directing, it remained professional despite all, and the quality of education was maintained at a very high level.

Structure and curriculum of drama schools in Poland under Communist rule (1945–1989)

From the early 1950s on, practical theater training in acting, ballet, singing, directing, stage design, puppetry, and literary management was concentrated in the professional, state institutions in Poland.

It should be noted here, that Polish universities do not offer practical theater courses; their theater programs are composed of historical and theoretical subjects: theater history, theory, sociology, psychology, aesthetics, and so on.

Theater training in drama schools during Communist rule was strictly professionally oriented. The goal was to train professionals: that is, those who will have only one profession and, therefore, only one job; for up till 1989, there was no unemployment in Polish theaters. Professional acting and directing departments were located in four multi-departmental schools of drama in Warsaw, Cracow, Lódz, and Wroclaw. There were a couple of stage designing programs in the Fine Art Academies in Warsaw and Cracow; and departments of film and cinematography in Lódz, and television directing in Katowice. Singers were trained in the singing departments of the Music Academies in Warsaw, Cracow, and Wroclaw, and dancers in the Ballet Studio at the Grand Opera in Warsaw. Additionally the Kielce studio offered acting, and the Musical Theater in Gdynia offered a combined acting and singing training, preparing its students for musicals and operettas.

In what follows I will concentrate on the acting and directing departments of schools of drama. They were operating (and still are) in the following schools:

(1) The School of Drama in Warsaw, with departments of acting, directing, literary management, and puppetry (the latter located in the city of Bialystok).

(2)   The School of Drama in Cracow, with departments of acting and directing.
(3)   The School of Drama and Film in Lódz, with departments of acting, film directing, and cinematography.
(4)   The School of Drama in Wroclaw (formerly affiliated with the Cracow School, but functioning as an independent campus) with departments of acting and puppetry.

All acting departments in these schools provided four years of intensive training. Admission was based on competitive exams (auditions) for high school graduates; the average number of candidates was about 200–300, and the average size of a freshmen class was between 15–20.

An acting program in each of the schools comprised of several classes; they were taught on a whole day schedule with an average of sixty class-hours per week; the students were neither allowed, nor able to work; though rare exemptions were given to students cast in leading roles in films or television. The classes were divided into practice and theory. Practice included acting, movement and dance, voice and singing, and physical training in various skills, including fencing, horse riding, and wrestling. Theory consisted of theater and drama history; in earlier years, Marxist philosophy and the Russian language were also mandatory, This complex program was followed for three years. During the fourth year the senior students played in three to four "diploma productions," produced by the school and directed by professional directors. Graduation was conditional on successfully playing roles in the "diploma productions," writing a final thesis, and passing the final oral exam. A graduate received a professional acting diploma and (if the written thesis was accepted) the Master of Fine Arts (MFA) acting degree also; it was equal to a five year university degree; but it was possible to finish the school without it. Only diploma holders could be employed in state, professional theaters.

The only alternative to the school of drama diploma was the "external exam," which was a narrow gate opened irregularly every few years. In the totalitarian state, which regulated all areas of life, the rule of employing only diploma holders was observed very strictly. As an exception, small provincial theaters could employ a limited number of non-professionals as "apprentices," for minimal pay; but the "apprentices" status was temporary: if they did not eventually pass the "external exam," they were forced to leave.

The programs of directing consisted (and still consist) of three major components: first, seminars and classes offered in the school; second, student assistantships with professional directors; and, third, directing in a professional theater, under the supervision of a professor. The classes taught in the schools included directing seminars taught by professional directors, a subject called "the director's work with an actor," stage design for directors, studies in playwrighting and writing adaptations, and seminars on the history and theory of theater, drama, literature, music, fine arts, and architecture. The assistantships, the second major component of the directing program, were practical assignments in which the students assisted directors in professional theatres at least once a year; the most ardent students could have up to four assistantships per year.

The schedule was generally divided into three segments: Morning to midday rehearsal in a theater (10:00 AM – 2:00 PM); an afternoon session of classes in the school (3:00 – 6:00 PM), and evening duties involving assisting or acting in a theater (7:00 – 11:00 PM). The schedule was very tight and all the students had scholarships, or were employed in theaters as assistants or actors.

The two major components of the directing curriculum (classes and assistantships) occupied the first two academic years of the program. The third year of studies consisted of independent work by students, who directed a play in a theater, supervised and advised by a professor who acted as mentor. This production was presented to the departmental committee as a "diploma production" and was supplemented by a written thesis; both of them were graded. The final oral exam followed. Directorial studies occurred only on the graduate level. An undergraduate university degree (in any discipline) was required as a precondition to a very competitive admissions exam, and the successful completion of a directing program led to the degree of Master of Fine Arts in Directing, accompanied by the director's professional diploma.

Theoretically, only professional directors who were diploma holders could be employed in professional theaters. This rule, however, had four major exceptions: first, any actor, writer, designer, or manager who had assumed the position of artistic director of a theater could direct in his/her own theater, without having the directing diploma; second, film and television directors, invited to direct in theaters were not expected to present diplomas in theater directing (they would have had directing diplomas in their own fields); third, the Poles who got their education in directing in the Soviet Union (something which happened quite frequently) had an automatic right to direct in Poland; fourth, the foreign directors, invited to Poland from time to time, especially after 1970, were, of course, not asked about their diplomas.

Blossoming of acting studios after 1989

The landslide electoral victory of Solidarity in the first (partially) free elections in Poland in 1989, which ushered in a Solidarity government, and the presidency of Lech Walesa, opened a new chapter in Poland's history. Communism was not eradicated and its heritage still lingered, as was evident when the post-Communist party regained power in the parliamentary elections in 1992 and won the presidential election in 1995; but the country had entered the path leading to full national independence, democracy, and a free market.

The old Shakespearian metaphor, "All the world's a stage," also suggests that the stage maybe a metaphor for the world. Developments in Polish theater after 1989, even within the narrow confines of theater education, confirm the validity of this metaphor.

The theater's context changed: it was freed from political manipulation and censorship imposed from above. But at the same time, it lost its political objectives as an anti-totalitarian force and its special social and financial status: that of being the national exponent of opposition to the regime, while being lavishly subsidized by the regime, as its propaganda tube; a paradox of the theater's situation in a totalitarian state. In its new circumstances, theater could and should have set for itself new, important, and useful objectives, and should have changed its structure. Some theater people did originate reforms, but the majority have preferred the "status quo" and have slowed any attempt at transformation. Generally speaking, the whole system of theater-life remained intact, including the laws pertaining to theater, the structure of theater as an institution, and the country's theater network. Theaters continued to be large institutions owned and subsidized by state or local administrations, and they carried permanent acting companies, technical crews, and administrative staffs.

But the state and local subsidies shrunk. The theaters were forced to search for new spectators, because the politically active segments of the traditional public turned their backs on theater and had to be replaced by members of the emerging consumer society, which was politically indifferent and aesthetically insensitive. This led to a lowering of artistic standards and shifted the repertoire towards shallow entertainment. At the same time, theaters had to trim the size of companies, previously overstaffed according to the Communist policy of full employment. This resulted, first, in actors' unemployment, and, second, in diminishing opportunities for acting school graduates.

Of interest to us is that acting instruction and rules for employment in the state/professional theaters were deregulated, not by law, however, but simply by life. The managers did not feel obliged any more to demand a diploma from an acting candidate; the supervising bodies were not able to enforce such preconditions; and the Actors' Union had no power to prevent theater managers from employing people without professional diplomas. These factors lessened the chances of acting school graduates from obtaining employment, because many managers preferred to hire young people without diplomas for lower wages. The barbaric rules of early capitalism started to run the theater job market.

The structures, institutions, and programs of theater education did not change. State funded schools of drama were at work as usual and continued to offer solid, reliable, and proven programs. They were still besieged by hundreds of candidates trying to pass a competitive admissions exam / audition, dreaming of stage or screen success yet conscious that it does not happen by chance or sheer force of talent but requires hard work and learning, and, therefore, a few years of drama school training. The faculty did not change; except, of course, for the inevitable retirements and their replacement by younger teachers. But generally the old masters remained entrenched in their old methods. It should be noted that old Communists, whose careers were boosted for political reasons years earlier, also continued teaching in drama schools. This epitomized the lack of decisive change in theater education.

The first sign of novelty was the wave of private acting studios which started to blossom in the early 1990s in major theater centers such as Warsaw, Cracow, Katowice, Gdansk, as well as in smaller cities like Szczecin, and towns like Grudziadz. All of them were run by rather young actors, who taught themselves, or employed well-known acting stars as teachers. The studios often had foreign sounding names (*Art-Play, Workshop, L'Art Studio*) or seductive Polish names (which translate as: *Ace, The Experimental Theater Studio, the Studio of Song and Acting*), and were advertised as "the school for stars" or "a springboard for professionals.

The studios usually offered two year programs, which were neither intensive nor systematic, and were based for the most part only on acting classes and the preparation for small cast productions. Both the classes and the rehearsals had to accommodate the regular work hours of the majority of students, and the tight schedules of the star teachers. The studios, unlike the state schools of drama, charged high tuition, which was their only source of income, and did not offer benefits, such as medical insurance. They received administrative licenses to operate (as any private business would), but they were recognized by neither the Actors' Union, nor the Ministry of Culture; consequently, they did not have the right to give their graduates the professional diploma, only a meaningless "certificate."

The theater establishment, including the faculty of the schools of drama, met these studios with a mixture of hostility and mockery. The theaters did not hurry to employ their graduates, although some of them — the most naturally talented — found parts in professional theaters. One by one, the studios started to collapse.

The studios wanted to participate in the general process of change in Poland: changes in mentality and attitudes, in ways of working and living;

they univocally rejected the past and boldly confronted the future; they pursued a new generation's dreams. Their work challenged the existing schools of drama and could have provided healthy competition. But the managers of the studios failed to control their own budgets, and underestimated opposition from the old guard. At the time of writing (Spring 1996) the few studios that still exist do not have a decisive influence on acting instruction in Poland, but they did open new avenues in the past and they may yet resurface.

Aesthetical and Ethical Perspectives of Theater Training in Poland

Challenges for Polish actors

Throughout the last two centuries, Polish theater has played a very important role in the defense of the Polish nation against foreign powers and their cultural impact. At the end of the 18th century, Poland was politically annihilated and divided by its three neighbors: Russia, Prussia, and Austria. This situation lasted until the end of World War I, when, thanks to both military and diplomatic efforts, Poland's independent statehood was restored. After twenty years of peace, a new partition, this time by the Third Reich and the Soviet Union in 1939, suppressed Poland's freedom. In spite of the defeat of Nazis' Germany in 1945 by the Allies, Poland did not regain independence, and remained under the Soviets' control until 1989.

During the 19th century, the struggle for cultural self-identification, especially under the Russian pressure for Russification and the German insistence for Germanization, resulted in formulation of the unique, individual, and independent character of Polish theater; the struggle for national identity included, as a side effect, the rejection of foreign influences.

When Poland's independence was restored in 1918, the national Romantic repertoire, which had been prohibited by the Russian and German invaders, became the greatest challenge for Polish actors and directors. The Polish Romantic plays are poetical and spiritual. Technically, they demand that actors play verse roles; psychologically, the actors must portray larger then life heroes; emotionally, they require that an actor be capable of attaining extreme intensity on stage.

Besides the Romantic poets, Adam Mickiewicz, Juliusz Slowacki, and Zygmunt Krasinski, the best Polish playwrights of the 20th century, Stanislaw Wyspianski, Stanislaw Ignacy Witkiewicz, Witold Gombrowicz, Tadeusz Rózewicz, and Slawomir Mrozek were poets, visionaries, or philosophers. They challenged both actors and directors with their nonrealistic structures and formalistic means of expression. But there are, of course, many realistic plays in different genres, including the socially and biologically conditioned realism of Gabriela Zapolska, the subtle psychological realism of Jerzy Szaniawski, the brutal and literal realism of Ireneusz Iredynski, the sophisticated and urban realism of Jaroslaw Abramow-Newerly, and Janusz Glowacki's realism which is both down to earth and figurative. A specific mix of psychology, emotionalism, and the archetypal universalization of character seems to be the ideal blend for the Polish actor to use in the various national plays.

Training in drama schools must provide students with the means of expression to meet these, specifically Polish, challenges. Needless to say, the students should be equally trained to cope with problems posed by the classical repertoire (for example the Greeks, Shakespeare, Molière, Racine, Schiller, and Goethe), twentieth century theater (for example, Chekhov, G.B. Shaw, O'Neill, and Brecht), and more recent challenges, such as those posed by the absurdists (Samuel Beckett, Eugene Ionesco, Arthur Adamov), the British "young and angry" (John Osborne, Harold Pinter, and Arnold Wesker), the American psychologists (Arthur Miller, Tennessee Williams, and Sam Shepard), and others. Generally speaking, Polish acting teachers, in their constant search for the originality of Polish theater, never fully adapted acting methods coming from Poland's eastern or western neighbors, such as Stanislavsky's system, Meyerhold's Biomechanics, or Brecht's Alienation. Paradoxically, Stanislavsky was never influential in Poland — although it had some proponents, in the 1920s, and later at the peak of the Stalinist period (1948–1955) — because he was first perceived as an exponent of the "Russian soul" which is alien to its Polish counterpart, and secondly, after World War II, he was viewed as yet another unwelcome Soviet ideological import. For the same political and cultural reasons, styles and trends with a German provenance, such as Expressionism, were not very popular in Poland. Of course, Stanislavsky, as well as Yvgeny Vakhtangov and Vsevolod Meyerhold, along with Max Reinhardt, Erwin Piscator, and Bertolt Brecht were well known in Poland, but Polish actors and directors utilized only selected elements of their acting or directing methods and styles, never accepting them entirely. Influences of French or English culture, including French playwrighting or English directing, were more readily adapted in Poland, although also filtered through the Polish tradition and sensitivity.

Faced with the complexity and richness of both Polish and foreign traditions, styles, and offerings, a student of acting in a Polish school of drama or a studio usually works successively with several different teachers-mentors and is taught several techniques and approaches, including:

Realistic/psychological techniques. These are treated as a basic foundation for any role. Their aim is to enable an actor to live truly under imaginary circumstances; the "acting truth" is required in any kind of character. Realistic/psychological acting in Poland is usually rather emotional and visceral. In the history of Polish theater there have been many actors with unusual realistic and psychological techniques. Examples include Karol Adwentowicz, an outstanding specialist in Ibsen roles, and Jan Kreczmar, an exceptional actor, able to explore profound psychological nuances; his best role was George in Edward Albee's *Who's Afraid of Virginia Woolf.*

Non-realistic, formalistic, or stylized techniques. These techniques are necessary for playing Romantic verse roles, the surrealistic characters of Witkiewicz, or the archetypal figures in Rózewicz's plays. Specific oral, vocal, and physical means of expression are sought here. The most famous Polish actors had their greatest successes in the romantic plays: examples include Juliusz Osterwa as the Constant Prince in the play by Calderon/Slowacki, or Józef Wegrzyn as Gustaw/Konrad, the hero of *The Forefathers' Eve* by Mickiewicz. Polish actors were also outstanding in Shakespeare (Jacek Woszczerowicz as Richard III) and Brecht (Tadeusz Lomnicki as Arturo Ui).

Personality revealing techniques. These techniques enable an actor to interpret a role personally, individually, and originally, exposing his/her own self, as well as building direct contact and generating strong interaction with the public. All acting students are taught to individually, personally, and creatively study and build a role, as well as to define their relationship with their audiences. As a result, many Polish actors are perceived by the public first of all as individuals: people, artists, educators, citizens, preachers, activist, and patriots. Some of them seem to play different roles as if by accident — they express themselves directly through their stage characters. If we consider this approach we should not be surprised that many actors in Poland have been in the forefront of its national and political struggles. To name only a few recent examples: Andrzej Seweryn is great star of both the Polish and French stages, currently a member of the Comédie Française, but as a student at Warsaw's School of Drama he was one of the leaders of the student freedom movement in Poland in 1968; he was arrested and persecuted for years. Halina Mikolajska, was one of the leading stars of the postwar Polish theater; her roles included Good Woman of Setzuan in Brecht's play, Lady Proctor in Arthur Miller's *The Crucible*, and Ranievskaya in Anton Chekhov's *The Cherry Orchard.* She was a founding member of the Committee for the Defense of the Workers (KOR-Komitet Obrony Robotników) in 1976, which led to the creation of Solidarity in 1980. Mikolajska was an actress, an opposition leader, and a political prisoner: a model example of an artist's ethos in Poland. In the first (partially) free Parliamentary elections in Poland in 1989, three outstanding actors or directors, Gustaw Holoubek, Andrzej Szczepkowski, and Andrzej Wajda were elected senators, and one, Andrzej Lapicki, a member of the *Sejm*, the House of Representatives. All the above-named artists were teachers in the schools of drama, and they influenced the younger generation, Lapicki was Rektor (President) of the School of Drama in Warsaw.

The Polish directing style and its instruction

From the 1930s to the present, the prevailing style taught in Polish directing departments has been what is called the "Polish Staging Theater." (In Polish: "Polski teatr inscenizacji," compared to German "Inszenierung Theater," and French "mise-en-scène théâtre"). The "staging theater" was the hallmark of the Great Theater Reform. It was based on Gordon Craig's idea that "theater is art," and his claim that the director must be a "theater artist" — "an author" of the theater work. This directing style, was practiced by Max Reinhardt, developed by Vakhtangov, Alexander Tairov, and Meyerhold in Russia and the Soviet Union, by Leopold Jessner and Erwin Piscator in Germany, and used by Gaston Baty in France and Emil Burian in Czechoslovakia.

This directorial style was mastered in Poland by Leon Schiller, founder of the Directing Department in the Theater Arts Institute in Warsaw. Through a blending of the Romantic and post-Romantic national traditions, Schiller developed the original, Polish form of a complex staging characterized by an elaborate mise-en-scène, literary and stage poetry, visuality, abundance of music, and expressive acting. Several directors in prewar Poland followed the same stylistic approach and in the postwar era it has remained a prevailing directorial trend.

Within the tradition of "Polish Staging Theater," the objective in teaching directing in Poland became to create a production as a whole, complex, yet coherent, artistic entity. The student director was taught to control all the elements of the performance, to be the sole and unique "author of the production" who creates all aspects of the piece. This control began with the text, he or she had to learn how to make adaptations, directorial versions of the classics, cuts, etc. and included acting, all the aspects of visuality and space (set, costume, and light design), and music. Students of directing in Poland were taught to be "theater artists," "total directors," or even "dictators of theater."

The three areas of directorial training (that is, directing seminars and various classes, assistantships, and directing practice) complemented each other, but all were oriented towards producing a "total theater artist, " who is a master of all aspects of theater. In the directing seminars, teachers expected students to prepare the entire mis-en-scène of a play, including the directorial interpretation of the text, the directorial "concept" of the production), which incorporated the choice of its aesthetic style, the edited script, the choreography and blocking; they had to prepare a lighting plot and build a model of the set, with tiny puppets or wax figures of the characters for in class demonstrations. The assistantships in theaters had to introduce student directors to all aspects of the practical preparation of a production, beginning with participation in the working sessions of the director and designer or composer, going through the whole process of rehearsal, ending with supervision of the evening shows, observing the public's reaction, and giving notes to the actors.

The total creative control of a production — the general objective of the whole program — is difficult and demanding; it requires knowledge, skill, ingenuity, imagination, and sensitivity to all of theater's areas. But, even the finest training has its limitations, and an intelligent student director who lacked imagination became what is sarcastically called in Poland "librarians " — directors who had a perfect bookish knowledge of all aspects of theater and who had prepared detailed mis-en-scène projects of the productions but were impotent as far as the theater practice was concerned; such directors mounted still-born productions, did not know how to inspire actors, and failed to excite the public. But when this complex program cultivated the fertile soil of a genuine talent, the results were sometimes astonishing. Indeed, Polish theater from the 1930s to the 1980s was centered on the work of directors. Directors were at the forefront of all major developments and Poland became a vibrant, strong, and internationally recognized center of "directorial theater."

The programs and methods of teaching directing in Polish schools of drama remained basically unchanged from the time of Leon Schiller, who headed the Warsaw department in the 1930s and again in the 1950s. Bohdan Korzeniewski, who replaced him as dean in Warsaw, followed Schiller's precepts strictly, as did his successors and the directing instructors in Cracow.

Gradually, the directing curriculum offered in the schools of drama seemed to petrify, and did not respond closely enough to artistic trends in world theater, nor to the political, cultural, and generational changes in Poland.

The new approach to directing was connected to the Second Reform of Theater. The latters' "theater of communion" between the actors and spectators, its postulate of collective creation, and its experimental use of space (including "flexible space" and "found space") did not influence the teaching at directing departments in Polish schools of drama, although some directors trained in these schools did participate in the avant-garde battles and skirmishes of the 1960s and 1970s. New approaches to directing were more visible in small, alternative student, and experimental companies.

Principles of teaching acting and directing in Poland

The long history of theater training in Poland, which begins with
Boguslawski's school in 1811, and continues in the contemporary
professional theater schools and studios, has been based on four
fundamental principles:

The principle of complexity. Acting and directorial training are
complex; they usually include both practice and theory, that is, a combination
of professional skills, techniques, and methods, as well as a literary, artistic,
cultural, and general humanistic education.

The principle of professionalism. Acting training is treated strictly
professionally: the teachers of acting and directing at the schools of drama
are-without exception-excellent professional actors or directors, very often
they are great stars. The students receive solid professional training, which
allows them to join professional theater companies as actors or directors
immediately after completion of the school's or studio's program.

The principle of the priority of aesthetic and spiritual values. Acting and
directorial training are treated as a preparation for artistic activity, which is
situated in the realm of high art and human spirituality. Although, in a
very natural way, "career," "money," and "success," have always been
appealing and attractive notions for theater people in Poland (as
everywhere), theater in Poland has been treated as a noble art, whose
objective is to create and convey both aesthetic and spiritual values.
Therefore, the aesthetic aspect and spiritual dimensions of theater play
important roles in theater training.

*The principle (or rather the awareness) of the ethical character and impact
of theater creation, paired with an extremely personal approach to theater work.*
According to this principle, a theater artist is treated, trained, and
understood first of all as a human being, a fellow of the human family,
aware of his/her role as a citizen and servant of society, and a patriotic
member of the nation. A theater artist's duty is, therefore, to serve, to
animate, and to energize the surrounding social group. The theater artist's
place within a society or a community is that of a spiritual, cultural, or
political leader.

Teaching and theorizing on acting, Osterwa introduced the notion
of the "sacrificial actor." It was also Osterwa and later the Byrskis, who
characterized acting as a "civil service," while Lech Raczak, the leader of
the avant- garde Eighth Day Theater, viewed acting as an "artistic/political
activity" influencing the course of history, and Staniewski taught it as a
"communal renewal" through the rediscovery, by the actors and participants
in the production, of the ritualistic roots of culture.

* * *

Based on a long tradition, practiced by many excellent artists, pedagogues, mentors, and masters of acting and directing, theater training has always been a very important factor in the development of theater in Poland, and has contributed extensively to the originality and uniqueness of Polish theater.

References

Antkowiak, Maria. (1978) "Studio Teatralne Iwo Galla." ["Iwo Gall's Theater Studio."] Wroclaw: Uniwersytet Wroclawski. A manuscript.

Braun, Kazimierz. (1989) "Wielkie role Haliny Mikolajskiej." ["Great Roles of Halina Mikolajska."] Przeglad Polski, July 6.

Braun, Kazimierz. (1996) *A History of Polish Theater, 1939-1989, Spheres of Captivity and Freedom.* Westport and London: Greenwood Press.

Chrzanowska, Izabella. (1979) "Teatr Laboratorium jako szkola aktorska." ["The Laboratory Theater as an Acting School." Wroclaw: Uniwersytet Wroclawski. A manuscript.

Hera, Janina. (1993) *Losy niespokojnych, [Fates of the Impatient Actors].* Warszawa: Semper.

Korzanska, Ewa. (1978) "Kieleckie Studium Teatralne I.T. Byrskich." ["The Byrskis' Kielce Theater Studio."] Wroclaw: Uniwersytet Wroclawski. A manuscript.

Michalowska, Danuta, (1991) ed. Trzeba dac swiadectwo. 50-lecie powstania Teatru Rapsodycznego w Krakowie. [*One Has to Testify. The Fiftieth Anniversary of the Teatr Rapsodyczny in Cracow*]. Cracow: Ars Nova-Zjednoczeni Wydawcy.

Mrozinska, Stanislawa. (1972) *Szkola Leona Schillera, PWST 1946–1949. [The School of Leon Schiller, State Higher School of Theater, 1946–1949.]* Wroclaw: Ossolineum.

Osterloff, Barbara and Committee, (1991) ed. *Warszawska Szkola Teatralna [Warsaw School of Drama]*. Warsaw: Panstwowa Wyzsza Szkota Teatralna.

Osterwa, Juliusz. (1990) *Reduta i teatr. [The Reduta and Theater].* Ed. Zbigniew Osinski. Wroclaw: Wiedza o Kulturze.

Skambara, Elzbieta. (1980) "Teatr i Instytut Reduty — aktorstwo jako powolanie. " ["The Reduta Theater and Institute — Acting as Vocation."] Wroclaw: Uniwersytet Wroclawski. A manuscript.

Smigielski, Bogdan. (1989) *Reduta w Wilnie. [The Reduta in Wilno]* Warszawa: Pax.

Wilski, Zbigniew. (1990) *Aktor w spoleczenstwie. Szkice o kondycji aktora w Polsce. [Actor Within the Society. Essays On the Situation of the Actors in Poland]* Wroclaw: Ossolineum.

Wilski, Zbigniew. (1978) *Polskie Szkolnictwo Teatralne 1811-1944. [Theater Training in Poland 1811–1944.]*

Wroclaw: Ossolineum. (A monograph with most complete bibliography on the subject.

2

THE HOCHSCHULE FÜR SCHAUSPIELKUNST "ERNST BUSCH" BERLIN: THEATRE TRAINING IN POST-GDR BERLIN

Steve Earnest

If one has the aspiration to become a professional actor in Germany, it is not a realistic option to simply enroll at a university and declare a theatre major. While most German universities have divisions of theatre, and many have practicing drama clubs, the approach taken by German universities is primarily academic, and one would not receive training in the performance skills necessary to tackle the demanding German repertory system. Most successful German actors and actresses have completed a program at a theatre *Hochschule*, a vocational school for the performing arts. Though it is possible to obtain a contract with a major theatre company without a diploma from a *Hochschule*, it has become increasingly rare, and those who do not receive training from a theatre *Hochschule* generally do not have the same mobility and longevity in their careers as do those with vocational training.

One of the most prolific theatre training institutes in Germany is the *Hochschule für Schauspielkunst "Ernst Busch"* (hereafter designated as *HfSK*), located in the Berlin suburb of Schöneweide. Known from 1951 to 1981 as the *Staatliche Schauspielschule Berlin*, the *HfSK* is important for several reasons. First, it is the direct descendant of the *Schauspielschule* (or acting school) of the *Deutsches Theater*, established in 1905 by Max Reinhardt. The *Schauspielschule* was one of the first organized attempts in Germany during the modern era to provide training for actors and other theatre personnel.

Secondly, the *HfSK* is located in Berlin, the theatrical capital of Germany, and is tightly intertwined with the Berlin theater system. For over thirty years there has been a continuous record of employment for students and graduates of the *HfSK* with major theatres in Berlin such as the *Deutsches Theater*, the *Maxim Gorky Theater*, the *Berliner Ensemble*, and the *Komische Oper*. In fact, of the 163 actors employed during the 1992–93 season by the first three theatres mentioned above, 77 were trained at the *HfSK*.[1] In addition, there

---

1. This information was compiled with the help of the *Deutsches Bühnen Jahrbuch* published in Hamburg by the *Genossenschaft Deutscher Bühnen Angehöringen*, 1992.

A performance of *Struggle of the Dogs and the Black* by Bernard-Marie Koltes at the Institut für Schauspielregie, Prenzlauer Berg, Berlin. Photo: Steve Earnest

has been an on-going system of exchange in the area of artistic personnel between the *HfSK* and those same major theatres. It is not uncommon to find Berlin's, leading directors and acting coaches teaching master classes at the *HfSK* or directing advanced students in studio projects. Lastly, the approach to acting at the *HfSK*, initially developed by Max Reinhardt, is pragmatic, problem/solution based, and has survived the many shifts in ideology of twentieth century Germany. It has been, and continues to be, exemplary in its ability to adapt to the repertory needs of the German theatre system.

Reinhardt established the *Schauspielschule* in 1905 and stayed with it, although at times from quite some distance, until 1933. With the emergence of the Nazi party, the *Schauspielschule* then passed into the hands of the party's cultural oversight committee, the *Reichsministerium für Volksaufklärung und Propaganda*, with Hugo Werner-Kahle installed as the school's leader. After World War II actor training resumed at the *Schauspielschule* under the guidance of the influential German stage director Wolfgang Langhoff until 1952 when the school was selected to become one of the four state theatre institutes of the German Democratic Republic, and was renamed the *Staatliche Schauspielschule Berlin*. The *Staatliche Schauspielschule* was moved from within the confines of the Deutsches Theater to a more suitable and spacious campus in the Berlin suburb of

A typical classroom space for acting and voice at the Hochschule für Schauspielkunst, Schöneweide, Berlin. Photo: Steve Earnest

Schöneweide. With the beginning of the 1981/82 semester, the *Staatliche Schauspielschule* Berlin was renamed the *Hochschule für Schauspielkunst "Ernst Busch" Berlin*. The name of the great German actor Ernst Busch, best remembered as one of Brecht's leading actors and a figurehead of the German Communist Party, was chosen to accompany the school's new title. The *HfSK* was named after him because of his unusual level of self discipline and work habits, his great acting talent, and his commitment to Communist ideals.

Many changes accompanied the conversion of the State Acting Academy to the *HfSK*. A better facility for full-length productions was included on the new campus and was named the *Studiobühne "Wolfgang Heinz,"* in honor of one of the school's leading acting teachers. The *Institut für Schauspielregie* (Institute for Directing), which had been associated with the State Acting Academy since 1974, was officially annexed as part of the *HfSK*. The Institute, located in Prenzlauer Berg just north of downtown East Berlin, produced a full season of productions and operated much like any of Berlin's other resident theatres with a full company and rotating repertory of plays. The new "Ernst Busch" school had a large "in-house" studio theatre on the main campus in addition to a fully equipped theatre and directing institute. With the addition of the directing institute it was possible to implement a goal that the school had long hoped to realize: a fourth year of study in which the actors could spend the entire year practicing their craft. By 1984 the school had a four-year program in acting, directing, and in puppet-theatre.

Although there were changes taking place during the period of my association with the *HfSK* (1992–94), it is accurate to say that the system for training actors in Germany was the one that had been in existence in the former West Germany since 1949. The East German schools, located in Berlin, Potsdam, Leipzig and Rostock, were still in existence, but had been incorporated into the educational system of the Federal Republic of Germany. In 1987, Professor Kurt Veth succeeded Hans-Peter Minetti (another figurehead of the Communist Party) as Rektor. Veth had worked with Brecht at the Berliner Ensemble from 1949–1954, and later directed plays in many of the major theatres in Berlin and Dresden. His association with the school dates back to the late fifties when he was an acting scene-study teacher at the *Staatliche Schauspielschule Berlin*. He brought to the school the Brechtian philosophy that,

> the young actor should learn to narrate and not to impersonate. They should learn, one *from* the other, and not one *or* the other to play. They should learn, to make the spectator watch the group of actions and not to be anxious for the end, to convey knowledge to the spectator and not experience, to address his activity and not his emotions.
>
> (Veth 1992)

Veth's association with and preference for a Brecht-based acting approach was evident in both the classes that I attended and the conversations that I had with him. He was strongly opposed to actors utilizing experiences from their own lives to create roles. Veth stated that when he works with student actors, he encourages them to stand outside of the characters that they play and not to make decisions for them. He stated, "Characters' lives are fixed; actors cannot impose their own experience onto the life of a character" (Ibid.). In acting classes that I witnessed he constantly asked that actors not "over interpret" the individual words which comprise the lines of a play. Given his Brechtian heritage, and the non-emotional acting style associated with Brecht, this was somewhat expected, but according to Veth there was a more practical reason. He pointed out that in real life people do not make it a habit of emphasizing key words and making them sound artistic. For Veth, actors should simply trust the action of the play, distance themselves from the situation, and rely on their imagination instead of their experience.

With his strong connections to the Berlin professional theatre, Veth was able to continue the tradition of placing graduates of the *HfSK* at the best theatres in Berlin. He told me in 1992:

I do not wish to brag, but I can safely say that between 1981 and today, we have trained practically all of the great actors in the Berlin theatre.

(Ibid.)

Veth retained the Rektorship of the *HfSK* from 1987 until 1993.

With all the changes taking place in German society after German reunification, many of the remnants of East German society were eliminated. In 1993 Veth was replaced by the noted dramaturg, author and director Klaus Völker. As a whole, the core of the program of study at the *HfSK*, with its emphasis on training for the German repertory system, was little affected by this change in leadership or German reunification. The most drastic changes came in the elimination of obligatory seminars in Marxism/ Leninism and World Economy. No new theoretical classes were added; those blocks of time were replaced with additional hours of instruction in acting, speech and movement. Practically all the former GDR professors who had remained at the *HfSK* after the fall of the Berlin Wall were of the opinion that the acting program had changed very little. Change of a greater magnitude came with the influx of western students who arrived after reunification, and the resultant change in student attitudes. There was no longer an emphasis on political issues and providing theatre for workers. The mixture of students from a variety of political and economic backgrounds resulted in occasional conflicts of ideology, but the overall feeling was a new freedom of expression. Students were more open to political dialogue and artistic criticisms[2].

Having undergone this series of changes, it is hard to imagine that one could discern any semblance of continuity from the days of Reinhardt until the final decade of the twentieth century. But the goal of the school has remained constant: the *HfSK* seeks to provide practical training in the performing arts modeled on the traditions of German theatrical history, and to provide highly trained artists to perform in the best theatres in the German speaking world. The school bills itself as a program centered around the theories of Stanislavski and Brecht – a philosophy that was engendered when the school existed as the *Staatliche Schauspielschule* and was still in place at the time of my visit. Despite the philosophical changes since the disintegration of the GDR, the administration believes that the theories of Brecht and Stanislavski remain the most significant influences on the German theatrical tradition, so the program description has been retained (Völker, 1993), The emphasis, however, is not on a particular theory or

---

2.   This information comes from several sources. Professors who made statements in this regard include Ulrich Engelmann, Eva-Marie Otte, Kurt Veth, and Veronica Drogi.

method of training; Brecht and Stanislavski merely represent the dialectic of presentational and representational performance aesthetics. Though it is evident, as spelled out in the instructional bulletin, that the course of instruction has a solid theoretical base, each of the division leaders made one thing very clear to me: the students learn by doing. Only a very small percentage of the coursework is given over to theoretical concerns. In fact, it was not uncommon for professors to state "there is no theory, no method, just good solid acting" (Engelmann, 1993). While theoretical viewpoints do occasionally creep in, the focus of the training is clearly on *Handwerk* or the craft elements of acting. Therefore, acting, movement, and voice classes constitute the bulk of the training program at the *HfSK*. More than providing training in Brechtian and Stanislavskian performance, the school presents a program much like that originally developed by Reinhardt – geared for the practical demands of the German repertory system.

The program in acting has two parts. The first two years of instruction are known as foundational studies (*Grundstudium*). During this initial period, the student receives a thorough grounding in rules and principles through a series of lessons known as *Regelunterricht*. The students are divided into groups of ten to twelve for improvisation, groups of from two to four for more personalized instruction in acting (scene work), voice and music, and finally in groups of from ten to twenty for movement and dance classes. According to Wolfgang Rodler, head of the acting program, it is most important that students begin, in their first year of study, to develop themselves physically and vocally, through the voice and movement exercises. In addition they are expected to learn to read, analyze, and perform scenes. Rodler stated:

> Yes, they can learn to simply recite words, etc., but the meaning, what is underneath it all, is what they must find. They must develop an appetite for discovering and showing human relationships. They must obtain a lust for playing.
>
> (1993)

During the first semester of study at the *HfSK*, students are enrolled in a course entitled the *Improvisations-Seminar*, a class which has been in existence under various titles since the Reinhardt era. The course meets every day for four hours and, as the title suggests, students are expected to develop their improvisation skills. It is perhaps in this course that it is easiest to witness the direction of actor training taken during the years of the GDR. Throughout the seminar, the dialectic between improvisation and the fixed score is explored, as it is felt that the creative process, invented during improvisation, can only be captured when the actor learns to repeat it unmechanically, and therefore creatively. Only by repeating the improvisation many times until it is fixed does the actor develop a rehearsal methodology. The methodology is realized through the creation of an improvisational process, which later can be transferred to the creation of a role from a written text. This process has several aspects. First of all, the actor has to make sure that the improvisation is based on reality, not metaphorical or fantastical elements. Settings should be from the real world and problems should be dramatized in a psychological manner. The focus in the improvisation should be on practical activity, such as the handling of properties, but not be an end in itself. Props should be evaluated with respect to the actor's own being, with meaning and motives. An example is summarized below:

> A purse on a park bench. A student passes by, notices the purse, goes over to it, takes a hurried look around, picks up the purse, sits down, and quickly opens it. He pokes around in it, finds nothing, and, disappointed, lays it back down on the park bench.
>
> (Ebert, 1988:4)

In this example the student attaches himself to an object. Elements of character may come into being, as he is viewed as a bum or a casual thief, while a course of motivational action emerges as the student makes a series of decisions based on his evaluation of the situation.

The entire improvisation process is characterized as: "observe-evaluate-react." According to Jeff Burrell, a third year student at the *HfSK*, this process is also described as the development of a "thinking act." Students utilize the basic rule which breaks down dramatic action into easily palpable sections, thereby focusing their thought processes and thus their stage behavior. If adhered to by the student actor, this formula provides the basis for concrete dramatic experience, therefore this rule is insisted upon by the faculty of the seminar. This simple formula has become one of the most important foundational components of the approach to improvisation advanced by the teachers at the *HfSK*.

Another important concept which is stressed in the improvisation seminar is the idea of a pivotal point. This is the point when the actor makes a discovery, is faced with the necessity to make a decision, and follows a course of action. Each pivotal point constitutes a block of action separated by the "observe-evaluate-react" rule. The changes of action at pivotal points are the results of decisions, or of new attitudes toward the situation. Therefore the dialectic between attitude and action becomes the actor's smallest building block.

Finally, the idea of self-projection onto a character is highly discouraged in the improvisation seminar. Students are not to confront situations at a personal level, but to experience them actively, and with a psychic awareness of the situation (Veth, 1992). If confronted at a personal level, students will become stuck at the level of emotionality. This, in turn, inhibits their ability to play within the established situation, and brings their personal lives to the forefront. Instead, they are encouraged to play from within a generalized, or archetypal self (Ebert, 1989:15).

The continual promotion of a de-personalized acting style along with references to archetypal or primordial behavior certainly bring to mind the theories of Carl Jung (in addition to Brecht) and his ideas of the collective unconscious. Though there was no mention of the study of Jung's theories at the *HfSK* (nor those of any other philosophers or psychologists for that matter), the idea of generalized behavior was most likely a legacy of the heavy theoretical base of socialist material studied during the years of the GDR. The separation of the individual from the creative process has been a theoretical position advanced by philosophers ranging from Plato to Jung, but can also be found in the study of Marx, who promoted a "self-movement" existing outside of the human mind. Because the mind, and therefore its ideas, emotions, and thought progressions are only a reflection of a greater process already in motion, personal experience would be valuable only as a point of reference. Students who tended to limit their characterizations to personal insight and experience were usually asked to read novels and other literature from the period of time that was closest to that of the character that they were playing. This information, though not the basis for concrete dramatic action, would stimulate the student's imagination, and allow him or her to see beyond their own realm of experience.

According to Daniel Morgenroth, one of the leading actors at the *Deutsches Theater* who studied at the *HfSK* from 1986 until 1990, students not only become more adept at improvisation, but also develop and utilize their skills of observation. They begin by sitting around and discussing situations that they have either witnessed or taken part in, later dividing into groups and reenacting the scenes. Later in the semester, they move into discussing situations in certain plays[3] and, without actually reading the script, work their way into extended improvisations based on a combination of their own experiences and imagination. Morgenroth stated:

---

3.   The *HfSK* maintained a list of recommended scenes for each year of study, and it was from the plays on the list that improvisations were developed. Two of the more recognizable titles were *Look Back in Anger* by John Osborne and *The Caucasian Chalk Circle* by Bertolt Brecht.

We did this for three months, but as it developed we got closer and closer to an actual play, and further away from our personal experience. Not only with the text of the play, but with our own text ... with the discoveries of how our own text and the situations related to us.

(1993)

In the second semester, the students continue with their established group and leader, and move to performing scenes from actual texts on which their discussion and improvisations were based. They also begin to perform scenes in smaller groups of two to four, working with other instructors to accomplish this. Students are responsible for two scene study projects, and one *Wahlrollenstudium* project (a role of the student's choice). After the selection is made, the student and the instructor meet for four hours a day twice weekly and work on the role, discussing and analyzing it. Later, monologues are selected and rehearsed and, in most cases, a partner is brought in for improvisations and scene work which are done in full costume with sets and properties. Both the scene study and *Wahlrollenstudium* projects last for six weeks. At the end of each session, the projects are performed for a panel of judges who decide whether or not the student "passes," meaning that the project is deemed acceptable. As is usually the case with artistic projects, the decision basically consists of a judgement call on the part of the committee. In the event that a student does not pass, he or she will be required to repeat the project, perhaps with a new instructor, new material, and/or a new partner. After two failures, the student could be asked to leave the program.[4]

As indicated earlier, students begin to work on short scenes from plays during the second semester. Those scenes are generally assigned by the faculty members[5] and are drawn from the contemporary theatre. Scenes are selected on the basis of the needs and desires of the individual students, and as a response to the following question: "What should we play – for whom – and why?" In the context of the education of an actor, the question "for whom" is different from that asked by the artistic director of a major theatre company. The "for whom" relates to the students, their needs as developing actors and actresses, their personal problems, and their productivity. The text that is chosen contains a large amount of *Assoziationsmaterial*, or material that the student has some basis for

---

4.   Professor Veth told me in 1992 that only on rare occasions have students been failed or removed from the program. The few instances he could remember were students who decided on other careers. Failed scenes are more common, but these are usually the product of personality conflicts and are resolved by assigning alternate partners and/or instructors.
5.   Occasionally students make strong requests to perform particular scenes and these requests are considered.

understanding. Ideally, the material would be drawn from the present-day, with, at least in the beginning of a student's study, everyday common occurrences as action. This allows the students to master simple actions in a recognizable environment before moving on to more complex actions from other periods. They learn, in conjunction with the improvisation seminar, the process for building action (observe, evaluate, react), as well as to explore the continuums between fantasy and discipline, and between spontaneity and a fixed score.

Movement, speech, and voice training exist solely as support programs for the division of acting. As of May 1993, there were eight full-time faculty members in the area of speech training, coordinated by professor Herbert Minnich. The faculty arranges meetings with acting and directing students during slots of time between the larger group classes (i.e., acting and dance). During the first year of study, each class consists of two students and one faculty member, with private lessons given to each student for the remaining three years. Students are strongly encouraged to switch vocal coaches throughout their training in order to get different perspectives. Though it is very taxing on the voice faculty to handle the large number of students in private lessons, it illustrates their commitment to one of their primary goals – to allow each student to find his or her individual voice (Minnich, 1993). It is felt that in large groups, students have difficulty developing their own voices sufficiently. According to the voice faculty at the *HfSK*, only through private, individualized instruction can students develop the desired subtleness and variety of vocal production.

Philosophically, the voice faculty contend that the basis of the speech program lies in the Brechtian theory of *gestic* language. *Gestus* in language has to do with a particular attitude adopted by the speaker towards others. Therefore the *gest* of a character determines his or her tone of voice, articulation, volume, facial expression and other characteristics of delivery. An actor's delivery should follow the *gest* of the character and acknowledge a change in *gest*. The reason for this, according to the faculty, is that all physical activity, including vocal production, is controlled by the *gest*. In other words, the voice should not simply be worked out for its own sake without relation to *gestic* activity of some kind (Ibid.). The basis for vocal training is: to allow the speech process to develop as part of the *gestic* through-line.

Movement classes in the *Grundstudium* portion of a student's training consist of three basic areas: acrobatics, dance, and movement for the actor. The philosophy of the stage movement program was formulated by Hildegard Buchwald-Wegeleben during the years of the GDR at the *Staatliche Schauspielschule Berlin*. The philosophy was primarily developed in opposition to what stage movement classes had been in Germany prior to the mid-twentieth century – classes which taught posturing, gesticulation, and stylized movement on stage in an effort to be "aesthetically correct" and beautiful (Buchwald-Wegeleben, 1991:199). This style of movement began to prove useless as a training style for realistic art, which was not always beautiful and aesthetically pleasing. Professor Buchwald-Wegeleben began to look at the content of the plays themselves, to determine what kinds of skills were required of the actor. From her investigation, she determined:

> only with highly developed bodily capabilities can the actor meet the demands of the plays. For our purposes, it is important we take the actor to a level that he can learn certain more advanced skills quickly. For example, the sabre dance of Eilif in *Mother Courage*, the fencing scene in *Romeo and Juliet*, the acrobatic feats of Truffaldino in *Servant of Two Masters* and so on ...
>
> (1991:200)

Movement faculty members Eva Marie Otte and Vera Neumann (both of whom studied at the State Acting Academy under Professor Buchwald-Wegeleben) attested that the basis of the method is: the concrete motivation and association of each movement to action. In the same way that the voice faculty claims not to teach "voice for voice's sake," the movement faculty does not teach movement for movement's sake. Throughout their movement training, students are forced to relate their movement to concrete situations.

To complement movement classes, students are given a second area of movement each semester. First year students take a two semester course in acrobatics which consists of basic tumbling, balancing, and fitness. During this sequence, they cover elementary stage combat exercises and beginning work on gymnastic apparati. As with the acting classes, students are encouraged to work with props, and to establish a motivation for all movements. Second year students take a two semester course titled *Tanz*, which covers a variety of dance forms. Students are given instruction in basic ballet during the fall semester, with less emphasis on strict form and more emphasis on freedom of expression. During the *Hauptstudium* portion of training, students are given specialized instruction in several different areas, as they move into more advanced classes such as stage combat, stage fencing, advanced dance, tap dancing, and dancing for musical theatre and opera. Because of the project oriented nature of the *Hauptstudium*, students are often introduced to particular skills as needed, and, during the final year of study, they have the option of skipping formal movement classes altogether.

The most positive aspect of the training program at the *HfSK* is the attention to *Handwerk*, or craft, that is, the tools such as voice, movement, and acrobatics needed by actors to perform their craft. When asked if they felt they were being well-prepared for their careers, the students who I interviewed in 1993 gave mostly positive responses, and recognized that there was only so much that could be accomplished in four years. Any negative aspects were prefaced by statements such as "there is no such thing as a perfect school." All students attend the *HfSK* for the same basic reason – to become a working theatre professional in Germany. When asked why they chose to study at the *HfSK* as opposed to some other theatre school in Germany, most students who responded said that they came to study at the *HfSK* because it had the reputation of being the best in the German-speaking world.

Despite its reputation, in a unified Germany the *HfSK* continually faces stiff competition for the best students. The *Hochschule der Künste (HdK)*, which is located near downtown West Berlin, presents a more centralized location to major theatres, far more plentiful and newer facilities, a budget almost double that of the *HfSK*, and much higher pay for instructors (Fragstein, 1993). Increased attention to theatres in western Berlin, such as the *Schaubühne am Lehniner Platz* and the *Freie Volksbühne*, may make attendance at the *HdK* more attractive to the better students. Though their record of placement was not that of the *HfSK*, the administration at the *HdK* assured me that while their graduates often had to begin in the "provinces," more than 80% of all their graduates were also being hired after graduation.

Time and money may make for a more even playing field as far as theatre schools in Germany are concerned, but none has the great actor training history of the *HfSK*. But history is just that, schools of theatre, like similar institutions of other disciplines, can only rely on reputation for a brief time. Concrete results bring accolades and it is only by adapting to the new set of circumstances in a unified Germany that the *Hochschule für Schaulspielkunst "Ernst Busch"* can continue to enjoy the same recognition and success that it has in the past.

References

Buchwald-Wegeleben, Hildegard. (1991) "Bewegung" In *Schauspielen Handbuch*, edited by Gerhard Ebert and Rudolf Penka, 199–221. Berlin: Henschel Verlag.

Deutsches Bühnen Jahrbuch. (1992) Hamburg: *Genossenschaft Deutscher Bühnen Angehöringen*.

Drogi, Veronica. (1993) Professor, *Hochschule für Schauspielkunst "Ernst Busch."* Personal interview by the author (May).

Ebert, Gerhard. (1988) *Improvisation und Schauspielkunst: Über die Kreativität des Schauspielers.* Berlin: Henschel Verlag. (1989) *Schauspieler Werden in Berlin.* Berlin: Berlin-information.

Engelmann, Ulrich. (1993) Professor, *Hochschule für Schauspielkunst "Ernst Busch."* Personal interview by the author (May).

Engelmann, Ulrich. (1992) Professor, *Hochschule für Schauspielkunst "Ernst Busch."* Personal interview by the author (May).

Fragstein, Thomas. (1993) Rektor, *Hochschule der Künste,* Berlin. Personal interview by the author (May).

Minnich, Herbert. (1993) Professor, *Hochschule für Schauspielkunst "Ernst Busch."* Personal interview by the author (May).

Morgenroth, Daniel. (1993) Actor, *Deutsches Theater.* Personal interview by the author (May).

Otte, Eva-Maria. (1993) Professor, *Hochschule für Schauspielkunst "Ernst Busch."* Personal interview by the author (May).

Rodler, Wolfgang. (1993) Professor, *Hochschule für Schauspielkunst "Ernst Busch."* Personal interview by the author (May).

Veth, Kurt. (1992) Rektor, *Hochschule für Schauspielkunst "Ernst Busch."* Personal interview by the author (May).

Völker, Klaus. (1993) Rektor (appointed October 1992) *Hochschule für Schauspielkunst "Ernst Busch."* Personal interview by the author (May).

3

MAPPING TRAINING/MAPPING PERFORMANCE: CURRENT TRENDS IN AUSTRALIAN ACTOR TRAINING

Barry O'Connor

Tracing a map of the actor training landscape in Australia reveals that training falls into two divisions: the private sector and the public sector. Private sector schools reflect single ideologies, such as Lecoq, Strasberg, and so on, while the public sector schools are more eclectic and generalist in their programs. The public sector may be viewed as three-tiered: (1) conservatories; (2) university drama departments; and (3) technical colleges. A survey map may be drawn, highlighting three techniques of autonomous acting: the "Yat" technique, which is practised in a number of training colleges; the Eric Morris system as it is taught by Leonard Meenach at the Queensland University of Technology; and Lindy Davies's Impulse Work, which she now brings to the Drama School of the Victorian College of the Arts following her appointment as Dean in 1996. These three techniques demonstrate processes whereby the actor may map his or her own work within the existing industry model which is dominated by the presence of the director.

The Training Landscape

Actor training in Australia is offered within the public and the private sectors. The former comprises tertiary level training in conservatories and universities, which provide full-time degree or diploma courses to students who have both matriculated[1] and been auditioned for their places. The private training schools offer part-time or after hours training to fee paying students of comparatively diverse ages and backgrounds. The private and public sector schools are not in competition: they cater to different clienteles, and offer diverse curricula. University actor training offers eclectic courses based on pluralist principles; schools in the private sector reflect, by

---

1. The conservatories waive matriculation requirements if they feel the applicant has a talent for acting.

comparison, specific philosophies of training the actor. The exception is the National Theatre School in Melbourne (the school and the theatre are national in name only), which offers part-time generalist courses in conventional theatre skills. More typically, private sector schools betray a singular ideological provenance. The Ensemble Studios, an extension of the Ensemble Theatre which was once Sydney's only theatre-in-the round, offers a specifically "American Method" based training, which has been nourished and adapted by founder and still principal, Hayes Gordon, an American who originally studied with Lee Strasberg and Sanford Meisner. "Access real feelings on cue" is one of the outcomes promised in the Ensemble's 1996 prospectus.[2]

Other private training schools include the Drama Action Centre in Sydney and the John Bolton Drama School in Melbourne, both of which significantly reflect the guiding spirit of Ecole Jacques Lecoq. This is especially true in the case of the John Bolton School, which, through a program of highly physical based work in mime, movement, mask and music, aims to equip students to "work in traditional theatre, the street, or the community."[3] The Drama Action Centre maintains its Lecoq tradition, (witness the frequent visits of Phillipe Caulier), and also runs workshops and weekly classes addressing a wide range of paratheatrical as well as theatrical practices. The Actors Centre, another private training initiative, began to upgrade and maintain the practice of professional actors in 1987, but it also conducts pre-professional instruction, including "The Journey", which is a one-year intensive acting course. The Drama Action Centre and the Actors Centre often serve as conduits for new ideas and practice, importing innovative practitioners from around the world, some of whose methods are absorbed into mainstream training.

Mainstream or full-time actor training is mostly located within universities, where it has occurred in two phases. The first phase saw the establishment of the major conservatories, which are largely based on the university drama departments, more or less following American models.

The first phase began in 1958, with the establishment of the National Institute of Dramatic Art (NIDA) on the campus of the University of New South Wales in Sydney. Although it found its home there, NIDA was not formally part of the university, drawing its funding directly from government sources. NIDA emulated the Royal Academy of Dramatic Art (RADA), and while it retains its preeminent position in the field of actor training, it has deliberately never espoused an ideology. By contrast, the Drama School of the Victorian College of the Arts (VCA) commenced in 1976 with a firm ideological base in community theatre. (Community drama is used here, not in the American sense, but in the Anglo-Australian sense

2.   The Ensemble Studios: School for Actors, (1996) *Prospectus*, p. 5.
3.   The John Bolton Theatre School, (1996) *Prospectus*, p. 1.

of socially and politically committed theatre.) 1980 marked the end of the first phase with the founding of the Western Australian Academy of Performing Arts (WAAPA) at Edith Cowan University. WAAPA replicated the NIDA model but diversified in 1984 with the establishment of its Musical Theatre program. NIDA, the VCA and WAAPA are in the first rank of training schools: apart from their reputations, what distinguishes them from all other schools is that they audition nationally for their student intake by sending out teams to most major capitals across the country.

The second phase was heralded in 1974 by the founding of the Drama Centre at Flinders University in South Australia. Flinders attempted to balance practice and theory in actor training, establishing a model whereby actors are trained alongside students studying drama as a liberal arts subject. The "intelligent alternative' has remained the Flinders' ideal, combining "the skill-based teaching of a drama school with the conceptual and intellectual training of a University."[4] From the 1980s onwards, actor training proliferated in universities, as new universities were formed by a process of amalgamations that has re-drawn the map of Australian tertiary education. At present, the following universities offer actor training (their programs variously reflecting the Flinders or the conservatory models): James Cook University in Townsville; the University of Southern Queensland in Toowoomba; Queensland University of Technology (QUT) in Brisbane; the University of Western Sydney (Nepean); the University of Wollongong; Charles Sturt University (Riverina); Ballarat College; and the University of Tasmania at Launceston.

In addition to the universities, tertiary actor training is also offered by colleges of TAFE. TAFE stands for Technical and Further Education, which, because of its tradition of vocational training is attractive to governments trying to address the problems of immanent unemployment. Actor training is not widespread among TAFE colleges, but it is taking hold. For example: the Centre for Performing Arts of the Adelaide Institute, which operates under the prestigious banner of the Helpmann Academy for the Visual and Performing Arts, and the misleadingly named Swinburne University of Technology (TAFE Division), which is located in Melbourne, offer intense practical courses with a high level of industry liaison. In addition, Swinburne conducts a program called "Showbiz," which, like the Actor's Centre in Sydney, offers professional upgrading courses for actors in camera technique, auditioning and so forth.

After three years of study in a TAFE, students graduate with an Advanced Diploma in Acting. Students in university courses of the same length graduate with a baccalaureate degree. Until recently the only actor training qualification was the advanced diploma; the 'degree' of training

---

4. "Drama at Flinders," Homepage: http://festival.hum.flinders.edu.au

has been a development of the last three years. There is little discernible difference between a diploma course and a full degree course. Ostensibly the TAFE courses are less academic. WAAPA still maintains the diploma status of its straight acting course (although its music theatre students graduate with a Bachelor of Musical Theatre), trying to preserve the longer established acting course from undue academic interference.

It is not so much a question of how academic the training of actors should be, but what kind of academic or theoretical preparation actors should receive. Typically, the academic component has been theatre history or dramatic literature courses, which have reflected Eurocentric and logocentric culture, thereby overlooking Australia's diverse cultural identity and the development of non-traditional theatre forms. I have written and spoken more extensively elsewhere on these matters (O'Connor, 1993, 1995). Here I want simply to pose the question: should the actor be a replicator of established culture or an innovator of new cultural forms? Because most acting schools seek industry credibility, training is conservative, serving to shore up the industry status quo. Students receive little opportunity to acquire a critical apparatus by which to theorise and interrogate their function as actors within the larger culture. The Drama Centre at Flinders University has expanded the intellectual platform of their course, adding a subject called "Theories of Performance" which studies the "structural, semiological, cultural, ethnic, psycho-analytical" theory that can inform performance making (Hartog, 1996). Ideally this kind of the training will produce actors who are not just agents of cultural reproduction but critical thinker-practitioners and cultural transformers.

Prominent Features on the Training Landscape

Acting schools in Australia essentially train actors to interpret scripts: to lift characters off the page, creating living and breathing incarnations in front of audiences and cameras. This means working with directors who, in the case of film and television, and, not infrequently, in the case of theatre, may not understand the creative processes and requirements of the actor. The actor needs to be in charge of the craft of acting, to be in possession of an artistic working method that can deliver on demand. Enter the autonomous actor who has ownership of the creative means of production. Discernible in the training landscape are three methodologies which place the actor at the centre of the craft, empowering the actor, affording the actor artistic integrity and control of creativity. These methodologies are: the "Yat" technique; the Eric Morris system as practised by Leonard Meenach, and Lindy Davies's Impulse Work. I want to consider each of these practices separately, identifying their particular contribution to the notion of the autonomous actor.

The "Yat" technique

Although the "Yat" technique has been around for thirty years it is not widely known and remains peripheral as a training methodology, except of course at its center of origin. The system was born in England in 1963, when Yat Malmgren and Christopher Fettes left the Central School of Speech and Drama to establish the Drama Centre, where Yat is still taught today by its originator. Malmgren, who is in his eighties, now enjoys guru status: surrounded by mystery in unprepossessing circumstances in Chalk Farm, he sits magisterially holding the "book" – which he has never allowed to be published – and from which his disciples learn, before going forth to spread the word throughout Europe, America, Australia, and beyond.

Drama Centre graduates established the Drama Studio in Sydney in 1980, where "Yat" was the basis of the training. The Drama Studio closed in 1990, but the "Yat" method is now taught as part of mainstream actor training at three key sites (the "Yat" teacher in each case is indicated in parenthesis): the Centre for Performing Arts in Adelaide (David Kendall); the Faculty of Creative Arts, University of Wollongong (Janys Hayes); and, most strategically, at NIDA (Tony Knight).

The system of movement psychology that Yat is based on may be traced back to the work of Rudolf Laban (1971, 1974), who is much better known than his disciple. The Laban movement and notation system, of course, are extensively published and used throughout the dance world. "Yat" is Laban movement analysis given the benefit of Jungian typological analysis. Late in his career at Dartington Hall in Devon, Laban, who was collaborating with Jungian analyst William Carpenter, equated movement with intentions, which in turn related to the Jungian personality functions of Thinking, Sensing, Intuiting, and Feeling. These functions were in turn correlated with Laban's Motion Factors – Space, Weight, Time and Flow. Laban's "equating movements with intentions and so with psychological [...] or personality types"(Hayes, 1996: 4) was only just beginning. The document containing his nascent theories was entrusted by Laban to Malmgren, who is said to have devised a practical methodology which he continues to refine. The result was a system which Malmgren prefers people to experience rather than study from books. David Kendall (1984: 157) believes that experience is the only way to comprehend "Yat."

How does the system work? It reduces all behaviour to character categories called "Inner Attitudes". There are six Inner Attitudes, or character analyses: "Near," "Mobile," "A dream," "Stable," "Awake" and "Remote" – in order of increasing complexity. For example, the inner attitude "Near" embraces appetitic senses demanding instant gratification; "Awake" comprises motivations directed towards problem solving and logical deduction (Hayes, 1996:8). The physicalisation of motivation, with a corresponding emphasis on the sensate body, is at the heart of "Yat'" as might be expected from a Laban influenced process. The actor analyzes character in terms of physical, movement-based images, which become icons of action (movement images) that the actor can back-reference in order to inform performance. "Yat" negates Cartesian mind-body dualism: the body is the mind; the mind is the body. Motivation travels from the mind to the body, just as it can journey from the body to the mind. Therefore a motivation can begin in an idea or a gesture; a reciprocity exists that means the one will necessarily stimulate the other.

This is reminiscent of Michael Chekhov's notion of psychological gesture, or even Stanislavski's concept of playing actions. Indeed , in the mid-80s, Malmgren's continuously evolving system underwent a name change from "Movement Psychology" to simply "Action," bearing evidence perhaps of the influence of Doreen Cannon, the Stanislavski teacher, and Malmgren's colleague at the Drama Centre. Since the 80s another name change has occurred: "Action" is now called "Character Analysis" (Hayes, 1996:8)

The "Yat" technique is a highly systematic process, which empowers the actor by providing a physical vocabulary of analysis. The actor has a paradigm of motivations at hand which appear to cover most situations. The technique also affords an independent and individual way of working. Once learnt, the actor does not require a director, nor even other actors, to practise the technique. The pedagogy by which "Yat" is learnt requires the student to present individually prepared work to the instructor,: the technique is acquired at the feet of a master. Significantly, the Drama Studio's student showcase was entitled "Solo," a touring show where the students presented their individual characters, which were rich, complex and highly physicalised. David Kendall (1996) admits that "Yat" training does not take place *en ensemble*, however, when two students of the system come together, their common training facilitates ensemble performance.

The Eric Morris system

Leonard Meenach's appointment as acting instructor at QUT last year has meant the introduction of Eric Morris's techniques to Australian actor training. Meenach credits José Quinterro, Arthur Lessac and Eric Morris as formative influences on his work, but he identifies Morris as the single most abiding influence (Meenach, 1996a:1). Indeed, Meenach convinced Morris, who was well enough known in West Coast acting circles, to introduce his work to academic teachers of acting (Meenach, 1996). Meenach's credo of acting is as follows:

> I don't believe in acting. I believe in reacting.
> I don't believe in acting style. I believe in acting reality.

I don't believe in concept. I believe in contact.
I don't believe in the idea of playing a character. Character to me is the product of playing.
I don't believe in product. I believe in process.
I don't believe in naturalism. I believe in truth.
I don't believe text creates truth in the actor. I believe the actor creates truth in the text.
I don't believe in doing. I believe in being.
I don't believe in facilitating a script. I believe in living it.
I don't believe in acting with the left brain. I believe in reacting with the right. I believe that truth can only come from truth and truth is what the actor is really feeling at any given moment. If an actor's behaviour is not truthful to what is really felt then there is a split between the behaviour he/she is expressing and what is really going on inside.

(Meenach, 1996a:2-3)

The work is clearly within the Stanislavskian tradition, but departs from it by insisting on the emotional realism rather than emotional illusionism – on self as focus rather than character. There is less of Stanislavski and more of Lee Strasberg in the Morris system.

Morris was not the originator of the approach which now bears his name. It began with Martin Landau, who had studied with Lee Strasberg at the Actors Studio in New York and started classes in Los Angeles, where Eric Morris, Joan Hotchkis and Jack Nicholson were among his students. Morris, Hotchkis, and Nicholson developed the work into a system, which divides into instrument and craft work. The instrument is the actor's psychophysical self and the craft is not technique, Morris does not use the word, but "the choices and approaches that lead [...] to fulfilment of the material. [...] Craft is a toolbox"(Morris, 1981:82).

Work on the instrument basically involves freeing or unblocking the impediments that, for whatever reasons, stand in the way of free emotional flow. "Instrumental blocks," says Meenach, "create a 'spilt' between how the actor is behaving and what he/she is really feeling in the moment"(Meenach, 1996a:4). The 'split' is corrected by identifying and working on the fear that stands in the way of truthful playing. There is a veritable battery of strategies for dealing with "splits," depending on whether they derive from the imagination, the ego, interpersonal relationships, or inhibited behaviour. Ultimately these strategies involve exercises which are exposing of the individual who performs them before the rest of the group. "First because being in front of people causes the blocks to expose themselves and second because working on a block under performance pressure is the best and fastest way to eliminate it from the actor's conditioning"(Meenach, 1996a:5).

The second part of the system is craft work, which is divided into three sections: "analysis of text," "choice," and "choice approach." Meenach points to the shortcomings in Stanislavski's text analysis which reduces the text to beats and actions. The "who, what, where, and why?" are important, but identifying an objective does not tell the actor how to play it (Meenach, 1996a:9). Meenach's criticism of the Stanislavski system is that it creates a gap between the actor's intellectual understanding of character and playing the moment to moment experiences of the character. Meenach found Stanislavski wanting on the matter of how to play an intention. His solution deserves quoting at length:

> I began working directly on the emotional state suggested in the text. I found that sometimes this would cause the actor to play an idea of the emotion instead of the emotion itself. After much exploration I discovered the problem was that the experience of emotion is different from how we 'think' it will be. The actor can never predetermine what the quality of the expression is in any given moment. Doing so creates result conscious behaviour not impulsive behaviour and thus bad acting. The myriad of possibilities is too complex. Trying to figure them all out beforehand only serves to keep the actor reverent to the idea of the experience. For the actor to say I will be angry is not enough. The idea of anger alone restricts the actor's playing of it. Being states are too complex to be reduced to just one quality of expression. Being states must be left in the realm of the unconscious. Still, we need a way of consciously deciding and communicating what it is we will play. I needed a way to define it, but keep the actor open to the spontaneity of the moment to moment experience of it. I created what I call the emotional cocktail, that is, a tool for spontaneously experiencing what the actor is to believably recreate. I call it a cocktail because the experience is usually a mix of emotions, not just one emotion. I find it keeps actors from emoting text if they have learned it is a combination of feelings that must be experienced, not just one emotion. It is best to describe the being state with at least three emotional or being state adjectives, for example:
> hurt/anger/rage;
> love/lust/need;
> thirst/exhaustion/despair;
> love/hurt/anger;
> joy/happiness/euphoria;
> disappointment/sadness/concern.

It makes no difference that some adjectives used are feelings
and others states of being. What is important is that the actors
have a target idea of what to shoot for when experiencing the
text.

(Meenach, 1996a:9-10)

Having found the right "emotional cocktail' for the being state, the actor
then chooses a strategy – sense memory, emotional memory, imaginary
monologues, to name a few – in order to personalize the experience. "The
actor must find a choice that will provide an organic stimulus to
action"(Meenach, 1996a:10). The choice can be animate or inanimate, but
Meenach prefers to work with the former: for example, relatives and lovers
make good choices. The actor talks to this lover or relative in front of the
class, directly revealing their feelings about them. When they achieve the
being state of the emotional cocktail, Meenach then has them "switch into
their material [the text] which brings them to the final section of the work"
(Meenach, 1996a:11)

The third part of the craft is "irreverence." The actor must be
irreverent to all but the stimuli he / she is reacting to and the expression of
impulses created by the stimuli. This means that the actor must also be
irreverent to text" (Meenach, 1996a:12). This does not mean that the actor
departs from the text, but rather if the actor is thinking about concepts,
themes, or other directorial matters then a split occurs. And this results in
bad acting. "Irreverence is the difference between obligated and reactive
behaviour " (Meenach, 1996a:13). Good acting is "when the actor is obligated
only to the stimulus that fulfils the needs of the being state the actor is
working for in the moment" (Meenach, 1996a:12). As with the rest of the
system, there are many strategies, all of which are clearly outlined in Morris's
books, by which irreverence can be attained.

The system, which is taught by Morris in the States and now
practised by Meenach in Australia, obviously betrays its roots in Stanislavski
and Strasberg, especially the latter, as far as removing psychophysical
inhibitions is concerned. Where Morris and Meenach depart from their
source is in the devising of set strategies to deal with problems of
performance as they arise. The system gives the actor a battery of devices
which enable self-direction and self-correction, thus ultimately affording
the actor the status of an autonomous creator.

Lindy Davies's Impulse Work

The notion of the autonomous actor is central to Lindy Davies's "Impulse
Work." "Autonomous" for Lindy Davies (1996a) does not mean ignoring
the playwright or the text. Quite the contrary, impulse work is closely text-

based, seeking to assist the actor to find the moment-to-moment impulses behind the dramatist's words. The work starts in the time honoured way with play analysis, discussing the play's meaning, themes and world; character study is not pre-empted as part of this process. Character in the Stanislavskian sense of a construct built on the foundations of "who am I? what do I want? how can I achieve it?" leads, in Davies's view, to a premeditated sense of character, emphasising the past and future to the detriment of the present.

Impulse work focuses on the present, trying to access the chaotic rather than the rational aetiology of behaviour. Beats, units and objectives are reductionistic and rationalistic, excluding all else in the name of intentionality. Plumbing the impulses behind words and actions, however, discovers a universe teeming with chaos and accident. Davies argues that this is a truer reading of life than one which is based on rationalism and determinism. So many forces are operating at any given time to produce a given moment that to reduce these to a single cause is to misrepresent the essence of the moment.

In impulse work, rather than premeditating the text – deciding who the characters are and what they want to achieve – the actor meditates the text. This process, which is called "dropping in," is a term which derives from Kristin Linklater. Lindy Davies has adapted the process and furthered it for her own ends. A state of neutral centerdness is first required, which is arrived at by relaxation and breathing techniques, so that the actor is fully available to the work. Lindy Davies paints a clear picture of the process in the following words:

> It is as though we are preparing a deep, still pond, filled with crystal clear water, and then into this pond we drop a pebble and the ripples pervade and pervade the water. In other words, we drop a word into the stillness of ourselves and the meanings resonate and pervade us until we find the impulse to speak from source.
>
> (Davies, 1996:5)

"Dropping in" can take place individually or in pairs, with the actors lying down in a state of relaxation induced by centering breath. The text is strategically located on a wall, either written on butcher's paper or a projected overhead transparency. The actor takes in each meaningful unit in order to make a "feeling of connection" with it (Davies, 1996a). The feeling of connection may be an association, a reference, inner experience whatever it is that personally prompts the actor to give utterance to the text. This procedure is called "sourcing." Sourcing reaches "completion' when the actor finds "satisfaction" or is happy that the true source of the word has been reached. The judgment that a connection has been made is entirely in the actor's own hands. A "pathway" is thereby established, which the actor will always return to, even during performance, in order to access the desired impulse.

The initial phase of dropping-in happens silently, in the meditative state of relaxed stillness and centerdness that must precede the process for it to be effective. It is not mystical: the actor simply finds, in his or her own life or in the life of the play, the impulse to give voice to the text. In the silence the impulse to speak is found: first in a whisper and then on in full voice. It is a kinaesthetic not an intellectual discovery. The pathways are not lost but carefully annotated for future reference and revision – the latter because the process is always open to adjustment.

The imagination is stimulated through seven "Fields of Impulse." These are: "Emotion/Feeling," complex emotional states producing anger, fear, pain, and so on; "Sensation," a physically registered response, tense arm, stiffened neck; "External Stimulus," the impact of the physical world, including interaction with other actors; "Image," still or cinematic mental impressions; "Thought," intellectual responses to the text; "Physical Gesture," bodily adjustments relating to others; "Action," which may be described in the usual way as to flatter, to stimulate, to excite. "Action" recalls Stanislavski, but the rest of the "Fields" demonstrate that acting is about more than rational linear cognition, it is potentially random and chaotic – kaleidoscopic rather than telescopic. Davies believes that action analysis may, on its own, account for what actors seem to be doing from an external observer's point of view, but it does not comprehensively account for what is going on in the minds of the actors themselves (Davies in Strube, 1995: 253).

When a text is scored as a result of the "dropping-in" procedure it can look something like this (the scene is from Caryl Churchill's *Top Girls*):

	TEXT	SOURCED TEXT
JOYCE:	So what's the secret?	I hate secrets.[F/T] I've got to know.[A]
MARLENE:	It's a secret.	No, don't block me off Marlene.[T]
JOYCE:	I know what it is anyway	I don't know what it is.[T] Dry the dishes.[A/PG]
MARLENE:	I bet you don't. You always said that.	No I don't ....[T]
JOYCE:	It's her exercise book.	A small green and white exercise book with spotty black pages[I] and secrets – lost of secrets.[F/T]

F = Feeling/Emotion; A = Action, I = Image; ES = External Stimuli; T = Thought; PG = Physical Gesture; S = Sensation (Strube, 1995:260).

The sourced text is from Joyce's point of view, showing that the sourcing is done both as speaker and as auditor. In terms of the impulse dynamic, an actor"s own statements are as important as the replies they occasion.

The next stage of the process, which Lindy calls the "abstract," involves an overt physicalisation of the imaginative work done as part of dropping-in. In the abstract, the actors play in space (Davies betrays her drama-in-education background here and her debt to Dorothy Heathchote), using symbolic junk and objects, which are chosen to suit the thematic concerns of the play. In her 1996 Chichester production of *Hedda Gabler*, Davies (1996a) used brocades and velvets, rich cloths, flowers, formal wear, pistols, and manuscript papers in the abstract stage of rehearsal. "Colors" textures, shape, height, width, depth, all of the coordinates of space start to become important"(Davies in Strube, 1995:188-90). The actors move about the space, rediscovering kinetic impulse through specific physical actions such as walking, running, and stillness – which Davies employs to help actors recover their fluency of impulse. Other actors feed in objects or lines of text, which are also projected onto the walls via overheads, keeping the actors' hands and bodies free of the script. The actors work physically, allowing their bodies to discover the text and recording these discoveries as part of the score already begun during "dropping-in." The abstract is purely for the actors: it enables their bodies to experience the text, to concretise the metaphors, and find illuminating gestures as a result; archetypical gestures are arrived at through this process.

"Blueprinting" is the final step. The actor internalizes the performance score arrived at in the two preceding stages, imprinting it within the body by refining and fine-tuning the abstract. Blueprinting is somewhat akin to conventional blocking, as Helen Strube (1995:137) observes, but it is driven by the initiative of the actor rather than the director. However, unlike blocking, blueprinting occurs only after the text has been fully and freely explored. Furthermore, blueprinting requires that the set be already constructed for it to happen, which enables the actors to build kinetic relationships with the space and the physical environment. In addition, the set becomes an integral part of the performance text itself: not only an environment for acting, but an environment that nurtures acting. Once the blueprint is found it is fixed, but the process of retrieving impulse continues for the actor, travelling down the pathways that have already been pioneered during the earlier stages.

Lindy Davies describes her Impulse Work as follows:

> I have established the aesthetics of performance in a very strong way. First of all, the aesthetic of working off the moment. Secondly, the aesthetic that language is a primary

source. It is language that ignites the imagination. And thirdly, the area of aesthetics in terms of the subconscious being important, not the rational self [...] The main thing [...] with the actors is not to appropriate what they are doing, to allow something off the wall to happen.

(Davies in Strube, 1995: 216)

Davies has evolved her methodology over a period of some twenty years or so. It has been a personal journey that began when a young actor was squashed by an autocratic director. That young actor was Davies. Davies' quest for an autonomous working process for the actor took her around the world and exposed her to many influences. In 1996 she took up her appointment as Dean of the School of Drama at the Victorian College of the Arts, which has a long tradition of empowering the theatre practitioner. Davies is now in a position to see that this tradition is maintained and developed according to her own lights.

Davies's Impulse Work, like the "Yat" technique, and Leonard Meenach's Morris practice, all place the actor in charge of the creative process. The three processes afford the actor the means to map his or her own performance, and revisit the map coordinates in order to rediscover the inspiration of the performance – whether it is termed "informing icon," "being state" or "impulse." The benefits are clear for the actor working in an industry which is still dominated by the figure of the director, whether in theatre or film. What remains to be seen is whether the actor who is empowered to map his or her own creativity, is also capable of remapping performance making in the future. This would mean breaking the industry influence on actor training.

Acknowledgments

The writer wishes to thank Lindy Davies, Leonard Meenach and Janys Hayes for permission to quote from their unpublished conference papers; and in addition to the three already mentioned, David Kendall, Lisa Scott-Murphy, and Dianne Eden (Head of Acting at QUT) for their generosity in allowing interviews, discussions, and e-mail correspondence.

References

Davies, Lindy. (1996) "The Act of Revelation: Language and the Presence of the Actor." *The Nagoya International Theatre Conference*. February 10-12.

(1996a) Personal interview. 30 August.

Hartog, Joh. (1996) "Professional Actor Training at Flinders." E-mail from Joh Hartog. 6 August.

Hayes, Janys. (1996) "Movement Psychology: the Yat Technique, A Method Training for the Nineties." *Together As One*: 5th Australasian Theatre Conference. Toi Whakaari: New Zealand Theatre School, Wellington, New Zealand. 7-10 July.

(1996a) <j.hayes@uow.edu.au> "Yat, Etc." Personal e-mail. 2 September.

Kendall, David. (1984) "Actor Training in Australia." *Meanjin* 43. 155-160.

(1996) Telephone Interview. 14 August.

Laban, R. (1971) *The Mastery of Movement*. London: Macdonald & Evans.

(1974) *Modern Educational Dance*. London: Macdonald & Evans.

Meenach, Leonard. (1996) Personal interview. 25 June.

Meenach, Leonard. (1996a) "The Being Process: a complete system for actor training." *Together As One*: 5th Australasian Theatre Conference. Toi Whakaari: New Zealand Theatre School, Wellington, New Zealand. 7-10 July.

Morris, Eric. (1981) Being and Doing: a workbook for actors. Ermor Enterprises.

O'Connor, Barry. (1993) "Actor Training and Cultural Identity in Austral/Asia." *Canadian Theatre Review*. 74, Spring, 22-26.

(1995) "Actor Training and Cultural Identity in Australia." Annual Conference of the International Federation for Theatre Research. *Actor, Actress on Stage: Body/Acting/Voice*. University of Quebec at Montreal, May 22-23.

Scott-Murphy, Lisa. (1996) <LSCOTTMU@earwig.ed.ac.cowan.edu.au> "Acting at WAAPA." Personal e-mail. 13 September.

Strube, Helen. (1995) "The Autonomous Actor: a case study of Lindy Davies." 2 vols. Diss. Queensland University of Technology.

4

ACTOR TRAINING IN THE UNITED STATES: PAST, PRESENT, AND FUTURE(?)

Ian Watson

In the collection of essays *Master Teachers of Theatre*, Jewel Walker, a leading teacher of movement for actors, makes a statement that reveals much about the American attitude toward performer training: "a bad actor has a better chance of becoming a great actor than does a very good actor" (1988:114). Walker's aphorism claims much for training. A "very good" actor has innate talent which either calls for little correction or allows the neophyte star to ignore classes, gurus, or an overdose of effort to achieve a modicum of success. The struggling "bad actor," who has few natural gifts, has to struggle through endless hours of study with teachers which, coupled with rigid discipline and hard work, gives him "...... a better chance of becoming a great actor." In short, according to Walker, and probably the majority of his American theatre colleagues, study combined with effort has the potential to transform ambition into Medea, Hamlet, Stanley Kowalski or Lady Macbeth.

Contrary to popular opinion, the perception in the United States that actor training is both necessary and potentially transforming did not begin and end with Lee Strasberg, the Method and Marlon Brando. Some twenty years before Konstantin Stanislavsky even founded the Moscow Arts Theatre with Vladimir Nemirovich-Danchenko, let alone developed his training system that was going to have a lasting impact on Strasberg and his colleagues, acting conservatories had been established in America because theatre people with vision recognized the importance of training actors. This recognition has persisted and in the ensuing years generated a variety of ways one can study acting.

A Brief History

The history of actor training in North America can be divided into four, somewhat overlapping, periods: repertory training that persisted from the beginnings of resident professional companies in the United States, during the latter part of the eighteenth century, until around 1875; the conservatory-type training developed between 1875 and the Moscow Arts Theatre tours in 1923 and 1924; the dissemination and Americanization of the Stanislavsky system from 1925 until the late 50s; and from the early 60s through to the present day, when the legacy of Stanislavsky's American disciples has come into question.

Repertory training

From the beginnings of theatre in the colonies, British actors dominated the American stage. They brought entire companies on tour, "stars" of the English stage mounted specially tours in which they performed with local actors, and the Boston Tea Party notwithstanding, English stage practices were the primary model for their Atlantic cousins. Given this influence, it is little wonder that the British training methods were adopted as local troupes began to emerge. Would-be performers were invited to play small parts in plays; as they learned through performing and by imitating their more experienced colleagues, they graduated to more important roles and eventually, following the European "lines of business" model, were assigned a set of character types that they were to play in the company throughout their career.

In the second half of the nineteenth century, resident stock companies were in decline in the United States. This decline was due to a combination of factors, the most important of which were: the supplanting of the repertory system (i.e., a company of actors that performs a season of plays) by the long run of a single play in which actors were only hired for each production; and the rise of combination companies in which a star and entire cast toured together with a fully rehearsed and designed production (as opposed to the previously popular format in which a star toured alone and did productions with local companies). The demise of the resident stock company meant that training opportunities for actors were limited. The awareness of this limitation, combined with what James McTeague, who has written the best and most thorough history of actor training between 1875 and 1925 in North America, describes as "....a deep desire to raise the standards of acting. because "....the theatre had a significant social and aesthetic purpose...." 1993:241), led to the formation of several professional training schools based on the dual premises that "....acting was an art and that it possessed principles that could be taught" (McTeague, 1.993:241).

The early conservatories

In 1871 Steele MacKaye, an actor, director, playwright, designer and inventor who had studied with François Delsarte in France, established the first professional theatre academy in America, the St. James Theatre School, in New York City. This school, which lasted a mere six months, was followed by at least seven others, four in New York City: the School of Expression (1877), The Madison Square Theatre School (1880), The Lyceum Theatre School (1884), and The National Dramatic Conservatory (1898); and three in New England: Emerson College of Oratory (1889), The School of Expression (1885), and The School of the Spoken Word (1904). Some of these conservatories survived a matter of months; one, The Lyceum Theatre School, became The American Academy of Dramatic Arts in 1892 and remains a major conservatory with branches on both the East and West Coasts of the country; two have since become university colleges: Emerson College of Oratory became Emerson College in 1936, while in 1943 The School of Expression, which was founded by Samuel Silas Curry, became Curry College.

In describing these schools, McTeague identifies several factors they shared in common that influenced and shaped their philosophy of teaching and the acting theory underlying it. The most commonly shared belief was that there was a body of knowledge and experience to be gained about acting prior to entering the profession. What this knowledge was, and views on how it ought to be taught varied. But, at least two elements of the various programs, the concept of a "system of acting" which could be taught and applied to performance and the curricular model of teaching, were foundation models for subsequent schools and training philosophies in the United States. The first of these owes its origins to MacKaye whose adaptation of Delsarte's system of acting, with its emphases on codification and bodily expression, was a major component of teaching in most of the New York schools since he was either the founder and/or a teacher, at all but one of them (The National Dramatic Conservatory). Even though MacKaye's adaptations were eventually discarded or altered so much as to be almost unrecognizable, they prepared the way for another "system" which was to have much more enduring repercussions, the Stanislavsky method.

MacKaye's legacy was also evident in the curricular model of teaching. He, along with Franklin Sargent, founded the Lyceum Theatre School and, even though MacKaye fell out with his partner and left the school prior to Sargent renaming it first the New York School of Acting (1885) and later the American Academy of Dramatic Arts (1892), he provided the model of a school guided by a single theory of acting. The American Academy of Dramatic Arts was founded upon this model but, as McTeague points out, rather than having one teacher, the Academy took the bold step of dividing offerings into areas of specialization taught by different instructors, all of whom tailored the content of their classes to the school's philosophy of acting (1993:69).

As one might expect, the eighteenth and nineteenth centuries' emphases on elocution and declamation in the theatre, evident in the stock companies of the day, was a factor in most voice and speech training in these early conservatories. The importance of speech and its links to oratory are evident in the names of several of the schools. The founders of the three New England schools, Charles Wesley Emerson, Curry, and Leland Todd Powers, who established The School of the Spoken Word, were all graduates of Boston University where they had studied oratory with Lewis B. Munroe. Each of their schools was initially established to teach oratory and only later added courses in acting.

More significantly, it was during this period that the pre-eminent role of the playwright in the rehearsal process was established. Prior to Stanislavsky's influence on American acting, Charles Jehlinger, a member of the first graduating class from the American Academy of Dramatic Arts who subsequently taught there for nearly forty years, was teaching the importance of the play text as the major source of information with regard to character and situation (McTeague, 1993:52). For Jehlinger, and eventually for most American theatre until it was questioned during the heyday of theatrical experimentation in the 60s and 70s, obedience to the "author's instructions," that is, the faithful transformation of the playwright's words to actions and interpreting characters as he conceived them, was the actor's primary task.

McTeague argues that this reverence for the playwright was not the only way in which the early American training academics anticipated Stanislavsky. According to him, the majority of the conservatories shared much in common with Stanislavsky's later psycho-physical concepts. Most, for example, shared the belief that relaxation was essential to both training and performance; similarly, in the vein of Stanislavsky's "circle of attention," they taught that the actor must accept the circumstances of the play as completely as possible; they believed that the actor must identify with the role by thinking and feeling "as if" he was the character in the situations of the play; and, in anticipation of "affective memory," at least three of the schools taught actors to use their own life as a source for the emotional experiences of their characters (1993;242-244).

Stanislavsky and America

Predicated pedagogy or not, America's early schools were hardly a match for the tidal wave of enthusiasm and interest that accompanied Stanislavsky's two visits to the United States in 1923 and again in 1924. Prior to the Moscow Art Theatre's (MAT's) tours, there had been considerable criticism of the commercialism of American theatre and unfavorable comparisons between it and the "superior" European models.

In addition, an entire issue of the influential *Theatre Arts Magazine* (October, 1920) had been devoted to Stanislavsky's company, billing it as the "world's first theatre," and a massive press campaign was mounted just prior to the MAT's arrival in New York. This campaign was more than matched by the unbridled enthusiasm for the company by critics and audiences alike. The obvious superiority of the MAT, combined with Stanislavsky's hectic schedule of interviews and appearances arranged by the press agent coordinating the tours, as well as the rushed publication of his first book, *My Life in Art*, in 1924, left the American theatre awash with "Stanislavsky-ism" and the demand to learn his "system." In detailing the Russian deluge, McTeague acknowledges the inevitable, the conservatories that had flourished prior to Stanislavsky's visit sunk in the flood (1993:251-252).

America owes no small debt to an opportunism born of its immigrant heritage and capitalist philosophy. This is as true in the theatre as it is elsewhere. It is little wonder then that an actor and actress from the MAT, Richard Boleslavsky and Maria Ouspenskaya, were encouraged to remain in the United States following the company's tour in order to head a new conservatory, the American Laboratory Theatre. This school, which remained open until 1930, was the first in the Americas to teach the Stanislavsky system. Significantly, among its approximately 500 students were Stella Adler, Lee Strasberg, and Harold Clurman, all of whom were going to play leading roles, not only in North American theatre, but also in the country's development of actor training.

Michael Chekhov was another expatriate Russian destined to influence the Americanization of Stanislavsky. Chekhov, who had been a leading actor with the MAT and headed its Second Studio, developed a system of acting that, as Mel Gordon puts it, emphasized "...... the super imaginative and intuitive sides of acting" (1987:118). Despite his interest in what other, less generous, critics have labeled esoteric and quasi-spiritual preoccupation's little concerned with acting, Chekhov's technique, which he taught in the United States during the 40s and 50s, has its roots firmly in the Stanislavsky system. Apart from giving private classes in post-War Hollywood, teaching at his own studio, the Chekhov Theatre Studio, in the North-East prior to the War, and the establishment of the Second Michael Chekhov Studio in New York in 1980 by a former student and colleague Beatrice Straight, arguably Chekhov's most important legacy in America lies in a 1935 lecture-demonstration of his technique sponsored by the Group Theatre. As Gordon reports, most members of the Group Theatre thought that Chekhov's ideas were too extreme and, given their reliance on the mystical, questioned how they could be taught. But, both Stella Adler and Robert Lewis, who were more impressed with Chekhov than their colleagues, incorporated aspects of his ideas, especially concerning character, into their teaching (1987:154-157).

The permeation of Stanislavsky's ideas were in their infancy with Boleslavsky, Ouspenskaya, and Chekhov. At least one other Russian, Vera Soloviova, an actress from the MAT who performed on Broadway with Chekhov's company the Moscow Arts Players in 1935, remained in the United States and taught. Lee Strasberg traveled to Moscow to observe Stanislavsky's work first hand in 1934, and Stella Adler studied with the master himself in Paris the same year. This direct or indirect contact with Stanislavsky's ideas were supplemented with a number of publications by Stanislavsky and fellow Russians who had worked with him. Stanislavsky's *My Life in Art* was followed by *An Actor Prepares* (1936), *Creating a Role (1936)* and *Building a Character* (1949); Boleslavsky's *Acting, The First Six Lessons*, based on what he and Ouspenskaya taught at the American Laboratory Theatre, was published in 1933, and Chekhov's *To The Actor* was released in 1953. These books, by the first generation of Stanislavsky teachers, have since been augmented with many technique-oriented books published by Americans greatly influenced by Stanislavsky. These books are beyond the scope of this paper, but a serious comparative chronological study of them and how they relate to Stanislavsky's ideas might yield a valuable understanding of the gradual Americanization of the Stanislavsky system.

The Group Theatre

Books and Russian masters aside, the first critical step toward an American technique of acting that had its roots in the Stanislavsky system lies in the formation of the Group Theatre in 1931. One of the inspirations for the Group Theatre was the Stanislavsky technique. Two of the company's founders, Lee Strasberg and Harold Clurman, had studied with Boleslavsky and Ouspenskaya, and at least one of the original members of the company, Stella Adler, had done the same. They, and co-founder of the group, Cheryl Crawford, were well aware that most American actors of the time had little exposure to Stanislavsky beyond seeing or hearing about the by now legendary MAT. So, an integral part of the Group Theatre's agenda included the teaching of technique. Strasberg, who is credited (or damned, depending upon one's point of view) with developing the Method school of acting, not only directed the new groups first production, Paul Green's *House of Connelly,* but he was also responsible for training. Armed with his fledgling interest in teaching, his classes at the American Laboratory Theatre, and his readings of Michael Chekhov and Yvgeni Vakhtangov, Strasberg began what was to become a lifetime journey that continues to shape the techniques and careers of countless American actors, mostly through the Actors Studio conservatory which, even though he did not found, he headed from 1949 until the early 80s.

The Group Theatre's actor training legacy is hardly confined to Strasberg. Apart from Adler, who eventually established her own acting studio, the company included Sanford Meisner who was to lead the Neighborhood Playhouse School of Theatre for decades, Robert Lewis, one of the original founders of the Actors Studio who eventually became a leading director and teacher, and fellow Actors Studio founder Elia Kazan who, apart from teaching, became one of the country's most important film as well as theatre directors and helped popularize the post-Group Theatre schools by making "stars" of many of their graduates.

Despite differences in their interpretations of Stanislavsky (Strasberg's Method, with its emphasis on emotional memory, and Adler's greater concern with actions and imagination rather than the personal life of the actor being the major such difference), these disciples of the master evolved a distinctively American style of acting. This style, with its emphasis on the psychological and emotional life of the character, justified motivations, and the subtext rather than the text itself, helped shape the heightened form of realism that came to dominate post-War American theatre and film.

Success breeds success, and dare one say, leads to excess? By the late 1950s Hollywood had turned graduates such as Marlon Brando, Montgomery Clift, Marilyn Monroe, James Dean, Kim Stanley, Geraldine Page, Eli Wallach, Paul Newman, Joanne Woodward, Shelley Winters, and Anne Bancroft into international stars. In addition, an army of teachers who, having studied with Strasberg, Adler et al., had begun teaching personal variations on their teacher's interpretations of the master's inspiration. Americanized Stanislavsky, of one form or another, was virtually the only type of training available in the United States. But, as the quintessential folk singer/rock star who frequently personified the pulse of America in his lyrics, Bob Dylan, was to record only a few years later, "the times they are a'changin'." This perennial present tense, born of protest, aimed at youth, and denying stasis, was as true for actor training as it was for the broader strokes of history's brush that Dylan was addressing.

Questioning Stanislavsky

A combination of reflection and developments in the theatre alerted actors, teachers, and directors to the limitations of post-Group Theatre actor training. The Group Theatre and its legacy was steeped in realism. The writer most closely associated with the company was Clifford Odets and the immediate post-War American theatre was dominated by the likes of Arthur Miller, Tennessee Williams, Kazan, the designer Jo Mielziner, and a production style most frequently described as "theatrical realism." But many were aware that, despite the slavish preoccupation with psychological truth, motivation, and emotional veracity displayed by Stanislavsky's American disciples, Stanislavsky himself had directed the MAT actors most familiar with his system in plays far removed from the realistic canon,

The interest in forms other than realism was prompted not so much by a reappraisal of Stanislavsky as it was by changes in the theatre, however. The late 40s and 50s saw the beginnings of regional theatre in the United States. Theatres were initially established in major cities such as Dallas, Houston (Alley Theatre), Washington (Arena Stage) and San Francisco (Actor's Workshop). These theatres began as semi-professional organizations which relied heavily upon volunteer help and amateur actors. But, in 1959 the Ford Foundation made sizable grants to many of these fledgling companies which allowed them to become fully professional. In the ensuing years, regionalism has redefined the American theatre. New York may remain the commercial center, but much of what is new, vital, and essential for the continued growth of the art is taking place in regional theatres. This is where many of the new writers are given their first hearings, where young actors invariably make their professional debuts, and where up-and-coming directors flex their artistic muscles. Artistic considerations aside, even though regional theatre has suffered loss of financial support in the economically troubled past years, most major cities boast a regional theatre of consequence. In addition to those already mentioned, some of the more important ones include the Mark Taper Forum (Los Angeles), the Guthrie Theatre (Minneapolis), Seattle Repertory Theatre, the American Repertory Theatre (Boston), Trinity Repertory Theatre (Providence), the Actor's Conservatory Theatre (San Francisco), and the Actor's Theatre of Louisville.

The growth of regional theatres has not only meant a shift in the artistic compass, but a similar shift in employment demographics. As Terry Schreiber, the head of the New York based Schreiber Studios and one of the country's leading acting teachers puts it, "most of the work for actors these days is out in regional theatre" (in Mekler, 1988:83). The majority of these theatres have, since their inception, presented a season of works that includes classics and plays outside the vein of realism. This repertory approach to theatre called for a reassessment of actor training since a technique which focuses almost exclusively on the psycho-emotional severely limits performers. Studios and teachers responded by re-addressing the importance of the movement, voice and speech components of training, as well as by teaching ways of approaching the works of Shakespeare, his fellow Renaissance playwrights, the plays of George Bernard Shaw, Molière, Goldoni and the like.

The growth of regional theatre has been accompanied by the proliferation of summer festivals which focus much of their attention on

Shakespeare's plays. Inspired by the success of Tyrone Guthrie's open-air Shakespeare summer festival in 1953 at Stratford, Ontario in Canada, Shakespeare festivals have sprung up around the United States, the most important being: Shakespeare in the Park in New York City; the Oregon Shakespeare Festival in Ashland; the Utah Shakespearean Festival in Cedar City; the Three Rivers Shakespeare in Pittsburgh, Pennsylvania; and the Illinois Shakespeare Festival in Normal. There are many more, and all call for actors trained in the classics.

Coupled with this renewed interest in the classics, was the work of contemporary playwrights which challenged realism and the actors' technique it was based upon. Writers such as Bertolt Brecht, Samuel Beckett, Eugene Ionesco, Jean Genet, Harold Pinter, as well as much of Edward Albee's and Sam Shepard's early works called for techniques that were different from the Americanized Stanislavsky that was being taught during the 50s. Clearly a change was called for.

As is often the case, the seeds of change were being planted before the true value of the crop had been realized. At the Yale Drama School, for instance, the acting curriculum during the 40s and 50s was shaped by Constance Welch who, according to John Wilk, had an "…. eclectic approach to actor training [which] was reputed to have run counter to the internal method acting" (1986:125) that dominated American training at the time.

The Drama Division at the Juilliard School in New York, founded by John Houseman in 1968, was based on training guidelines developed by Houseman's founding co-director Michel Saint-Denis. These guidelines emphasized training for the classics, extensive voice and movement classes, and performance in a theatre attached to the training institute. Apart from The Acting Company, the theatre company that grew out of the training program at Juilliard which employs graduates, a major focus in training is to prepare actors to work in the "established repertory companies" around the country (Charles, 1993:114).

But, repertory companies have hardly been sitting on their hands waiting for graduates to emerge from Juilliard. A number of them have established their own training programs. The most famous of these, the Actors Conservatory Theatre (ACT), founded by William Ball in 1965, has been a model for many of them. Interestingly, Ball, whose initial vision included a training program attached to his theatre, was, like Juilliard, greatly influenced by the ideas of Saint-Denis (Wilk, 1986:121); and it is no accident that two of Welch's students from Yale, Robert Goldsby and Allen Fletcher, were the first two directors of the ACT conservatory program.

It was also during this period that movement classes began to become an accepted part of actor training in universities with pre-professional training programs. In 1964 Jewel Walker was invited to join the faculty of Carnegie Mellon University (then called Carnegie Tech) which, in a similar adventurous move, had instituted the first university degree granting program in theatre in the country in 1914. Walker's success at Carnegie Mellon, followed by his teaching at the University of Wisconsin-Milwaukee and more recently at the University of Delaware, Newark have promoted movement studies so successfully that they are now an accepted part of most conservatory-inclined university programs.

Vocal training has undergone a similar resurgence since the late 50s. As one might expect from a training grounded in nineteenth century declamation with links to schools of oratory, speech was always an important part of training prior to the Americanization of Stanislavsky. The Group Theatre and the teaching that grew out of it moved attention away from the mechanics of speech and onto the inner-justification for how one's character spoke. But, the pendulum swung back with the likes of British trained Kristin Linklater, Edith Skinner, and Cecily Berry. Their classical training, influenced by the psycho-physical concerns of Americanized Stanislavsky and movement schools such as Alexander, has led to an eclectic approach to vocal and speech training that reflects all its various influences.

The 60s and 70s in America was a period of intense experimentation in the theatre. Just as there was reaction to the domination of the Method and other American interpretations of Stanislavsky's ideas in traditional training institutions, much of the avant-garde of the period had roots in exploring alternatives to psychological-based theatrical realism. Several of these experimentalists were concerned with the actor's process, both in rehearsals and during performance. Through workshops, developing new training methods, and performances, artists such as Joseph Chaikin at the Open Theatre and Richard Schechner at the Performance Group explored alternatives to the Stanislavsky-ism of the day. Chaikin, Schechner and others with similar concerns owed their allegiance to the likes of Vsevolod Meyerhold, Antonin Artaud and their Polish contemporary Jerzy Grotowski, rather than to Strasberg, Adler or Lewis.

In their attempts to discover alternatives to realism and psychological based acting, Chaikin and his contemporaries researched new forms of expression. This research included examining the sonorous qualities of the voice, investigations of various movement and body techniques, exploring the links between mental imagery and physical as well as vocal expression, and experiments with collective creation. Since much of this research called for skills which were outside the domain of conventional teaching at the time, training became an integral part of groups such as the Open Theatre and the Performance Group. These companies devoted much of their time to workshops and training sessions which combined researching new techniques with the learning of equally new skills. As evidence of their success, a number of the training strategies and techniques have been incorporated into mainstream contemporary actor training which, to generalize, is a combination of Americanized Stanislavsky, British classical training filtered through the legacy, of the Group Theatre, and the 60s and 70s experiments with alternative techniques.

Types of Training

Actor training in America focuses on four areas: acting, voice, speech, and movement. This is not to say that any one of these areas could not include a number of different classes (acting often consists of various specially studies such as technique, improvisation, and theatre games, for example), but that the primary goal in each area is to develop a particular skill which, when combined with the other skills, produces a fully-rounded performer.

Acting classes vary from one training institution to another. In addition to the instruction in improvisation and theatre games already mentioned, most include classes in sensitivity training designed to encourage students to relax vocally, physically and psychologically in order to free their expressive instrument. These classes are the ones which have been most influenced by the experimentalists of the 60s and 70s, since many of the exercises developed by the likes of Chaikin have been incorporated into them. On the other hand, technique classes (which encompass areas such as text analysis, character, creating and controlling emotions, motivation, and psychological action) invariably dominate an acting curriculum that can vary from between two to four years, depending upon the institution.

In addition to teaching how to analyze and realize a text, technique classes include the study of how to apply these skills. "Scene Study" and what are often referred to as "Styles" classes are seminars in which students attempt to employ their newly acquired technique on scenes from plays. Scene Study classes tend to focus on what students are most familiar with, contemporary American realism, since the emphasis is on skill application to the exclusion of most everything else. Styles classes have a broader agenda. As their name implies, they explore a variety of theatre genres. It is in these classes that the classics, Absurd Theatre, farce, the Comedy of Manners etc., are explored.

Acting classes usually also include performances in front of an audience. This part of the acting curriculum varies greatly, some institutions incorporate performance from the beginning of an actor's studies, others do not allow it until the final year. Most schools fall somewhere between these extremes. Whatever the programmatic schedule, performance is generally viewed as a two-part training in which one part is concerned with the rehearsal process while the other is seen as an opportunity to apply all one is learning in a situation similar to that which will face the actor upon graduation. Consistent with the pedagogical intent of these performances, actors are cast in different types of roles during their studies and are required to perform in a variety of plays.

The more professionally oriented comprehensive training schools frequently offer specialist seminars in specific areas. These can include things such as make-up, audition technique, the compilation of a portfolio for an agent, and acting for the camera.

Since acting classes are not subject to federal, state, or in many cases even institutional curriculum requirements, classes are invariably shaped by the individual teacher's training, experience, and adaptation of what s/he has been taught. Thus, despite reaction against the post-Group Theatre mindset, American interpretations of Stanislavsky still shape technique classes because most of the leading teachers are products of it. This is not to say that other factors, such as a concern for the classics, do not influence training, but leading college teachers like Robert Benedetti (who taught at Carnegie Mellon University as well as the University of Wisconsin-Milwaukee, was chair of the Acting Program at Yale University, and has been Dean of the California Institute of the Arts), William Esper (head of the Acting Program at Rutgers University's Mason Gross School), Michael Kahn (who heads Juilliard's Drama Division), and Dale Moffit (the head of theatre at Southern Methodist University for many years) have all studied, and in some instances even taught with, the Group Theatre teachers (Mekler, 1988). Similarly, the leading private acting teachers, such as Michael Howard, Michael Schulman, Terry Schreiber, and Ed Kovens, have all been influenced by years of study and/or teaching with either Strasberg, Meisner, Lewis, or Adler (Mekler, 1988). And, as of September 1994, the Actors Studio and the New School for Social Research in New York have offered a degree program which includes seminars headed by luminaries of the Actors Studio such as Paul Newman, Al Pacino, and Alec Baldwin.

Voice and speech are frequently classified together in discussions of actor training, but they tend to be studied separately in the United States. Voice classes focus on the vocal instrument. They are concerned with areas such as vocal resonators, voice projection, diaphragm control and correct breathing, pitch, musicality and rhythm. In recent years, this area has been especially influenced by the likes of Kristin Linklater whose concern with the psycho-vocal relationships between the body and the voice as well as imagery and the voice owes an admitted debt to Alexander movement techniques (Linklater, 1976:2 and 4), and possibly a similar debt to experimental theatre directors such as Chaikin and Grotowski, both of whose experiments included extensive exploration of the links between imagery, voice, and the body. Speech classes, on the other hand, are primarily concerned with pronunciation, Shakespearean scansion, poetry and dramatic verse, meter, and the International Phonetic Alphabet.

Despite the differences between the study of voice and speech, the two areas overlap a great deal. To use a metaphor, the voice is the instrument while speech is the music played on it. For this reason, they are often taught by the same person, and many of the exercises used in one class are, with subtle variations in their goals, equally valid in the other.

As might be expected in a country that looks to Britain as the standard against which to measure itself with regard to the classics, England has had a major impact on speech and voice training following the questioning of the Group Theatre hegemony in the late 50s and early 60s. Linklater and other leading influences on current training, such as Edith Skinner and Cecily Berry, were all trained and began teaching in England. Similarly, Elizabeth Smith, the renowned Julliard voice teacher, is British trained, and one of the most important summer workshop training opportunities for professional actors and teachers of voice and speech has been the annual master classes organized by the Illinois Shakespeare Festival which are taught by David Carey and Jane Boston from London's Central School of Speech and Drama.

As with the resurgence in the teaching of voice and speech, the importance of movement training specifically for actors was only generally recognized in the early 60s. Since then, it has become a standard component of most actor training programs. Movement classes, which are often taught in conjunction with dance departments, are essentially of two types: those geared to train the actor's body for performance, and specially skills classes. The body-oriented classes are concerned with teaching methods of relaxation, flexibility, expressiveness in gesture and the trunk, as well as techniques for physicalizing character. The best movement teachers tend to be eclectic both in what they teach and the influences that have shaped their teaching. Jewel Walker, for example, cites many sources for his work including, among others, yoga, the Pilates Method developed by Joseph Pilates, Françoise Delsarte, Michael Chekhov, Rudolph Laban, Etienne Decroux, the Rolfing form of body massage, Tadashi Suzuki, and various types of gymnastic jumps using a mini-trampoline or Reuther board (in Hobgood, 1988:114-115). Other teachers may add Moshe Feldenkrais, F. Matthias Alexander, T'ai Chi, and experimentalists like Chaikin, and Grotowski to this list.

Speciality skills offerings vary considerably among schools but can, depending upon the availability of teachers, range from mime to period dance, circus skills (juggling, clowning, slapstick etc.,) to mask work, as well as from combat techniques, like fencing and T'ai Chi, to gymnastics.

Survey or not, it would be unfair to give the impression that the only form of actor training available in the United States is for mainstream dramatic theatre. A number of conservatory-type programs offer singing and dancing in their curricula in order to enhance the versatility (and hence the job prospects) of graduates. These offerings tend to be elective rather than required classes and are limited in scope. But, there are at least two schools in New York, the Musical Theatre Works Conservatory and The American Musical and Dramatic Academy, that have programs specifically designed to train performers for musical theatre.

Similarly, there are several institutions which focus on body oriented training and/or what might best be described as a more experimental form of theatre. The Dell'Arte School of Physical Theatre in northern California, for instance, which is described as "...... the only institution in the United States offering full-time programs in physical theatre styles" (Charles, 1993:12), provides courses in Commedia Dell'Arte, mask work, pantomime, silent comedy, and clowning. The Ringling Bros., and Barnum and Bailey Clown College offers somewhat related courses focused primarily on training circus clowns.

Tangentially the legacy of the 60s and 70s experimentalists has never been entirely abandoned. The Experimental Theatre Wing at New York University, for example, was established to nurture experiment among student actors. As well as the training provided by its permanent faculty, guest teachers have included Ryszard Cieslak, Eugenio Barba, Robert Wilson, Richard Foreman and Augusto Boal. A related venture, with a somewhat greater emphasis on public performance, The New World Performance Laboratory, has sprung up in recent years at the University of Akron under the leadership of a former assistant to Grotowski, James Slowiak. And Tadashi Suzuki has had an important presence in the United States since the early 80s when he first taught at the University of Wisconsin in Milwaukee. Graduates of his teaching both in America and Japan, like Teresa Kim and Eric Hill, have in turn become teachers, while Suzuki himself continues to teach when his schedule allows it.

There is a healthy interest in Asian theatre as well as Western theatre in the United States. In terms of teaching, this interest is centered on universities and tends to have a scholarly rather than practical thrust. There are, however, places that teach courses in Asian theatre performance techniques. Unquestionably, the leader in this field is the University of Hawaii at Manoa which has a Master of Fine Arts (MFA) in Asian performance and periodically offers courses in forms such as Kabuki, Noh, and Chinese Opera. Despite the fact that these latter courses invariably involve training with an Asian master and culminate in a performance, their primary aim is as a complement to academic studies; the training is not designed to prepare professional actors for traditional Asian stages.

Where to Train

The major ways in which one can train to be an actor in the United States range from individual coaching through private classes to conservatories and universities. Independent teachers, such as Michael Howard in New York and Eric Morris in Los Angeles, teach individuals and/or small groups in private studios. Their students tend to be experienced actors who have trained elsewhere and wish to continue master classes. Students are usually attracted to these classes through word of mouth, the reputation of the teacher, and/or advertisements in trade papers.

A number of these "independents" have been so successful that they established larger studios not dissimilar to conservatories. The Schreiber and Marjorie Ballentine Studios in New York are typical of these. The former, headed by the actor/director Terry Schreiber, and the latter, under the leadership of the actress Marjorie Ballentine, include faculties of teachers and offer courses in, among other things, technique, voice, speech and movement. These types of studios tend to be dominated by the training philosophy of their director. But, there are several legendary studios which remain rooted in their leaders' visions, even though the leaders have passed on; the two best known examples being the Actors Studio headed by Strasberg, who died in 1982, and The Adler Conservatory of Acting whose founder, Adler, passed away in 1992.

Traditional conservatories are somewhat different from independent studios in that they are more institutional in nature and are rarely guided by one individual's vision of performance. Some conservatories, like The American Academy of Dramatic Arts (with branches both in New York and Los Angeles), The American Musical and Dramatic Academy (New York), and The Lorrie Hull Workshop and Theatre Conservatory (Los Angeles), are independent of any theatre or educational institution. Many conservatories, however, have a professional performing wing and/or are affiliated with a university. Those associated with professional theatre companies, such as the Actors Conservatory Theatre (San Francisco), The National Theatre Conservatory (Denver), The Circle in the Square Theatre School (New York), and the Trinity Rep. Conservatory (Providence, Rhode Island), incorporate their play season into the training of student actors. They require observation of select rehearsals and all productions, small roles are cast from among students in the middle stages of their training, senior students are frequently cast in larger roles, and graduates are often invited to join the company.

The advantage of conservatories with theatres being connected to universities is that they are able to offer degrees rather than diplomas to their graduates. These degrees, though of little value in winning a role, are invaluable if one wishes to teach at a university (a major source of employment for qualified people) since most universities demand that professors or lecturers have a terminal degree (i.e., usually a MFA in performance for acting teachers, though some teachers may have a more academically oriented doctorate).

Despite the general trend towards graduate study at theatre-linked conservatories, probably the best known conservatory/university affiliation in the country is the undergraduate program at New York University's Tisch School of the Arts. Students in the program attend the university two days a week during which time academic subjects such as theatre history and dramatic literature are taught. The other three days are spent at one of a selection of studios or conservatories in New York: the Stella Adler Conservatory of Acting, the Lee Strasberg Theatre Institute, the Circle in the Square Theatre School, Playwright's Horizon's Theatre School, or The Musical Theatre Works Conservatory.

Arguably the most prestigious conservatories in the country, The Institute for Advanced Theatre Training at Harvard University, Yale School of Drama, and the Drama Division at Juilliard, though not strictly university programs, offer fine art degrees and provide a rounded schooling that is generally regarded as amongst the best available. Given their reputations, entrance into any of the three programs is highly competitive; but, once accepted, students receive a thorough, extensive training from excellent teachers, and, upon graduation, join an alumni which boasts many actors well-established in the profession who are walking advertisements for the programs.

Actor training at universities is common in the United States. Oscar Brockett, one of America's leading theatre historians, maintains that as early as the mid-60s there were over 1500 universities offering theatre studies of one sort or another in the United States (1991:575). This training is generally divided into one of two types, either fine arts or liberal arts. Actor training in a school of fine arts is closer to a conservatory model than to a traditional university education in humanities because it, like other university-based vocational fields such as engineering, business, law, and architecture, is regarded as a pre-professional training.

Most fine arts actor training programs offer undergraduate (Bachelor of Fine Arts, BFA) and/or graduate (MFA) degrees. Even though the BFA has a conservatory bent, it often includes basic survey courses in theatre history and dramatic literature, as well as some study outside of theatre subjects in areas such as history, civics, and English. The MFA programs tend to minimize academic study, preferring instead to focus almost exclusively on practical training. Both degrees have performance requirements in addition to a full array of technique, styles, voice, speech, and movement classes. These requirements usually, involve performing in productions directed by faculty or professional directors hired especially for the occasion and are presented in theatres on campus. A number of programs, such as those at the University of California – San Diego, Boston University, Wayne State University in Detroit, and the University of North Carolina at Chapel Hill, are also affiliated with professional theatre companies which have a training function much like their conservatory counterparts.

In addition to classes and performances, fine arts training can also include study with professional artist who are resident at the university for extended periods. In 1993, for example, the Argentine theatre group Diablomundo was in residence at the University of Tennessee in Knoxville teaching their collective creation methods, and the Florida State University School of Theatre has an ongoing residency program that in 1994 included Ann Reinking, one of America's leading musical theatre performers and dancers.

Actor training in a liberal arts school is generally limited to the baccalaureate (Bachelor of Arts, BA) degree. There are some graduate (i.e., Master of Arts, MA, and doctoral, Ph.D, programs) like those at the University of California at Berkeley, the University of Wisconsin-Madison, and the University of Hawaii at Manoa, which allow for a practical component in their degrees, but their primary focus remains academic.

Academics also play a greater role in the liberal art bachelor's degree than they do in fine arts' undergraduate programs. Unlike most BFA sequences, The liberal arts degree has a general education requirement that makes up approximately half of all courses. These requirements are the same for all undergraduates regardless of their major field of study and usually include electives in subjects such as math, English, science, at least one foreign language, and the social sciences. In addition to these subjects, a student interested in acting would major in theatre.

A student majoring in a particular area has to successfully complete a fixed number of courses in that field, some of which are mandatory subjects while the rest can be chosen from a selection of class offerings. A student interested in acting, for example, would have to take a number of academic subjects in theatre, such as dramatic literature, performance theory, and history courses, in addition to technique, movement and voice classes. Thus, given the general education requirements and the academic component of a theatre degree, the undergraduate acting student in a liberal arts school does far fewer practical courses that her colleague in a BFA program.

Unlike the fine arts baccalaureate degree, the BA in theatre is not viewed as a pre-professional training. Those interested in becoming actors are expected to pursue graduate school or further professional study. Despite what appears to be a clear distinction between the BA and a BFA in performance, there is contention among educators as to the ultimate value of the degrees. Some maintain that the goals are quite separate, the BFA is training actors while the BA provides a general humanistic education with an emphasis on acting. Others argue that the BFA is not a proper grounding for the professional actor because, even though it may provide a solid training in the craft of acting, it is too limited in scope to nurture the budding artistic spirit. The advocates of the BA argue that this nurturing calls for a broad education, post-university life experience, maturity, and further study.

Some Final Thoughts

The BA/BFA discussion hints at a much broader issue in the philosophy underlying actor training. Mainstream theatre throughout the United States is predicated upon the role of the writer, who is generally viewed as the first creative artist in the theatre. It is the function of the actors, in conjunction with the director, designers, and technicians, to realize the writer's pertinence for their particular audience. Actors are viewed as craftspeople who must be taught particular skills in order to interpret the writer's ideas. Projects in which actors are involved in writing and/or collectively creating a play, either from scratch or through workshop/rehearsals of an existing text, are few and far between. Hence training like the Diablomundo residency referred to earlier, in which the emphasis is on actors learning creative rather than interpretive skills, is rare.

Even though there is a range of training opportunities open to young actors, training in the United States is characterized by its inherent conservatism. This is especially true with regard to technique classes which remain rooted in Americanized Stanislavsky. Despite the questioning of the post-Group Theatre gurus in the late 60s by experimentalists and those who realized the importance of the classics, the focus on psychology and the inner processes of character still dominate technique classes. The Schreiber Studio in New York is typical in this regard. In a recent open letter Schreiber described his program as, "..... an eclectic approach to the work [i.e., training] that we feel combines the best of Strasberg, Meisner, Lewis, and Adler techniques, along with our own ideas of helpful acting exercises, body dynamic work, and vocal training for the actor" (1994).

To be fair, the experiments of the 60s and 70s that might have laid the foundation for a lasting alternative to Americanized Stanislavsky, failed to develop a system of acting which could be taught, applied, and passed on in the same way that the Russian master's could. In keeping with the anti-establishment sentiments and the prominent role of the human potential movement during those years, Chaikin, Schechner, Grotowski et al., were more concerned with alternative forms of dramaturgy and exploring each member of their ensembles' abilities as a performer than they were with systematizing an approach to acting which all actors could apply. Their work had a profound influence on the theatre of their day and on those who worked with them, but its legacy in terms of contemporary training is scant.

If McTeague is correct, history as well as missed opportunities and conservatism may be a factor in America's preoccupation with the psycho-emotional component of acting. In concluding his study of early American actor training, he maintains that the majority of schools, and the philosophies underlying them, laid great emphasis on what he terms the actor's "inner technique." An "inner technique" which he argues is little different from Strasberg's interpretation of the Stanislavsky system (1993:245)

The concern with inner technique is further encouraged by the nature of the acting profession. One of the major sources of employment for actors is television and film, mediums whose dramatic fair has been shaped by realism and graduates of the realistic school of acting. The close-up, as well as the director's ability to focus attention on minute detail through lighting, the camera, and editing has, in America, popularized a style of screen acting which favors psychological-based techniques over more physically or vocally oriented approaches to acting. Schreiber touched on the success and limitations of this approach in an interview with Eva Mekler where he discussed the work of several actors, including one of America's most successful screen actors, John Malkovich: "I was amazed when I saw Shaw's *Arms and The Man* at Circle in the Square [a leading Off-Broadway theatre]. The problem with American actors was laid out in front of me. Whereas Raul Julia, for instance, took on that material and was absolutely wonderful, John Malkovich and his [ex] wife, Glenne Headley, were much too small for these roles. Their work was honest and real and it was good acting, but it belonged in somebody's garage. It never rose to the size of the material" (1988:83).

Criticized or not, Malkovich and Headley can count themselves lucky that they continue to be employed, most actors are out of work. This is hardly a problem limited to the United States, but it nevertheless raises serious questions about the purpose of training. Despite the fact that the best programs are highly competitive, even they, let alone the myriad of lesser institutions that churn out graduates at a giddy rate, produce more actors than there are jobs for them to fill. Should schools stop training? Should the majority of students be guided into a different profession? Should training be adapted to better equip graduates for finding work in other fields? There are no simple answers, but the biggest problem is not so much that these questions are left unaddressed, it is that since vested interest is involved, namely insuring that student intake remains high since budgets tend to be enrollment driven, few institutions even raise them.

Unemployment, under-employment, and the lack of creative outlets have long been the bane of the arts in general, and the acting profession in particular. They have not brought an end to the profession, and it is unlikely that they will bring an end to training. In fact, far from hinting at demise, actor training has planted several new seeds which may hold promise for the future. One such seed is the development of international cooperation in training which is part of a general trend in American education toward internationalism. A number of conservatories and universities offer training that includes a portion of study at an institute in another country. The majority of these programs reflect America's training heritage, sending students to either one of two countries: Britain (in which classical training is emphasized) or Russia (where the focus of study, is invariably Stanislavsky,'s legacy). The British American Academy in conjunction with Juilliard and various universities has a summer school arrangement in Oxford, for instance, the National Theatre Institute requires students to spend part of their training in England, Trinity College in Hartford, Connecticut has a summer program that offers training in both Russia and Bulgaria, while Carnegie Mellon University has a program that sends students to both Cambridge, England and the Moscow Art Theatre School for part of their training.

The international influence on American training is not limited to traveling abroad. As in the past, when Michel Saint-Denis was sought out as a guiding influence on the newly formed Drama Division at Juilliard, Columbia University's recently established division of fine arts invited Andre Serban, the Romanian-born director who worked for several years with Peter Brook at his International Center for Theatre Research in Paris, to create and head the MFA acting program. As one might expect of Serban, given his contact with Brook and his reputation for experimentation, he has designed a curriculum far removed from the tradition of technique classes dominated by American interpretations of Stanislavsky. In his first semester he divided students into groups working on Greek tragedy. Each group, which was led by a director and dramaturg, was assigned a script to "research" and asked to present the results to their colleagues. This "research" was supplemented with voice and movement training consisting of Kathakali dance and Indian chanting which was incorporated into the work on the Greek plays (Istel, 1994:27).

The Saratoga International Theater Institute (SITI), discussed at length in this volume by Eelka Lampe, is another experiment with potential for the future. The Institute, headed by a leading American director, Anne Bogart, and the Japanese experimental director and teacher Tadashi Suzuki, conducts workshops which focus on the intercultural nature of dramaturgy, the rehearsal process and training. Since it was founded in 1992, SITI has produced a number of productions including *Orestes* by Charles L. Mee Jr. and *The Medium*, both directed by Bogart, and Suzuki's adaptations of *Dionysus, The Tale of Lear* and *Waiting For Romeo*. Productions are hardly Bogart's and Suzuki's only concerns at SITI, however. Both are committed to alternative acting methods and are in the process of organizing an expanded training program led by master artists from various performance cultures around the world. These sessions will augment their present focus on the Suzuki Method which combines traditional Japanese performance techniques with rigorous physical and vocal disciplines.

Japanese, Indian, Greek, Romanian, Russian, British and possibly more influences filtered through the American theatre experience are coming together to shape the actor training programs of those with vision. Is this an indication of an intercultural bent in tomorrow's training, or is it merely one more cycle in history's windmill? Time will be the judge. But, the very fact that an Ivy League bastion of conservatism, Columbia University, sought out Serban indicates that there are some who feel the need to offer alternatives to contemporary training programs so that Jewel Walker's aphorism about the good and bad actor remains true into the next century.

References

Adler, Stella. (1970) "The Actor in the Group Theatre," in *Actors on Acting*. Edited by Toby Cole and Helen Krich Chinoy. New York: Crown Publishers.pp.602–606.

Bethune, Robert W. (1989) "Describing Performance in the Theatre: Kabuki Training and the Western Acting Student," *The Drama Review*, Vol 33, No 4 (T124):146–166.

Brockett, Oscar. G. (1991) *History of Theatre* (6th Edition). Boston: Allyn and Bacon.

Charles, Jill. (1993) *Directory of Theatre Training Programs*. Dorset, Vermont: American Theatre Works.

Edwards, Christine. (1965) *The Stanislavsky Heritage*. New York: New York University Press.

Gordon, Mel. (1987) *The Stanislavsky: Technique: Russia*. New York: Applause Theatre Books.

Gunter, Gregory. (1994) "Bogart Tunes in: What's Her line?", *New York Theatre Workshop News*, (Spring):2–3.

Hobgood, Burnet M. (Ed). (1988) *Master Teachers of Theatre*. Carbondale: Southern Illinois University Press.

Istel, John. (1994) "Andrei Serban: Educating Properos," *American Theatre*. Vol 11, No 1 (January):27, 80–82.

Lampe, Eelke. (1993) "Collaborations and Cultural Clashing. Anne Bogart and Tadashi Suzuki's Saratoga International Theatre Institute, *The Drama Review* Vol 37, No 1 (T137):147–156. Linklater, Kristin (1976) *Freeing the Natural Voice*. New York: Drama Book Publishers.

McTeague, James. (1993) *Before Stanislavsky: American Professional Acting Schools and Acting Theory. 1875–1925*. Metuchen, New Jersey: Scarecrow Press.

Mekler, Eva. (1988) *The New Generation of Acting Teachers*. New York: Penguin Books.

Munk, Erika. (Ed). (1966) *Stanislavsky and America: An Anthology From Tulane Drama Review*. New York: Hill and Wang.

Schreiber, Terry. (1994) Letter to the author, February 8.

Strasberg, Lee. (1973) "Russian Notebook (1934)," *The Drama Review*. Vol 17, No 1 (T57) March:106–121. (1970) "The Actor and Himself," in *Actors on Acting*. Edited by Toby Cole and Helen Krich Chinoy. New York: Crown Publishers. pp. 621–629. Wilk, John R. (1986) *The Creation of an Ensemble*. Carbondale: Southern Illinois University Press.

PART II

THE EAST AND EXPERIMENTS

5

INVISIBLE TRAINING IN BALINESE PERFORMANCE

Ron Jenkins and I Nyoman Catra

Introduction

> "I was thinking about our duty as human beings. We live here
> on the island of Bali. When we compare our island to other
> islands it is very small. Now if we are so small and we don't
> want to go to war, we will be dominated by larger islands ....
> What can we use as a weapon ... Yadnya is what we can use
> as a weapon."

This rambling meditation on politics, geography, and survival was improvised by a Balinese actor named Ketut Kodi in the village of Banjar in the summer of 1996. The speech accompanied his stage entrance at a festival to celebrate the building of a new temple. Kodi's character wore the clown mask of a "penasar" and was expected to provide the audience with laughter and enlightenment tailored specifically to the moment. His opening reference to the power of yadnya provides an important insight into his complex performance of metaphysical slapstick and the skills required to successfully pull it off.

"Yadnya" is the fulfillment of ritual obligations performed by all Balinese as part of their Hindu/Buddhist/animist religion. By invoking the significance of yadnya in his first speech, the clown immediately connects to the audience's reason for coming together. They are building a temple where yadnya can be practised. Their gathering in support of the temple is itself an act of yadnya, as is the willingness of the performers to donate their skills to the event. Before the evening is over the clown and his comic collaborators will have made puns about the name of the village, invoked the deeds of Bali's ancient Kings, joked about the upcoming Presidential elections, satirized the rise of tourism, and bantered about their geographical relationship to the sacred mountain "Agung" in a routine whose staccato rhythms echo the cadences of Abbot and Costello's "Who's on First?"

This kind of multi-layered joking is part of every Balinese temple festival. In fact, the name of the clown character, penasar, (meaning foundation), implies that this type of sacred laughter is fundamental to the ceremonies. The penasar's performance is both a demonstration of and a lesson in the meaning of yadnya. The audience watches the penasar participate in an obligatory ceremony that links them to their gods, ancestors and tradition. At the same time the penasar's jokes, songs, and religious quotations provoke reflection on the practical and spiritual significance of yadnya in a variety of contexts. The artists who succeed in playing the penasar are highly esteemed throughout the island, but the multiple skills required to orchestrate performances of this nature are difficult to master, and even more difficult to categorize.

There is no formal training that can prepare a Balinese performer to become a great penasar. Like all other masters of Balinese performance, they follow the rigorous apprenticeship of dance training that provides them with the physical virtuosity that the island's demanding audience have come to take for granted. In addition to this relatively straightforward acquisition of physical technique, a penasar must master subtler theatrical and linguistic skills that will enable him to intertwine ancient religious texts with improvised contemporary dialogue in an entertaining and provocative style that mixes song, dance, and slapstick, while shifting back and forth between several languages. The audience would be satisfied with nothing less.

While it is impossible to specify the formative experiences that lead to this sophisticated level of Balinese theatrical virtuosity, conversations with the islands most highly respected actors suggest three primary sources of informal theatrical education that are crucial to the development of a penasar:

1) Lingkungan – Attentiveness to the environment
2) Sastra – Written chronicles of religion and history
3) Penonton – Interaction with the audience

Lingkungan

The Balinese performer assimilates incalculable bits of information and technique simply by paying close attention to his environment (lingkungan). One master of penasar said, "I learned to sing by listening to the women who picked flowers in my village. I stopped my work to listen to them." Exposure to random encounters of this nature enables performers to develop skills outside the parameters of formal training.

Performers who live in a family of artists have the advantage of watching their relatives perform over and over again. The complex rhythmic patterns that link dance, song, and spoken text become second nature to

I Nyoman Catra performing in the comic mask
of the old man. Photo: Ron Jenkins

I Made Bandem in comic mask.
Photo: Ron Jenkins

Close-up of Gusti Windia in comic mask.
Photo: Ron Jenkins

them without the necessity of formal study. Apprentices from outside the family get similar experience when they work as assistants, carrying masks and costumes for a master performer as he travels from village to village to practice his craft. Simply watching performances is also instructive, as demonstrated by the localization of artistic specialties in Bali. The village of Sukawati is famous for the number of high quality shadow puppet masters ("dalangs") who live there. Singapadu is known for its topeng dancers, maskmakers, and penasar. The proliferation of performances in one area gives young people the opportunity to see a great many plays as part of their natural environment and facilitates their mastery of the art.

The functions of Balinese performance are similar to the functions of yadnya ritual obligations. They provide symbolic representations of ideas and events that create harmonic balance between humans, their gods, their demons, and their environment. To create performances that promote a balanced relationship with one's environment, performers must be keenly aware of their surroundings. It is the responsibility of the penasar to invent metaphors that provoke the audience into a deepening awareness of their environment. The late Kredek, one of the most respected penasar in Singapadu, wrote songs about the importance of the sandat flower that grows in abundance in his village. His songs suggested that it was advisable to emulate the sandat, which was not as beautiful as the hibiscus, but lasted longer, and was more useful because of its scent. Even when it looked wilted and old, the sandat was treasured for its aroma and practical value as a key ingredient of expensive perfumes. The flashier hibiscus, on the other hand, loses its bloom quickly and is soon forgotten. Kredek's son, I Made Bandem, (who now lives on Sandat street in Denpasar), sang his father's songs about the sandat flower when he performed as a penasar and uses the principles of the song's message as a guide to his own career as a member of Parliament and the director of Bali's national university of the arts. Other penasar of his generation, including Ketut Kodi, also of Singapadu, still sing songs that remind their audiences of the metaphor of the sandat flower as a model for modesty and true value. The example of the sandat song is only one of the countless references to the social and natural environment that are embedded in Balinese performance.

Sastra

In addition to scouring their environment for performance subjects and techniques, a Balinese penasar must study the ancient historic and religious writings that are preserved in ancient languages on manuscripts made of dried palm leaves. These palm leaf manuscripts are called "lontar" and collectively the cultural heritage of written wisdom that is preserved on them is known as "sastra." All the stories staged in Balinese dance/drama are drawn from these historic and religious manuscripts that chronicle Bali's spiritual development. It is the responsibility of the penasar to sing songs taken from these ancient texts and translate them into a modern vernacular for the audience in a way that their relevance to modern choices is made clear. Referring to a story preserved in a text of the Hindu epic Ramayana, I Made Bandem parallels the building of Hanuman's bridge to Sri Lanka with the metaphoric bridges that modern Bali is forging with cultures and technologies of the Western world. It is a reference that Bandem has used in both his performances as penasar and his speeches as a member of parliament.

When Ketut Kodi called for the use of yadnya as a weapon to preserve Bali from destruction by the larger islands that surround it, he was referring not only to the ceremonial rituals of yadnya but to the ancient religious texts (sastra) that give those rituals meaning. Moments before Kodi had made his entrance that evening, another performer had reminded the audience of the fifteenth century King Kepakisan, who was not accepted as a legitimate ruler of Bali until he agreed to restore the archeological remains of Bali's ancient temples and abide by the teachings of its sacred texts.

Shortly after the reference to King Kepakisan, another character enters the stage singing a song that is quoted directly from one of the lontar manuscripts. Although the character that sings it is a buffoonish lout that entertains the audience with silly walks and slapstick falls, the song itself is a lyrical and abstract meditation on the necessity of freeing oneself from the illusions of the world. A world that prevents human beings from differentiating between spiritual truth and the traps of the material world. The song reminds the audience that good and evil are interwoven into the fabric of life, and that it is important to see past the surface value of people and events that one encounters in the world. It ends with a zen-like enigma, "Let us go now to search for that which is contained in emptiness." ("Jalan jani ruruh isin ne suwunge.") Songs like this are interspersed into every penasar's performance.

Penonton

In addition to lingkungan and sastra the third intangible element of a Balinese performer's training is an ongoing interaction with the audience ("penonton"). Balinese performances are usually staged in close proximity to an audience crowded around actors in a temple courtyard. The actors continually change their improvised dialogue in response to the moods and needs of the audience, so that no two performances of the same story are ever equivalent. Each performer is obligated to tailor the evening's story to the specific needs of the event.

The principles by which a performer is expected to adapt each performance to the needs of the audience are known as "Desa, Kala, Patra." Desa means village or place. Kala means time. Patra means situation. The choice of which story will be told in any given performance is always based on the history of the place in which the play is being acted. And the way in which the story is told depends entirely upon the circumstances in which the audience finds itself. In the story quoted above, Kodi's reference to yadnya as a weapon that is essential to the cultures survival is a response to another character's mockery of tourism. Balinese and English words were used to create bilingual puns, setting up a tension between the island's traditions and influences from outsiders. Kodi's endorsement of yadnya is introduced as a reassuring path to keeping that tension in balance. The influence of tourism on Balinese traditional culture is an issue of crucial importance in the late nineteen nineties and the performers acknowledge this by inserting these modern puns into a story that begins with the reign of a fifteenth century king who achieves legitimacy by preserving the teachings, rituals, and temples of the past.

The interweaving of time frames is used by the penasar to connect the audience to a story that might otherwise seem distant. It is the audience's laughter and encouraging response to this type of frame-breaking that encourages the penasar to go further in adapting a story to the particular circumstances of the audiences. As the penasar gets positive feedback for his joking references to the name of the village, the names of local politicians in attendance, and the topical issues of local concern, he subtly takes the performance in the direction that the audience wants to go. One segment, for instance, is full of sexual innuendos, related to the ruling political party's election slogan encouraging voters to "stick it in the middle'" (this party's place on the ballot is in the center between the other two party choices). The more the audience laughs at these double entendres, the more the clowns provide. Because the performances are improvised, these types of audience-inspired side-tracks are common in Bali. Plots are sometimes reduced to excuses for entertaining and informative diversions that bond the actors and the audience in an interactive exploration of topics both trivial and profound.

As the penasar shifts the dialogue in response to the audience's urgings, it is not only the play that is being shaped. The performer himself is being trained by the audience to respond to its impulses. This is an aspect of performance training that happens primarily when the actor is onstage, but even before a play begins actors have the opportunity to eat and chat with their hosts. Shrewd performers use this social warm-up to gather tidbits of gossip and current events that they incorporate into their onstage improvisations. Early in their careers it becomes clear that some actors are better than others at listening to the audience and creating a performance that rises organically from the interaction between the spectators and the players. These are the ones who go on to long and respected careers, and are invited back repeatedly to perform in villages where they have succeeded in establishing a rapport with the public.

Conclusion

While western observers often focus on the physical virtuosity of Balinese performance, and the corporal training required to achieve that high standard, the Balinese themselves are equally interested in the more intangible linguistic, philosophical, religious, historical, and topical elements of the performance which require a subtler kind of training that is almost invisible.

These less tangible elements of Balinese performance are inextricably intertwined with the culture's adherence to yadnya, the complex web of activities that fulfill their obligations to their gods, ancestors, and natural environment. A Balinese performer in training must be intimately familiar with the rules of yadnya and the ways in which they link a village community to its heritage, and help the culture at large survive in the face of destructive influences from outside Bali.

Even though it is impossible to trace a precise training path that will enable a performer to translate the complexities of yadnya into entertaining and thought-provoking theatrical terms, a few essential elements can be specified. First, an actor must have the opportunity to assimilate skills from his natural and social environment (lingkungan) , and develop the sensitivity to remain attentive to information his environment is providing him. Second, an actor must study the historic and religious teachings preserved on palm leaf manuscripts (sastra) . And third, and actor must learn to interact with an audience in a way that connects them both to the immediacy of the issues being dramatized in the play.

When a Balinese performer succeeds in integrating all these skills and techniques into a performance that captivates an audience at the same time that it connects them to their cultural heritage, that performer is said to have "taksu." This is the highest compliment a Balinese actor can receive. Taksu literally means, "the place that receives the light", and it is appropriate praise for a performer whose virtuosity lies not so much in what he can do, but in how receptive he can be to the multiple influences of spirituality, environment and community that give Balinese performance its primal power.

6

A STUDY IN MOTLEY: THE ODIN ACTORS

Janne Risum

(Auto)biography

"Motley's the only wear."[1] In his memoirs from the years 1917-22 in Russia, *Sentimental Journey*, the formalist critic Victor Shklovsky warns us, that if we did not try so hard to make history all the time, but rather tried to be responsible for the single events of which it consists, we might succeed in making ourselves less ridiculous. "We should not make history, but biography." He substitutes concrete thinking for abstract, and so adds the dimension of personal ethics.

A study in motley is a study in syncretism. When discussing the intercultural aspects of acting and actor's training in contemporary multicultural theatre groups such as the Odin Teatret, let us remember theatre is intercultural in its very approach. The stage of Ancient Athens was a sacred playground for worship and dance, consecrated to a powerful migrant god from Asia Minor. Here, after the Persian wars, Aeschylus staged contemporary tragedy, *The Persians*, in front of his victorious compatriots in 472 B.C.

Let us not cheer, or lament, the more recent products of modern migration unduly. Steamships, airplanes, and multicultural coexistence have certainly speeded up the process of cultural exchange. Yet they cannot invent, or prevent, what was already there: social intercourse.

An actor's biography, in the sense of Shklovsky, consists of personal actions. As a genre, autobiography emerged around 1770, when Rousseau wrote his *Confessions*. So did the first autobiographies written by European actors. As a genre, they testify to the close relations between autobiography, storytelling, and travelling. They have close ties to the educational novel (*Bildungsroman*), and to different types of novels based on diaries, letters, and travels. Working within an established convention, traditional actors more often than not portray their lives as having two phases: a local or stationary period of learning, and a more mobile period of accomplishment, which may include international touring. Marco de Marinis has investigated

---

1. Jacques in *As You Like It*, Act II, Scene 7.

a selection of actor's autobiographies in traditional theatre, from the first that were published to more recent ones. He summarizes their typical narrative macrostructure as "the double journey":

> the form that unites it resembles a **double journey**: the actor accomplishes the first through the different stages of his career, let us say from his début to his success; whereas the second is not symbolic, but his journey through the world, his tours, and – it is worth noting – this journey usually begins when the first has been completed, or almost been so.
>
> (De Marinis, 1995: 180)[2]

Sociological observations such as these highlight the main phases in the normal professional development of a traditional actor. They also point out the degree to which the writing actor simultaneously shapes his or her personal life, at least in retrospect. Yet they do not quite face the (inter)cultural and personal varieties of this development. While not forgetting context, we should center our study in the relation between poiesis and individuation when studying actor training. Actors write their most reliable artistic autobiographies while training, rehearsing, and performing.

If we compare the professional autobiographies of Zeami, Mei Lan-Fang, or Stanislavsky, we may read them as three different ways of recounting artistic lives in the context of a home culture. Yet if we look more deeply into them, this reveals itself as being only a partial truth, however valid it might be locally.

Most innovators in the fields of acting and performer training in the twentieth century are not confined to cultures of origin or the local language of single nation states. They have succeeded in substituting theatre as business and as a public institution with an international and intercultural archipelago of nomad and independent workshops, studios, laboratories, and groups. These may have no primary intention of public production. They may have no productions at all, only one production at a time, or might dissolve after having accomplished single theatrical events (Cruciani, 1985). Yet from these studios a new kind of theatre production has sprung, thoroughly dependent on personal signatures embedded in an intercultural approach. The corresponding actors' autobiographies are cultural hybrids.

Odin Teatret is a late offshoot of the intercultural landslide running through the studios of Stanislavsky and Copeau, Meyerhold and Decroux, Craig and Grotowski, Artaud and Hijikata, all of which merge various conventions of theatre into a new hybrid of personal forms. Coming to terms with the shocks of this landslide, we cannot limit ourselves to aesthetics.

---

2.   Translated by the author.

None of them did. Nor can we limit ourselves to cultural studies. None of them did. To paraphrase Shklovsky once more, their various choices rather suggest how to make our present artistic history equally viable, indeed worth living, by adopting the motley wear of complex contemporary biography.

After Four Weeks, We Were But Five

For many years Barba called himself and his actors autodidacts. They certainly are. But no more so than all the other hippies. Any actor starts like the Odin actors. From scratch. Eugenio's experience came from his years with Grotowski.

In Opole Eugenio had mostly watched, but in the performance *Akropolis* (1962) he worked as Grotowski's assistant on the sound montage and the rhythms of the actors' feet in the production. He assisted again in the 1963 production of *Dr. Faustus* (Watson, 1993:14; Kumiega, 1985:60, 66, 67). In the same year, Eugenio visited the Kathakali Kalamandalam at Cheruthuruthy. On his return, he introduced Kathakali exercises into Grotowski's training. The next year he formed Odin Teatret in Oslo. He summoned some young inexperienced people, who had applied in vain for admission to a theatre school. The idea of basing a theatre on a radical intercultural approach was still an almost complete novelty. Eugenio 1982:

> We are typical autodidacts. Nobody wanted us. When we began the theatre in Oslo, on the one hand there were some young people between seventeen and nineteen years old who applied for admission to a theatre school, but had failed. And on the other hand there was me, who had been to Poland, but only seen other people work. I had seen the work of Grotowski, but I had never worked practically myself. So in the beginning the most important thing for us was to learn something.
>
> (Barba, 1982)

This is Torgeir Wethal at seventeen, a well-behaved young Norwegian living with his middle class parents, having an appointment in a restaurant in Oslo with a stranger who called himself Barba on the phone and wants him to join a theatre group he plans to start. This is also Eugenio at twenty-seven, the immigrant son of one of Mussolini's officers who died shortly after the war, juggling at a restaurant table to attract his young listener. He shows him pictures of Kathakali exercises, and of Grotowski's actors training acrobatics and martial arts, or playing Faust standing on one leg. The voice that told the story of the pictures seduced Torgeir. Since he was nine, he had always acted as much as he possibly could. But certainly not in this way. Torgeir 1983:

> The dark little man with the blue jacket and the correct tie had set the **Dagbladet** [newspaper] to one side and spread the strangest pictures out over the table-top. (...)
>
> Close-up shots of two men using their fingers to spread their eyes wide open. A woman, making the most frightful grimaces. A man in white robes, standing on one leg on a table. A man lying on the floor with his legs spread in the air, while another man flew between them. Two men, hitting each other with sticks. (...)
>
> Madness - pure and simple madness, but exciting - and above all, excitingly told. A table as a performing area! Neither I nor anyone I knew had ever seen a theatre without a stage. And flying actors! And psychotechnique!? (in Christoffersen, 1993:41-42)

As her girlfriend told Else Marie Laukvik about Barba on the phone, "It's going to be really hard, it's very Oriental." This is Else Marie Laukvik at twenty-one, the daughter of an engineer, beginning her training with Eugenio after having been rejected twice by the Theatre School in Oslo. The time is 6p.m., October 1st, 1964. The place is a classroom in a school in Oslo:

> Like a frightened rat, I looked carefully around the classroom filled with people in black tights. (...) I began to do the same exercises as the people in tights. In the following months, I never asked myself whether this was better or worse than theatre school, whether it was good or bad.
>
> (Ibid: 28–29)

Eugenio sat on a stool and told them what to do. The exercises were purely physical and highly demanding. Else Marie:

> I remember that we had to crouch down and roll our shoulders at the same time. But it was impossible for me to roll my shoulders as much as a millimetre, in spite of the fact that Eugenio sat there on a stool like a pillar of salt and repeated over and over again, 'Up with the shoulders'. (...) I thought, 'You'll never manage this'. I was so stiff and sore, I could hardly go up and down stairs.

There were various kinds of exercises in those first months. There were Kathakali exercises, eye and hand exercises, there were some yoga exercises from Grotowski's training, there were mime exercises, ballet training.

(Ibid: 29-30)

Torgeir:

When I started with the Odin I had a body like a stick and no experience of physical theatre. Learning to do headstands and somersaults was so difficult ....

(in Watson, 1993:46)

After a few days Eugenio introduced improvisation. He asked them to follow whatever came into their minds, and react to it. Tiredness began to set in. The people in black tights began to leave. After the first week the group had been reduced by half. The number of those who stayed amounts to the fingers of a hand. Else Marie:

There were eleven of us when we first started, but after five or six days, there were only six of us left, and after four weeks, we were but five.

(in Christoffersen, 1993:29)

Eugenio recommended that the actors read the works of Stanislavski and Meyerhold, and study available material on Asian actors, especially Noh and Kabuki, and particularly postures documented in woodprints and photos. From this grew what they called their stock of *études*.[3]

Presenting their first performance *Ornitofilene* by the contemporary Norwegian author Jens Bjørneboe one year later (1965), the actors had been reduced in number to four. When Odin Teatret left Norway for Denmark in 1966, only three of them travelled along with Eugenio. In 1994, thirty years later, two are still with him. Else Marie and Torgeir. This process of selection through personal determination has been repeated in the life of the group ever since.

Training

Training at Odin Teatret was never only technical. From the beginning it was an autonomous and time-consuming daily work that had to be developed in steps that could not be forced. It was protected above anything else. As the group's greenhouse, or laboratory for growth, the training

---

3.   See Barba, 1979: 49; Watson, 1993.44.

created the inner resistance that made the performances possible. It is the apparent paradox of the Odin Theatre, that the training was always considered essential to the performances as their very foundation. It changed, however, according to their needs.

Arriving in Denmark in 1966, the Norwegian actors taught what they knew to their new Danish apprentices. Iben Nagel Rasmussen, who joined in 1966, remembers how much the inspiration from Asian theatre affected the exercises. Iben 1989:

> When I came to Odin Teatret, Eugenio's model for our education was that of the Asian actor. He used expressions like 'the Chinese principle' to indicate that a movement or an action should always begin in the opposite direction: if I want to go to the right, I begin with a step to the left. There were exercises for the face which had clearly been influenced by Kathakali. There was stick-fighting, which had a Japanese name. Eugenio explained how he had been fascinated by Kathakali when he was in India, and not only by the suggestive night-time performances, but particularly by the Kathakali actors' attitude towards their work. (...) As our work developed over the years, it was clearly not bringing us any closer to the East; on the contrary, the results were typically the fruit of our own time and situation. (...)
>
> In the technical preparation of our productions, those principles with the exotic names are still to be found, but not as foreign elements. They are the joints and nerves of Odin Teatret's body.
>
> (Ibid: 102-4)

Denmark also meant starting up a new and lasting activity: intensive training seminars with European and Asian actors at Odin Teatret in Holstebro, starting in 1966 with a seminar conducted by Grotowski and his leading actor Ryszard Cieslak. Barba expanded this activity in 1979 with his formation of the research network ISTA, the International School of Theatre Anthropology. When ISTA had its first session in Bonn, Germany, the Odin actors were already more than familiar with Asian acting techniques and continued their explorations in the new context of ISTA. Each of them had their own selective affinities and personal choices as to how useful the Asian actor techniques were for their work in light of the principles they had always built on since their very first day at the Odin.

Torgeir sums up the experience of the first years' training. It consisted of fixed elements. Many exercises came from the physical and plastic training that Grotowski's theatre laboratory had developed. Yet despite always doing those exercises with an imagined motivation, they slowly became caught up in their own psychic clichés. Torgeir 1983: "When we became aware of this, we chose to go the opposite way (Wethal 1983:18). "We chose to go the opposite way." What did this mean to the group of young actors then? It meant working on physical actions, and on what they called their score, or what Meyerhold called movement design (*risunok dvizenij*). It also appears that it meant going too far in the opposite direction at first. With Meyerhold, for example, we may call the Odin's most radical phase a case of "meyerholditis."[4]

In the years before 1970, the group frequently trained eight to twelve hours a day, six days a week. Each day was divided in two, teaching new actors and individual work. It became a cultivation of the body and an acquisition of skills comparable to the training of circus artists or professional athletes. Working to the breaking point or beyond; this meant building a personal endurance in the sense of psychophysical stamina. Torgeir 1983:

> It was hard. I don't believe it taught us anything as actors (but it was undoubtedly one of the reasons for the aggressiveness and inner competition which characterized the *Ferai* company). And yet some of us developed a psychic conditioning. If you could manage to survive that period, you could survive anything.
>
> (Wethal, 1983:18-19)

This changed after *Ferai* (1969). Until then all actors used a common stock of principles and skills in their training. However in 1970, Iben began to break away from this. To explore the quality and needs of her own voice and body, she developed a series of personal training experiments. Iben 1989:

> Energy can flow like a wave. The first time I understood this was when I saw Japanese actors. I understood purely intuitively that they modulate energy as a continuous wave.
> I had earlier had a natural resistance to training because it was so tiring. Later I developed a form of training which had a continuity, based on my own elements. various ways of sitting, of losing balance, of falling on the floor, of jumping

---

4. "On the 14 March, 1936, Meyerhold spoke in Leningrad on the theme 'Meyerhold against Meyerholditis': far from admitting his mistakes, he accused his imitators of propagating 'meyerholditis,' the plagiarising and indiscriminate application of his formal devices with no comprehension of their logical motivation" (Braun, 1986:61).

and turning in the room, establishing oppositions in the body and various directions in space by means of a concentration of energy in a direction opposite to that of the action's final goal. Like when you reach back with the arm before throwing something (sats).

I discovered that training has 'shadows.' work with the exercises but they also work with me. A clear example of this is the exercises based on failing. If they are done correctly, there is a little moment of lack of control where the body is off balance. At this moment, it is easy to see if the actor is cheating, if she is attempting to control the whole process herself.

(in Christoffersen, 1993:104-5)

Iben's example led to a gradual shift in direction. Torgeir 1983:

The biggest surprises which have occurred in the development of our training have come about because of the actors who, in spite of what Eugenio and the other actors thought, insisted on developing new work because of their own needs. Working against the group and for themselves, they brought us all further.

(Wethal, 1983:19)

My Father's House (1972) was a much more collective process. All roles had their equal share. The training for this performance was concerned with flow. Else Marie 1989:

The training was much shorter, more intense and freer. It was no longer skill training but impulse training, which is a warm and expressive training, a wave flowing through the body (...) with variations (...) just like in music. (...)

Neither Torgeir nor I trained very much during that period. We were tired after all the perfection training. But Iben continued to work and found new possibilities.

(in Christoffersen, 1993:36)

According to Else Marie the new softness in *My Father's House* was "in reaction to five years of discipline training: a kind of liberation."

For complex reasons, *My Father's House* stands out as the group's *rite of passage* to a first stage of maturity. Discipline matured as flow. All actors began to develop a personal training. Between 1972 and 1973, collective training was abandoned altogether, and Eugenio began to stay away from the training sessions.

In Torgeir Wethal's films from 1972 *Physical Training* at Odin Teatret and *Vocal Training at Odin Teatret*, you see five grave and committed people. They do not smile even once. They are Eugenio, Torgeir, Iben, Tage Larsen, and Jens Christensen. The actors are thin and highly-trained. The male actors have bare chests and very long hair. In the first film, they take turns demonstrating their exercises. With remarkable precision, they perform impressive acrobatic feats. It looks like a drill. They begin to improvise more freely, with a partner or alone. Iben joins them on the floor. They repeat patterns such as pushing the chest of their partner with their foot. The influence of martial arts and of Meyerhold's Biomechanics is obvious. The improvisations in pairs are concerned with absolute confidence in the partner. The solo improvisations are concerned with flow. The grave introversion of their presence is as great as the perfected extroversion of their actions. The only one who speaks is Eugenio. He is tense and concentrated. As if speaking from a state of deep introspection, he hardly looks into the camera. He says that this is not a theatre school. There is nothing to "learn." The actors' training is personal. Its aim is not to perfect skills, but to develop goals and capacities as human beings. Eugenio 1972: "Training is an encounter with the reality which one has chosen. Whatever you do, do it with your whole self" (in Wethal, 1972). He speaks the *credo* of his theatre. The performances have done nothing but embody this in various ways.

The chosen reality has not always been quite the same, however. In the white rehearsal room in 1972, it was very grave and committed indeed. Iben 1979:

> There is a moment in the Odin voice-training film where, after my improvisation, I sit down beside Eugenio and he strokes my hair. Certain people have seen this as an image of a girl who, having finished her improvisation, returns to the role of docile instrument in the hands of her director, kneeling beside him. Some have compared Eugenio's gesture to that of a trainer after an animal has properly performed its exercises.
>
> But the quality of a work-relationship is not merely defined by original techniques and artistic results, but also by exertion, fatigue, and human warmth. All of this is clear to me. Yet people who talk so much of 'different' and 'more profound' human relationships, when actually face to face with the difference of such relationships, think merely of zoos and asylums.
>
> (Rasmussen, 1991)

Joining in 1974, Roberta Carreri was the last actor to be trained by Eugenio. Roberta 1989:

> For the first twelve years of the group's work, Eugenio was in the room every morning when the actors trained.
> I came in the tenth year. This means that after the first two years of my apprenticeship, during which time Eugenio followed my work very closely, I was left to myself in the training. I learned very quickly to train alone. Eugenio watched my training every once in a while and gave me certain key words with which to work further.
> I was the last actor to be trained by Eugenio himself, from zero. Other actors came after me but then it was some of the older colleagues who took on the responsibility for teaching them. Iben and Tage started what became called adoption.
> The theatre was formed during those first ten years.
>
> (in Christoffersen, 1993:60)

Roberta 1993:

> We have different experiences. Torgeir had been with the Odin for ten years when I joined the group. He stopped training shortly after I arrived. The training during the first decade was so brutal that he didn't want to train anymore. Iben came eight years before me. She and another colleague had developed a personal training, a language which was their own. When I came, I just learned what Torgeir and Iben knew, they taught me. Then I began elaborating my own training. My elaborations were inspired by other cultures.
>
> (1993:17-18)

Roberta sums up the basic training principle during the first two decades as: expressivity in space. Roberta 1989:

> The first eight years of my work at Odin Teatret were concentrated on how to send energy out into the space with large movements, on trying to fill the space with energy. This had become quite automatic. I would work without using my brain. My body knew how to work by itself. The training carried me. I was not directing it. My body flowed with the stream of energy that it had been my goal to dive into for many years.
>
> (in Christoffersen, 1993:150)

Carpignano 1974. Like an Emotional Meteor Let Out Into Open Air

Their voices are young and soft. Their cheeks still have the roundness of youth. The men have long hair. The women have short haircuts falling in soft curves. They are from Norway, Denmark, and Italy. Dressed in bright colours, the actors make acrobatic exercises and dance with flags in the wind in a deserted courtyard. Eugenio goes to and fro and directs them. He has grown an impressive full beard that gives him the sinister appearance of a mask, which almost, but not quite, succeeds in concealing his quick eyes and his youthful agility. They all have an energetic, determined, and vulnerable look. The acrobatic skills of some of the actors are impressive. Others are quite inexperienced. This is an Italian television documentary on Odin Teatret's stay in Carpignano, Southern Italy, in 1974.[5] It is a little uncanny to meet them in this way on a video.

Their rare smiles stand out. To a committed person, there was little to smile at in Europe in 1974. The speed with which we were confronted with global political disasters was a shock to our values. The war in Vietnam, The *golpe* in Chile in 1973.

At sunrise the actors walk out to practice in the landscape. With its olive groves slowly being colored by the first rays of the sun, it is extremely beautiful. Each actor does his or her own individual exercises and vocal training. They move as trees among trees, or like animals passing softly. In their words to the microphone, they already look back upon their short lives.

With the typical appearance of a male left-wing highbrow in the 1970s, a stern professor who calls himself Eugenio Barba looks into the camera from behind dark-rimmed spectacles. He is trying to explain what they are doing here in this deserted village.

> Training is the only possibility that the actors have to demonstrate that they want to transform their intentions into actions. It's difficult to put into words. It's like an emotional meteor that cannot be halted. But they have only one possibility. To demonstrate that these intentions may be transformed into actions through their training. It's the proof of a conviction, of a necessity to transform personal needs into actions. There is a need, through theatre, to break this layer and see the flesh, the blood. It may not be a pretty sight, but it's alive and it makes us react.
>
> (in Ripa di Meana, 1974)

---

5.   See Ripa di Meana, 1974

They still have a long process of individuation ahead of them. But in their voices and behaviour you already see the contours of their mature personalities.)

The actors train in a deserted factory. The room has pillars and green walls. It is filled with a strong, indirect light. The sun must be blazing outside. They follow their own individual rhythms. Iben moves backwards. She repeats a short sequence of physical actions. Her hair is very short and partly wet. Her eyes and her voice seem to entreat an invisible person in front of her. Suddenly she moves her head backwards to the right with a sharp jerk. Her short wet hair spreads and stands out from her skull. She conveys a transitory image of a female victim, faintly reminiscent of the face of Maria Falconetti in Dreyer's *Jeanne D'Arc*. Almost imperceptibly Iben makes a short stop, as she converts her movements by beginning to move backwards again repeating her plea.

Her improvisation is a pattern of repetitions. She explores a score that has not been quite fixed yet. Each gesture is born anew, as in an improvised solo by a jazz musician. She is working on that project which is perhaps the core of the group's work: how to keep the improvisation impulses alive in a repeated pattern. Her improvisation still pulsates as impulses and spontaneous reactions. The uninterrupted speed with which she moves supports the flow of her movements.

Eugenio tells the camera that after *My Father's House*, they don't know what their next performance is going to be. All he can say is that it is about seven people starting out on a journey to discover something within themselves. Other theatre groups have announced similar things when they really didn't know what they were about to do. In retrospect, what did they find after creating the dance performance *The Book of Dances* (1974) in Carpignano? If you saw *Come! And the day will be ours* (1976), it is difficult not to connect an exercise like Iben's, the strong and vulnerable jerks of her head in the deserted factory, with her character of the Indian shaman she plays in the latter.

In her white half-mask, Iben also goes alone to several villages with her drum to make barters in the streets and houses. In some cases Torgeir follows with his camera, documenting for his film *Vestita di bianco* (*Dressed in White*). During a new solo barter in Sardinia in 1975, Iben states the fundamental likeness between such barters and what she already knows, improvisation:

> To begin with, I thought it was the first time I had done something like this, alone, but afterwards I decided that it was similar to an improvisation. It involved the same way of facing a situation, with no idea of a beginning, but remaining open only to what happens. It is not that one thinks of being

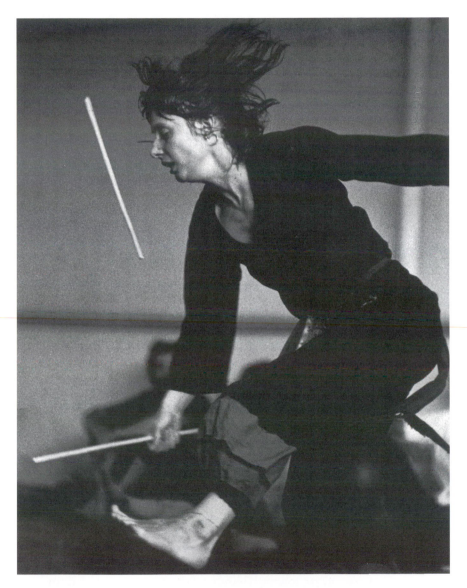

Iben Nagel Rasmussen training with small sticks. Photo: Odin Teatret

open, it is simply a matter of being so. In both instances it is like a journey which has only a certain point of departure and whose destination I don't know. It is a matter of being ready.

(in Watson, 1993:79)

Et in Arcadia ego. The long summer of barters in Carpignano, May to September 1974, has the Utopian quality of a dream coming true among olive trees in the middle of nowhere. A professional theatre cannot live in Utopia forever, but it can camp there for quite a long time. Carpignano was only a beginning for the Odin. Here in the olive groves and narrow streets the usual boundaries between training, rehearsal, performance, and community were radically suspended in favour of new combinations that made a return to the former status quo impossible. It was, in fact, an old dream come true. Eugenio's impressions of the Kathakali actor's devoted life materialized as a self-made Western counterpart with classical European roots. Iben 1989:

> When I look back at one of the strongest, most beautiful and most important fruits which our work has produced, it strikes me that I recognize in it many of the elements that had fascinated Eugenio twenty years before [watching the night-time performances of Kathakali and the Kathakali actors' attitudes toward their work], but it has gone through such a transformation that no one, certainly not Eugenio himself, has noticed it.
>
> I'm thinking about our stay in southern Italy, where we made *The Book of Dances* and *Johann Sebastian Bach* [a clown performance]. There, under the Italian sun, and with all the daily problems, I think that the last thing on our minds was Asia and Asian actors. We wanted to be ourselves, fully and completely, and yet it was as if Eugenio's old dream melded both with our daily life and also with the dream that certain young Scandinavians had of being able to live and work in a way that was different from the usual.
>
> Vocal training began at 5.00 a.m., outside town or by the sea. After breakfast, we continued training, After training came performance work. In the evenings we did barters in the surrounding towns. These barters could sometimes, in one single evening, bring an otherwise divided and disparate village back together. We lived together and the practical work in the house was part of the daily programme.

(in Christoffersen, 1993:103-4)

This social model: the utopian artistic community going out to meet the schisms of the surrounding culture, is perhaps the closest one can get to a definition of actors and acting according to the Odin performers then. Paradoxically, it had catapulted from almost total seclusion in the middle of other nowheres: training underground in an air raid shelter in Oslo, or in a converted farm in Holstebro.

In Carpignano, Torgeir performs a vigorous acrobatic dance with a stick. He already wears the pale pink half-mask, in which he is going to appear for many years to come, as a sort of cock in a Latin American cock fight. Four years later, in 1978 in Ayacucho, Peru he performs his cock in a new way – always jumping around in a squatting position. The character is a pink dwarf carrying a whistle and a walking cane that he uses as a drum-major's baton. On film, Torgeir's pink dwarf cock, courageously advancing with his cane and his whistle in the streets of Lima in 1978, is extravagantly crazy when it tries to resist and attack the black, giant representatives of death and dictatorship on stilts. It is the world turned upside down. The Odin actors insist that they are visiting strangers obeying the law to the letter. In doing so they commit a more sincere worship of the spirit of carnival, than any dictatorial restrictions of carnival, theatre, and human rights ever dreamt of prohibiting. Obviously they were idealists, thinking that the social ritual of theatre mattered and might outwit its own prohibition on moral grounds.

Reduction

When the Odin actors began to construct their scores by using videotapes of their improvisations, rehearsals changed. They began to work with the director only in the final montage of the performance. Iben 1989:

> During the first years, Eugenio watched everything. He observed all the training and all of our improvisations. The actors wrote down the various improvisations and Eugenio took part in their reconstruction. Later, when we began to use video to reconstruct the improvisations, particularly during the work on *Come!...*, we were often alone. It was the first step. Eugenio began to withdraw from the actors' preparatory work and training.
>
> (Ibid:1993:97-98)

Around 1977, the Odin actors began to change direction in their training, from working on stimulus-response, to working on energy. The former emphasis on expressivity in space gave way to an exploration of

segmentation and reduction of expression. This gradual development did
not involve a break with past training principles. On the contrary, the actors
began to distill their basic principles even more and to apply them for new
purposes. Torgeir 1985:

> To stand on one's head involves mastering particular technical
> skills such as placement of the hands, legs, and head, and the
> adjustment of body weight and balance. It also involves the
> principle of shifting the body's weight quickly so that one is
> off-balance, finding a point of equilibrium which is held for a
> period, and returning to the normal body position. Standing
> on one's head is a skill that has to be learned, the principle
> underlying it, meanwhile, can be applied to many situations
> including walking, sitting, and working with a requisite.
>
> (in Watson, 1993.63)

Roberta 1989:

> In 1981, when Eugenio returned from ISTA in Volterra, Italy,
> he presented us with a new exercise. We were to sit on the
> floor and move one joint at a time. wrist, shoulder, elbow,
> neck, the eyes. We called it the segmenting exercise.
>
> (in Christoffersen, 1993:150)

Training with the Japanese Nihon Buyo Dancer Katsuko Azuma during
the first ISTA in 1980 in Bonn, Germany Roberta had already started to
move in this direction. Still she found the transition hard in 1981:

> I had to force myself not to move. So I sat down in a chair. (...)
> I worked at moving only one joint at a time. Right down to
> the smallest details like the eyes: first seeing only 5 metres in
> front of you, then 10 metres, and then 100. The exercise became
> part of my daily training.
>
> (Ibid:150)

From her daily segmenting exercise in the deck chair slowly emerged her
solo performance *Judith* (1987). She states in 1989:

> In fact, it is possible for an audience to feel the smallest change
> in tension just as if it were being shown on a huge cinema
> screen.
>
> (Ibid:155)

Individual training at the Odin Teatret. Photo: C. Falke

Torgeir 1983/1989:

> For a long time, I didn't take part in the training. I stopped
> several years ago, for certain very specific reasons. I wasn't
> getting any further with it, it had become barren ground for
> me. It wasn't something which held me. It had slowly become
> more difficult to materialize ideas and needs as 'sprouts' in
> the training situation.
>
> (Ibid:107)

The performances kept him in shape. However, rehearsing and touring *The
Gospel According to Oxyrhyncus* (1985), he performed a physically very static
character and realized he was getting out of shape. He began training again
on his own terms, working with motivation as well as with reduction of his
actions. Torgeir 1989:

> So at the moment I am trying to go back to a combination of
> good old acrobatics and basic physical training. (...)
>   But at the same time, it's also very exciting right now to
> find out what possibilities I have to fill a space with presence

by using very limited physical actions, with less activity than before. This is a point one should first permit oneself to be fascinated by after having gone through the opposite. Purely technically, it is the same as it is with any form of training or expression. It has to do with certain tensions, certain directions in space and, most of all, with a combination of various directions at the same time. An action which is unequivocal and which follows only its own speed and direction will never be as fascinating as the action which contains built-in oppositions.

With respect to these minimal physical actions, I am currently training with a 'why' for every single movement. I extend my hand and turn my wrist because I am touching or want to touch something specific, rather than just doing the action. If you begin to work in this way, you begin to develop small action patterns which have a simple basis above and beyond the technical.

You choose a principle: I work with at least three directions in the body at the same time, all of which must have a specific basis.

(Ibid: 107-8)

The training has remained individual. The actors work with various principles and investigations, following their own personal choices. They can work with anything, including motivation. Torgeir 1989:

Today, the training is based on an almost cold, technical analysis. Eugenio will never interfere in the actor's 'why,' he is only interested in the set action patterns and in the usable energy which they contain. It is left completely up to the actor himself to fill out and motivate his action, or not.

(Ibid. 50)

Iben 1989:

Ballet dancers, for example, stop dancing quite early. Is the same going to be true for us? Or can we do something exciting, something which is not just an unsuccessful repetition of the efforts of our youth? This is something I was very interested in during the work on *Marriage With God* [with César Brie, performed 1984-90].

> In Asian theatre, the masters are often 50 or 60 years old or older. If you are trained into top form when you are young, then it is possible to keep the energy in your actions when you are older. The release of energy in space can be diminished without the same thing happening to the intensity. (...) It is relatively easy to take an action which has occupied a lot of space and diminish it, but the opposite doesn't apply.
>
> (Ibid:107)

In the beginning of the 1990s wear and tear also forced some of the older actors to reduce their training. Not all of them train regularly, and they often pursue quite different goals.

Distillations

In 1985 Barba wrote a central essay, *The Dilated Body*. He compares the quantum leaps in the work of an actor and director with their personal and artistic developments. He speaks of experiences which all serious actors know. One sentence especially speaks in a familiar voice:

> In the course of my experience as a director, I have observed an analogous process occurring in me and in some of my companions: the long daily work on physical training, transformed over the years, slowly became distilled into internal patterns of energy which could be applied to the way of conceiving or composing a dramatic action, of speaking in public, of writing. (1985:15)

It speaks of the individuation that Eugenio senses taking place in the actors and himself as they work and mature together. He shares this knowledge with Stanislavsky. The core of it is that as an actor you work upon yourself. This professional privilege is a personal chance to resist a mutilation, corruption, or inflation of your personality, and to develop some of the rich and mature creativity that human beings are capable of.

Julia Varley proposes that the different aesthetic values of contemporary theatre groups, as they appear in their performances, are not primarily due to an abstract choice of aesthetics, but to the personal needs of the members of the group, as well as the social structure and way of working they have found to meet their needs the most. Julia 1990:

> (...) theatre groups have created some generally identifiable procedures which are more connected to a group's social

Roberta Carreri and I Made Bandem during a work demonstration at the International School of Theatre Anthropology (1987). Photo: Tony D'Urso

structure than to aesthetic values. So the dramaturgy that can
be recognized in the performances of these groups is more a
consequence of the ways of working, of the needs which have
brought the persons together in search for a sense in their
profession, than the other way around.

(1990:8)

The Odin actors have developed a plurality of competences. They cultivate
their professional competences as actors in training and performances. As
in Commedia dell'Arte, since 1974 the Odin actors have created their own
original set of stock characters, or alter egos. Each character is a crosscultural
hybrid. Wherever they tour, they go out in the street to improvise with
them. Some are still performed by the actor who created them, while others
have been passed on to new actors. The actors also present work
demonstrations, conduct training seminars, work as organizers on special
projects within the theatre, work as directors, or write articles and edit books.
All of them speak several languages.

The dancer as the director's puppeteer. I Made Bandem and Eugenio Barba during a work
demonstration at ISTA in Salento, Italy (1987). Photo: Tony D'Urso

All experienced Odin actors present solo work demonstrations. Iben Nagel Rasmussen, *Moon and Darkness*, on her training and creation of scores (since 1979, filmed 1981), and *White as Jasmin* on her vocal work (since 1995). Roberta Carreri, *Traces in the Snow*, on her technique in building a score or a character (since 1989, filmed 1994). Julia Varley, *The Echo of Silence*, on her vocal work (since 1991), and *The Dead Brother*, on her work with poetic text (both filmed 1993). Torgeir Wethal, *The Paths of Thought*, on his creation of scores as motivated montages (since 1993). Iben, Julia, and Else Marie especially, have worked as directors several times.

All Odin actors have written, or given interviews, about their work. A selection was published in 1993 by Exe Christoffersen in the book *The Actor's Way*. Else Marie, Torgeir, Iben, and Julia have also published essays on their own work.

Travelling with Socrates

When the Odin Teatret was founded in 1964, an intercultural theatre group in Europe was a novelty. It no longer is. In the Nordic theatre laboratory in rural Holstebro the migrant actors have matured, while even society at home has been catching up with the theatre.

As members of a theatre with high artistic standards that travels constantly, the Odin actors have never really separated their two *"journeys."* Their artistic and geographical journeys have been concentric. They multiply personal crosslights by cultural-crossroads. I would not call that an easy artistic life, but definitely a coherent contemporary one. Intercultural from the outset, the training at Odin Teatret has enabled its actors to go between cultures, by presenting them with a motley but closely-knit bundle of personal cultures.

References

Barba, Eugenio (1979). *The Floating Islands*. Holstebro: Drama.
    (1982). Interview with Stig Krabbe Barfoed. In **Barfoed: Et vestjydsk verdensteater** (A World Theatre in West Jutland). Danish television.
    (1985). *The Dilated Body. The Gospel According to Oxyrhyncus*. Rome. Zeami Libri. The essay is reprinted in Barba 1993 and 1995.
Braun, Edward (1986). *The Theatre of Meyerhold*, London: Methuen (1979).
Carreri, Roberta (1993). "Interculturalism and the Individual Performer. An Interview with Roberta Carreri", by Ian Watson, New York, 25 January 1993. Ms., 24 p. Printed as "Territories of the Body. A Conversation". in: Hastrup (ed.) 1996, pp. 106-113.
Christoffersen, Erik Exe ed. (1993). *The Actor's Way*, London and New York: Routledge.

Cruciani, Fabrizio (1985). *Registi pedagoghi e comunita' teatrali nel novecento*, Firenze: Sansoni.

De Marinis, Marco (1995). *"Maschere allo specchio. Appunti per un'indagine sulle autobiografie degli attori fra XVIII e XX secolo"* (1990), in: *Annali della facoltà d di lettere e filosofia* (1992-93), Università di Macerata, 1995, p. 173-202.

Gordon, Mel (1987) *The Stanislavsky Technique: Russia: A Workbook for Actors*, New York: Applause Theatre Books.

Kumiega, Jennifer (1985). *The Theatre of Grotowski*, London and New York: Methuen.

Rasmussen, Iben Nagel (1991). "The Mutes of the Past: Responses to a Questioning Spectator." In the program of her production Itsi Bitsi. Translated by Richard Fowler.

Ripa di Meana, Ludivico (1974). In *cerca di teatro. L'Odin Teatret di Eugenio Barba nel Salento*. A 16 mm film made with the collaboration of Claudio Barbati, Mario Raimondi and Ferdinando Taviani. RAI.

Stanislavski, Constantin (1981), *Stanislavski's Legacy*, Elizabeth Reynolds Hapgood, London: Methuen (1958).

Varley, Julia (1990). "Venturing on a foreign ground (*Reflections on stage directing*)". ms., 1990, 10 p.

Watson, Ian (1993). *Towards a Third Theatre. Eugenio Barba and the Odin Teatret*. London and New York: Routledge.

Wethal, Torgeir (1983). *"Et kapittel til Odin Teatrets skuespilleres bok"*, ms., 1983. 70 p.

[director] (1972). *Physical Training at Odin Teatret/Vocal Training at Odin Teatret*. 16 mm films and video cassettes co-produced by Odin Teatret Film and RAI.

7

AMBIVALENT POSITIONINGS: GROTOWSKI'S ART AS VEHICLE AND THE PARADOX OF CATEGORIZATION

Lisa Wolford

Jerzy Grotowski is hailed as one of the foremost stage directors and performance theorists of the twentieth century, despite the fact that he created public performances for only a short portion of his multi-faceted career. As leader and artistic director of Poland's Teatr Laboratorium, Grotowski directed eleven original performances over the course of ten years, establishing an international reputation for himself and for the actors of his company. In 1970, two years after the premiere of his acclaimed masterwork, *Apocalypsis cum figuris*, Grotowski announced that he no longer intended to develop new productions; rather than repeating his prior achievements, he preferred to shift his professional activity toward hitherto unexplored areas at the intersection of performance, anthropology and ritual studies. "My work as a director, in the classical sense, was something beautiful," Grotowski mused, years later. "But a certain automatism had begun to encroach. What are you doing? *Othello*. And after? After, I.... One can become mechanical" (Thibaudat 1989:36)

Rather than quietly disappearing from the cultural landscape or returning to his erstwhile craft as a stage director, Grotowski has maintained an active and continually evolving exploration into the range and boundaries of performative phenomena. This research has coalesced in the form of four distinct projects: Paratheatre or Theatre of Participation (1969-1973), Theatre of Sources (1976-1982), Objective Drama (1983-1986), and Art as vehicle (1986-present).[1] Each of the disparate phases of Grotowski's post-theatrical research shares certain basic elements, specifically a focus on the immediate, physical presence of the actor (in the etymological sense of "one who does"). Each project has been shielded, to greater or lesser extent, from public view; during each phase of his activity, Grotowski has reconfigured or marginalized the conventionally passive role of the spectator.

---

1. See Osinski, 1991 for a brief overview of Grotowski's theatrical and post-theatrical work.

Grotowski himself finds nothing shocking or self-contradictory in the unusual course of his creative journey:

> In appearance, and for some people in a scandalous or incomprehensible manner, I passed through very contradictory periods. but in truth [...] the line is quite direct. I have always sought to prolong the investigation, but when one arrives at a certain point, in order to take a step forward, one must enlarge the field. The emphases shift. [...] Some historians speak of cuts in my itinerary, but I have more the impression of a thread which I have followed, like Ariadne's thread in the labyrinth, one sole thread. And I am still catching clusters of interests that I had also before doing theatre, as if everything must rejoin.
>
> (Thibaudat 1995:29)

Grotowski sees the various phases of his work as being unified by certain consistent desires and questions, interests that have fascinated him since childhood, long before he ever thought of pursuing work in the field of theatre. He suggests that the underlying impulses of his work would have remained much the same even if he had chosen to pursue a career in a different field.

From Grotowski's viewpoint, theatre, in the conventional sense, is something pertaining to his past, a practice with which he has not occupied himself for more than twenty years. From a different perspective, however, it is necessary to acknowledge a certain ambiguity in terms of Grotowski's position vis-a-vis the theatre, since it is impossible to deny that the generous institutional support accorded his post-theatrical research was given at least partially in deference to his status as cultural icon, a position he achieved by means of his accomplishments as a stage director, as well as his contributions as a teacher, writer and acting theorist. Further, it seems clear that however Grotowski himself may attempt to situate his work, a majority of his collaborators (as well as a majority of persons who maintain interest in his research) are theatre professionals; despite Grotowski's longstanding efforts to distance himself from conventional forms of theatrical production, it is the theatre, first and foremost, that concerns itself with his ongoing work. Among persons who have followed Grotowski's work from a relative distance, two basic questions seem to recur: What is Grotowski actually doing? And what – if anything – does this work have to do with theatre as it is normally practised?

An Itinerary in Verticality

The three most recent phases of Grotowski's research, while by no means identical in terms of their goals and objectives, are united by a shared emphasis on performative behaviors derived from the ritual traditions of various cultures. Grotowski posits that certain performance elements (e.g., particular songs or ways of moving) can exert a tangible impact on practitioners, affecting the physical, psychological and energetic state of the doer(s) in precise and measurable ways. Through extensive fieldwork and applied practice, Grotowski has sought both to identify such elements and to understand the process by which they function.

"Art as vehicle," which Grotowski describes as the culminating stage of his lifelong research, is a practical work developed since 1986 at the Workcenter of Jerzy Grotowski in Pontedera, Italy, under the auspices of the Centro per la Sperimentazione e la Ricerca Teatrale. According to Grotowski, Art as vehicle focuses on "actions related to very ancient songs which traditionally served ritual purposes, and so can have a direct impact on—so to say—the head, the heart and the body of the doers" (Thibaudat 1995:29). Grotowski's work is founded on the premise that these special songs, which he refers to as "ancient vibratory songs," can serve the practitioner as a tool for activating a process that creates a transformation from one quality of energy (gross) to another (subtle). He speaks of this inner process as a type of "itinerary in verticality":

> Verticality – we can see this phenomenon in categories of energy: heavy but organic energies (linked to the forces of life, to instincts, to sensuality) and other energies, more subtle. The question of verticality means to pass from a so-called coarse level – in a certain sense, one could say an "everyday level" – to a level of energy more subtle or even toward the higher connection. [...] There, there is another passage as well: if one approaches the higher connection – that means, if we are speaking in terms of energy, if one approaches the much more subtle energy – then there is also the question of descending, while at the same time bringing this subtle something into the more common reality, which is linked to the "density" of the body.
>
> (Grotowski 1995:125)

Art as vehicle explicitly shifts the locus of meaning away from its conventional place in the perception of the spectator, relocating it (and it is precisely in this respect that Grotowski's recent work most closely corresponds to traditional ritual practices) in the experience of those who do. The basic impulse of the work is autotelic, concerned with performative elements as a tool by means of which the human being can undertake a work on her/himself. Grotowski attempts to reconstitute a type of performance which he describes in terms of "art as a way of knowledge" (Sullivan 1983:42), a form of art that is in itself an initiatory practice.

The name by which Grotowski refers to this body of investigation is taken from a talk delivered by Peter Brook in 1987, "Grotowski, Art as a Vehicle." Brook observes that Grotowski is looking for "something which existed in the past but has been forgotten over centuries and centuries; that is, that one of the vehicles which allows man to have access to another level and to serve more rightly his function in the universe is – as the means of understanding – the performing art in all its forms" (1988:34). Brook articulates Grotowski's concern with performance as a means to an end similar to the way in which certain orders of monks have historically used music or the making of liqueurs to give form and structure to their inner search. Speculating on the implications of Grotowski's current research for professional theatre, Brook asserts that the hidden work of the laboratory exerts a strong and vital influence on other forms of theatre work, even if this influence appears indirect. In stating his conviction regarding the "living, permanent relationship between the work of research that is without public witness and the immediate nourishment that this can give to the public work" (1988:33), Brook suggests that the relation of Grotowski's Workcenter to the broader realm of theatre is analogous to that between the monastery and the Church. While Brook never goes so far as to say that he believes Grotowski's current practice can be understood as theatre, he maintains that such a rigorous investigation into the mystery of the actor's art as that conducted by Grotowski and his collaborators will have far-reaching influence, even if only a small number of persons come into direct contact with the work.

Horizontal and Vertical Dimensions of the Performance Score

The day-to-day activities of practical work in Art as vehicle concentrate primarily on the development and execution of performance pieces, what Grotowski and his collaborators call Actions – repeatable, precisely-scored works that are dissimilar to a theatrical production in terms of structure and detail. Working under the direction of Thomas Richards, Grotowski's essential collaborator and primary doer in the structures created by his group, members of the research team in residence at the Workcenter develop a set score of physical actions which support the more elusive and internalized process of work on the vibratory songs; these songs, derived primarily from African and Afro-Caribbean traditions provide the axis of the structure, since they are the tools that serve as catalyst for the subtle process of energy transformation. The Actions developed at the Workcenter are perhaps more easily apprehended as a variety of dance theatre than as narrative performance, though a fragmentary story is discernible in certain Actions, and passages of text (derived from scriptural rather than dramatic sources) "interspersed with musical materials. These performance structures, which are rigorously rehearsed, are developed over relatively long periods of time, sometimes several years.

Both Richards and Grotowski emphasize that in the practical, day-to-day work of Art as vehicle, there is no discussion of qualities of energy or the question of a "vertical itinerary." "In our work, it's much more that we simply sing and work on the line of actions around the songs" (Richards 1995:53). The language of daily work is a language of craft, overtly directed toward developing participants' acting skills. The more subtle elements of the ritual songs are never directly addressed; the attention of the practitioners, especially in early stages of work, is focused much more explicitly on the external structure of the performance, elements that comprise an "acting score" in a fairly conventional sense of the word. Richards notes that is possible for a given song, as a result of its particular impact or energy signature, to suggest a specific usage or life-situation; this can provide the basis for development of a corresponding fragment of the acting score. He observes that one of the songs in the cycle with which the group is currently working is clearly a funeral song. "We see that this song is a funeral song, so we approach it, as one possibility, like actors working on the situation of a funeral" (Richards 1995:26). Richards suggests that an acting score which is to some degree in accord with the energy impact of the song can serve the doer as a support for the subtle inner process, since the performance score, once thoroughly structured and memorized, "begins to have its way of contacting certain associations, awakening something in you from your life and memories" which can augment the specific response created in the doer by the song:

> The acting score has already been dominated, memorized, and the body – and not just, is doing the line of actions. But you are going with this vertical journey simultaneously, as if you have your horizontal score, related to your line of actions, related to the contact with your partners, the order of actions – and something like a vertical score which is related to this "inner action," your vertical itinerary, what quality of energy is with you now. So you have two levels which can begin to be working simultaneously.
>
> (Richards 1995:28)

Thus the external score of the performance, constructed in such a way as to stir up associations which harmonize with and accentuate the energy impact of the musical material, can be seen as a tool to help the doer accomplish the vertical itinerary.

Action: The Objective Correlative

During my most recent visit to the Workcenter in summer and autumn 1995, the research team in residence consisted of four actors, three men and one woman, working under Richards' leadership.[2] The performance then under development was initially shown to invited witnesses in July 1995; presentations of the work are ongoing, although the composition of the group changed in August 1995 and again at the beginning of 1996. The structure not only features a relatively straightforward narrative and certain elements that can be understood as "character," but also includes a number of sequences that are distinctly presentational in style, sequences which Grotowski himself acknowledges are primarily intended to suggest specific meanings to the spectator.

The performance, which Grotowski and his collaborators title simply *Action*, depicts two contrasting life cycles. The first, which is presented as a kind of framework, is the story of a man who is born, grows to maturity, and subsequently dies. It is performed by a single actor, related entirely through action and spoken text.[3] After the death of the body, the man's spirit undergoes a trial in which he is judged by a caustic Sphinx, the Guardian of the Threshold, who denies him the possibility of an afterlife since the Guardian sees in the deceased no sign of his claimed descent from the Living Father. The basic premise of the frame story calls to mind the classic Oedipal riddle, except that in this case the Sphinx wins, crushing its petitioner beneath one disdainful paw.

The second story, which constitutes the major portion of the performance, is depicted through actions developed in relation to ritual songs, with only brief interpolations of spoken text. This song-action tells the story of a man born old (played by Richards), who progressively becomes younger and finally attains the state of a child. I understand this transformation from old man to child as a type of "objective correlative" for the inner process activated by the songs. By accomplishing the vertical

---

2.   A fourth actor, who had been in residence at the Workcenter for approximately eight months, had not yet been integrated into the performance structure.

3.   At the time I first witnessed *Action*, this role was performed by French actor Jerome Bidaux. Following Bidaux's departure from the research team as a result of prior professional commitments, these text-based actions were performed by Mario Biagini, an Italian performer who has been in residence at the Workcenter since shortly after its inception in 1986.

journey," bringing into the body a greater proportion of subtle energy, the protagonist reverses the cycle of aging, ending as an infant with a rattle— but an infant gifted with a sublime and penetrating wisdom, one who knows how to enter a state of perfect harmony and peace.[4]

Interpreted as a parable, the narrative structure of *Action* suggests that the natural cycle of life may well lead from birth to the grave, but that the human being can actively defy degeneration by re-*membering* its relation to the Living One, its origin in/as Light. Abolishing the structure of linear time, tracing the life cycle back to the point of origin, the soul contemplates its own pre-existence. Different traditional techniques provide various ways to accomplish such remembering; for Richards and the other practitioners of Art as vehicle, performance of the ancient vibratory songs is the particular means they have chosen. This practice is concrete and precise, dependent on embodied action rather than belief for its efficacy.

Elements of Craft

Despite the admittedly esoteric dimension of their work, both Grotowski and Richards emphasize that the basic elements of Art as vehicle are the same as those of the actor's craft. "When I say 'elements,'" Grotowski notes, "I am thinking of physical actions, of tempo-rhythms, of composed movement, of contact, of the word, and above all, of the ancient songs with their vibratory qualities" (Grotowski 1996:90). Richards explains that a substantial portion of the practical work conducted by his group

> is oriented toward the creation of a comprehensible performing structure through the montage of a series of basic little reactions and actions, and finally – which from the point of view of acting seems fundamental – looking for the development of the ability to repeat a performing score hundreds of times and each time maintaining its precision and truly alive process.
>
> (Richards 1995:20)

"The people involved here," Richards clarifies, "are almost exclusively actors" (1995:19). I was somewhat surprised, on first visiting the Workcenter in December 1992, to discover the extent to which the daily work of the research group resembles the mundane and familiar activity of rehearsal. Richards and his collaborators work through fragments of melody and sequences of action with an extraordinary degree of precision (continually

---

4. For a more detailed description of the performance structure currently under development at the Workcenter, see Wolford, 1996.

interrupting, adjusting, repeating, adjusting again), requiring the actors to make minute corrections in quality of pitch or vibration, or to look more attentively for details in a specific moment of the acting score. My first impression of the work was that it resembled nothing so much as a particularly demanding choral rehearsal—which, on one level, it was.

The form of physical training I witnessed when I first visited the Workcenter was by no means dissimilar in either its structure or objectives from certain forms of training I have seen employed by other experimental groups. The actors engaged in a series of exercises designed not only to help each performer overcome his/her individual physical limitations, but also to enhance their ability to respond to their partners in the space.[5] Whatever other aspects the training structure may address, either directly or indirectly, on one level it simply constitutes a forum within which the actor can develop the pre-expressive bases of her/his art through work on such fundamental elements as strength, speed, stamina, responsiveness and receptivity. It is a time and place for the actor to focus on the development of her/his instrument. While the type of training structures practised at the Workcenter undeniably cultivate certain qualities rather than others (emphasizing fluidity and organicity, for example, over acrobatic virtuosity), the knowledge and skills acquired through such a process can be applied in a wide variety of aesthetic/performative situations.

On one level, the level of structure and craft, artists trained in a certain type of experimental performance tradition would find nothing particularly unusual in the day-to-day activities of the Workcenter. A number of the basic principles which characterize Workcenter culture are by no means unique: a commitment to daily training, a conceptualization of performance as a legitimate field for ongoing research, a sense that a performance should be presented "when it is ready" rather than in accordance with pre-imposed deadlines.

---

5.   During an earlier period of the Workcenter's operation (1987–1993) a second research team was in residence, under the direction of Maud Robart, a Haitian ritualist who collaborated with Grotowski during both Theatre of Sources and Objective Drama Research. Robart's group was even more explicitly *theatrical* in its orientation than the group under Richards' direction; at one point, the group working with Robart created a physical training structure modeled on that employed by the Teatr Laboratorium. I did not witness the physical training conducted by Richards' group during the period of my extended residence at the Pontedera Workcenter (summer and autumn 1995), though I understand from Richards that the current approach to physical training is somewhat different from the structure I had witnessed some years earlier, with a primary goal being the elimination of certain contractions (which Richards describes as "physical but not just physical") that block the internal process for which the ritual songs can serve as a tool. "[T]he way to work now is much less to find the stream of dynamic vitality but the task of the leader is much more to prepare the body – of himself and of the group members –for this 'empty channeling'" (Richards 1995:82). It is difficult for me to visualize what form this takes in terms of concrete tasks and activities.

Dynamics of Reception, Structures of Exchange

During the period immediately following the establishment of the Pontedera research center, the ethos surrounding Grotowski's activity seemed impenetrably closed. "Only the participants systematically working here and the visitors invited by Grotowski can know this work," wrote Zbigniew Osinski after having witnessed a session at the Workcenter in 1988 (1991:105). Early witnesses, conscious of their own privileged status, spoke of the absolute necessity for such work to be protected from public view or media appropriation. While I would not deny the truth of this, I suspect that Grotowski's initial reluctance to make the work accessible to outside view and the extreme care he exercised in selecting invited participants were motivated, at least in part, by a much more pragmatic concern: the former stage director was well aware that a creative/artistic process ripens at its own pace and is at its most vulnerable in early stages of evolution. When Grotowski and his colleagues developed a performance structure which they felt was ready to be shown, they began to present it, first to invited scholars and theatre professionals, then to groups of young theatre artists. *Downstairs Action*, a performance structure developed at the Workcenter during the late '80s and early '90s, was presented in this way for several years until the departure of a key member of the group made it unfeasible to continue.[6] Following this event, the Workcenter entered another relatively closed period, during which time presentations were suspended while Richards and his collaborators continued the development of their research. They selected and trained new actors, integrated these artists into the research group, and above all worked to deepen their own capacities in relation to the subtle inner process for which the songs can serve as tools. All this while searching to discover how a new and different performance structure could germinate from the process, one that would support the doers in accomplishing their "vertical itinerary." It was more than two years later, in July 1995, when Richards and Grotowski agreed that the new structure had arrived to a point where it was ready to be presented.

Soon after their initial impetus to open their activities of the Workcenter to outside view, Grotowski and his colleagues discovered that a format of barter or work exchange with other theatre artists provided the most amenable dynamic for reception of their work. They realized that fellow artists were for the most part better prepared to receive and

---

6. This Action is documented in the film *Workcenter of Jerzy Grotowski* by the late Mercedes Gregory. Periodically screened at conferences and symposia throughout Europe and the Americas, always with commentary and interpretation by Grotowski himself, this film has been a primary means by which individuals who have not witnessed the work of Art as vehicle in person have been introduced to Grotowski's current research.

comprehend their work, since a common basis in performance craft gave them a point of entry for interpreting what they saw. Richards, discussing the benefits of this dynamic of work exchange for both the Workcenter research team and the visiting groups, emphasizes that the basic elements which comprise the foundation of his work "are the same as the basic elements of acting. And on one level, the level of craft, the work is the same for the actor in public theatre and the person who is doing this work" (1995:20).

Grotowski and Richards began to invite ensemble theatre groups – some relatively well-known, others more obscure – to travel to the Workcenter in order to demonstrate their training and creative work and in turn witness the performance structures developed by Grotowski and his collaborators. Members of the visiting group cover their own expenses for travel and lodging, but no other costs are involved. The visiting companies do not work actively with artists from the Workcenter, their exchange is discursive, dialogic, based on the creative work of the separate groups (Grotowski 1995:131). A typical work exchange can last for as long as three days, with the Workcenter group presenting their opus and physical training on the first day, the visiting group reciprocating on the second, and the two groups meeting informally over a meal to discuss their observations of one another's work over the course of a third evening. More than ninety theatre groups have visited the Workcenter since Grotowski and his collaborators initiated this form of meeting. While I have never heard this stated directly, it has always seemed to me that an important element in the dynamic of work exchange by means of which Grotowski and his collaborators make their practice accessible to a larger (if admittedly hand-selected) public has to do with a desire to infect the visiting artists with a sense of extraordinary rigor and meticulous self-critique in the realm of performance craft. (By stating this, I by no means wish to suggest that the visiting groups are all lacking in this area, or that Grotowski's work team has any sort of monopoly on artistic excellence.) Although Grotowski and his collaborators apparently presume that artists working in public theatre have other goals in mind than those toward which their own practice is aimed (the activation of a type of yogic or transformational process by means of performance), they suggest that basic principles of craft and scenic presence are a common concern for all types of performing artists, despite differences in style, genre, and conditions of production.[7] Grotowski asserts that the dynamic of work exchange demonstrates one way in which his current practice, "more or less isolated, can still maintain an alive relation in the field of theatre" (1995:132).

---

7.   Such an assertion, I am well aware, is subject to debate, since the issue of what constitutes "craft" in performance is by no means neutral.

Ambivalent Positionings

Although the external structure of the work conducted at the Pontedera research center can be apprehended as a performance, the creation of a performance event for the sake of its reception by random spectators lies outside the primary goals of Grotowski's current work. Grotowski describes the internal process of energy transformation, which comprises the essential element of Art as vehicle, as "a direct practice not intended for spectators":

> During my period of theatrical work in the proper sense of the term... the actor's Act was at the same time a challenge vis-a-vis the spectator. But in my present work, in Art as vehicle, in principle, *the spectator doesn't exist.*
> (Grotowski 1996:89 [my emphasis])

Obviously, this is a somewhat drastic and exaggerated claim, not entirely accurate in terms of the actual functioning of the Workcenter. When challenged on the statement Grotowski went on to explain that this did not mean that spectators were not given access to the work, but rather that the research of Art as vehicle was not conducted primarily for their benefit, and could be fully accomplished even in the absence of outside observers.

One might argue that the director, as Grotowski himself has claimed, functions as a type of professional spectator (1980); consequently, the praxis developed at Grotowski's Workcenter is always conducted under the watchful eye of some observer, even on those occasions when the work is not accessible to public audiences. Given this qualification, as well as the obvious importance Grotowski and his collaborators place on the dynamic of work exchange, it might be more accurate to suggest that the presence of the outside witness is not *essential* to the purpose of the work, rather than claiming that the spectator's role has been fully abolished.

Richards makes a similar claim when he relates the work of Art as vehicle to that of the Bauls, yogin-bards of India whose spiritual practice takes the form of songs and dances that can be appreciated on an aesthetic level. Richards suggests that the Bauls, by means of their ritual songs, accomplished "something that was like performing, but it's not just that they were doing theatre [. . .]what they were doing really was related to the work with their teacher, to this something 'inner' " (1995:44). Speaking at a semi-public meeting held at the Workcenter in August 1995, Grotowski also referred to the tradition of the Bauls as an analogy for the practice of Art as vehicle.

This comparison between the work of Art as vehicle and the tradition of the Bauls highlights the ambivalent nature of spectatorship in relation to Grotowski's current work. When Richards spoke to me about the Bauls, he noted that they would often travel from village to village to sing for the people they met (1995:43). If the presence of the outside witness was truly perceived as irrelevant to their work, then why did the Bauls bother traveling from one place to another to sing in the villages? Conversely, why would the villagers bother to come and listen, if the work did not touch them in some way? Of course what the Bauls were doing was not, as Richards suggests, "*like* Performing"— it *was performance*, whether or not it required the presence of anyone except for their guru (and presumably God) to attain its full meaning. The yogin-bards may well have been, as Richards claims, more concerned with some type of internal work related to self-transformation than they were with how the villagers interpreted their songs (1995:44), but I venture that the people standing around the village square found their own way of coming to terms with what they saw.

Seen in light of a desire to separate their work from conventional notions of performance-as-mimesis while claiming for it an efficacy and sanctity associated more with ritual than with theatre, formulations as drastic as those advanced by Grotowski and Richards in their attempts to peripheralize the spectator's role reveal a certain logic. The assumption that performance exists for the spectator, that it is a consumable product, the value of which can be assessed only in terms of its effect on an outside observer, is sufficiently prevalent that Grotowski must struggle to articulate a different set of criteria for the evaluation of his work. The occasional extremity of his rhetoric is intended precisely to destabilize such expectations. Richards clarifies that *Action*, the structure developed around the ritual songs, "is in some way a performance."

> It can be seen. But is it just for – to be seen? No, because the moment it's – just for to be seen, just for this, it would lose the contact with its original intention, with the reason for doing. *Action* is on that edge-point, which is like what I can imagine, from my orientation, as "primary performance. " It's finding its value in the act of doing, and that act of doing exists in a structure which accepts the fact that someone is there watching, and also that there is not someone watching.
>
> (Richards 1995:45)

Art as vehicle is not a mimetic enactment of ritual performance; it is ritual, even if it is possible to discern the seams where Grotowski's practice is grafted onto the roots of ancient tradition – even if one can argue that those roots seem to have been tampered with: transplanted, excavated, hybridized perhaps even partly imagined.

In a recent interview, Grotowski used the term "laic [or lay] ritual" to describe the practice of Art as vehicle. He suggests that this expression is "both tactical and true," noting that during the early period of his work in Communist Poland he had to "pass between Scylla and Charybdis, that is in some way between the atheist state and the Polish Church," without simultaneously antagonizing both forces (Thibaudat 1995:29). Such a process required an acute tactical sensibility, a strategic mindset that has remained with Grotowski even in situations when external circumstances seem not to warrant excessive caution. The term "lay ritual" positions Grotowski's current praxis at the threshold between sacred and secular realms, belonging fully to neither. If one allows Grotowski's ambiguous definition to prevail, then Art as vehicle is not mysticism, in the sense of a sectarian or doctrinal practice. It is also not not-mysticism, in so far as Grotowski accepts and even on occasion promotes Brook's monastic analogy (1988:34) as a description of the work.[8] Conversely, the work is not theatre. Speaking of the ritual songs of Afro-Caribbean tradition which provide the basis of investigation in Art as vehicle, Richards maintains that "they simply were not made for doing a 'public performance' as we can conceive of this term now" (1995:16). And yet it is not not-theatre: when witnesses come to view the activities of the Workcenter, Richards acknowledges that "they're observing a group of actors working in a precise performative structure ... they are seeing something done" (1995:17). Thus, in Grotowski's and Richards' definition, Art as vehicle is neither: not-theatre and not not-theatre nor not mysticism and not not-mysticism. And at the same time it is both, or at least this appears to be the meaning Grotowski and Richards attempt to convey.[9]

The performative framework of Art as vehicle is by no means extraneous to the interior agenda of the work, but functions as an essential component of the practice. As Richard Schechner observes,

> Grotowski's rhetoric is spiritual while his practice combines "ancient ritual techniques" (or ones foreign to most Europeans and Americans) with theatre exercises long known to students of Konstantin Stanislavski or Vsevelod Meyerhold.
>
> (Schechner 1993:248)

The combination of an esoteric agenda with an overtly Stanislavskian approach to performance craft distinguishes Grotowski's current work from

---

8.   I borrow the double negative construction from Schechner, 1985.

9.   See Grotowski, 1995 and Richards, 1995 *passim*, for further development of this concept. Both discussions are carefully crafted to emphasize the precarious balance Grotowski attempts to maintain at the cusp of performative and esoteric practices.

more familiar forms of ritual/performance discipline. Art as vehicle is simultaneously a performance and a form of embodied esoteric practice. The latter aspect, however, can only be realized if the former is well-accomplished. Consequently, the meditative or interior element of Art as vehicle is dependent on a certain mastery of the performative framework for its actualization, its coming into being. The two aspects cannot be separated, and any attempt to assess the validity of Grotowski's current praxis by privileging one over the other – whether categorizing the work purely as mysticism or conversely, purely as performance – would be incomplete and potentially distortive.

Rather than allowing himself to be labeled either as a theatre practitioner or an esoteric teacher, Grotowski prefers to occupy an ambiguous, paradoxical position at the intersection of the two domains, moving within a field of action he himself defines. Drawing on structures and techniques derived from traditional esoteric systems, yet striving to balance on a precarious cusp between aesthetic performance and ritual practice, Grotowski appropriates the techniques of the former (including substantial emphasis on a Stanislavskian tradition of actor training) and the transformative aspects of the latter. It is an undeniably privileged position, one that only someone with his extraordinary intelligence (not to mention his prior accomplishments) could successfully negotiate.

People of the theatre have tended, by and large, to view the post-theatrical phases of Grotowski's work as somewhat suspect, self-indulgent, and elitist, having more to do with therapy or alternative spiritualities than with art. How is the value of such work to be judged if it is not assessed by spectators and critics? What and whom does it serve, if its primary purpose is not to communicate with an audience? What is the use of the actor's talent if the work does not culminate in a publicly-accessible production? Despite the apparent isolation and esotericism of Grotowski's current activity, I would argue that the relation between Art as vehicle and the wider realm of theatre practice is "symbiotic rather than parasitic. Grotowski and his collaborators strive to make the results of their research accessible to an ever-widening circle of professional colleagues, both scholars and performance practitioners. The influence of Grotowski's teachings is further disseminated (albeit in a somewhat indirect and quasi-anonymous way) through the work of a small but widely-dispersed group of young actors and directors who, upon completing their contracted periods of residence at the Pontedera Workcenter, pursue their careers in a variety of professional/artistic circumstances. Although it seems reasonable to assume that the conditions of production most of these artists encounter in the course of their subsequent activities have little in common with the relatively protected environment of the Workcenter, the inscription of a Grotowskian "performance culture" – a particular type of bodily and mental habitus acquired through endless months of rigorous work on craft – remains with them, subtly coloring their independent practice. Some become teachers in their own turn, not proselytizing a so-called "Grotowski method" or founding isolated laboratories with aims similar to those articulated by the Workcenter, but rather imparting their understanding of basic principles of craft through a far-flung network of educational and alternative theatre settings in Europe, Asia, and the Americas.

Perhaps most significantly, Grotowski's Pontedera research center influences the artists who come into contact with the work either through long-term residence or in the more casual dynamic of work exchange in so far as it models a type of performance practice which defines itself as intransigently separate from the pressures of theatre-as-industry. It is an almost impossibly (and some would suggest irresponsibly) utopian vision of the actor's art, one that attempts to (re)vivify the ritual efficacy Grotowski associates with ancient Mystery Schools and the archaic roots of theatre, yet strives to accomplish this within the framework of an undeniably twentieth century approach to performance craft. By attempting to reconfigure the boundaries of theatre practice, moving beyond the conceptualization of theatre-as-mimesis, Grotowski has successfully actualized (albeit within a limited and protected scope) an alternative vision of performance and what it can be used for.

References

Brook, Peter (1988). "Grotowski: Art as a Vehicle." *Workcenter of Jerzy Grotowski.* Pontedera, Italy: Centro per la Sperimentazione e la Ricerca Teatrale: 31–35.

Grotowski, Jerzy (1993). "The Director as Professional Spectator." Trans. Farahilda Sevilla and Fernando Montes. *Mascara* 3.11: 47–55.

(1995) Appendix. "From the Theatre Company to Art as a Vehicle." Trans. Thomas Richards and Michel Moos. *At Work With Grotowski on Physical Actions.* By Thomas Richards. New York: Routledge.

(1996) "A Kind of Volcano. Trans. Magda Zlotowska. *Gurdjieff. Essays and Reflections on the Man and his Teaching.* Ed. Jacob Needleman and George Baker. New York: Continuum. 87–106.

Osinski, Zbigniew (1991). "Grotowski Blazes the Trails." Trans. Halina Filipowicz and Anna Heron. *TDR: The Journal of Performance Studies* 35.1: 95–112.

Richards, Thomas (1995). Interview conducted by the author at La Rotta, Italy, August 15.

Schechner, Richard (1985). *Between Theatre and Anthropology.* Philadelphia: U of Pennsylvania P.

(1993) *The Future of Ritual.* New York, Routledge.

Sullivan, Dam (1983) "A Prophet of the Far Out." *Los Angeles Times*, October 2: 1, 42.

Thibaudat, Jean-Pierre (1989). "Gurutowski." *Libération*, 1 March: 35–36.

(1995) "Grotowski, un vehicle du théâtre." *Libération*, 28 July: 28–30.

Wolford, Lisa (1996). "Action: The Unrepesentable Origin," The Drama Review, Vol 40, No. 4: 134–153.

8

BECKETT IN KYOGEN STYLE: LESSONS IN INTERCULTURAL TRANSLATION

Jonah Salz

How can Japanese theatrical forms be used to interpret Western texts? How do professionals trained in orthodox, time-tested techniques of rote repetition manage to create new works outside their ancient repertoires? How are such experiments received from within and without the tradition? As director of the Noho Theater Group in Kyoto, Japan since 1981, I have confronted such problems continually, working primarily with actors from the Shigeyama family of Kyogen, stylized classical comedy.[1] In order to elucidate the frictions and creative solutions that nurtured our intercultural enterprise, I will focus on the rehearsals and development of Samuel Beckett's *Act Without Words I*, a solo mime, that I directed in 1981 featuring Kyogen master Akira Shigeyama that became our most successful intercultural experiment.

Chance Encounters

I arrived in Japan in January, 1980, following a degree in English literature, and a year's administrative work at Inter-Action, an arts and education center in north London. I had planned to spend three months in Japan, observing the thousand-year panorama of its dance, ritual, and theatre, somehow assimilate their techniques, then return to the U.S. to begin a career as a professional director. I decided that I had to go to the source of that stylized grace and dramatic power in a quasi-scientific quest for a potent theatrical "isolate." If I could discover essential, universally-moving elements in such a distant theatrical culture so distinct from the Western tradition, with only slight historical mutual influence, then they might be used, in different contexts, to create powerful, new theatre capable of moving people from many countries.

Attending Ichikawa Ennosuke's 1977 Kabuki tour to New York inspired my decision to go to Japan. Even without knowing the language, I

---

1. I use a sociolinguistic model of a pidgin-creole continuum to identify the range of interpretation of theatrical cultures I call the "entre-garde" (Salz, 1997b).

found that I could not only understand the plot, but I was deeply moved. But a chance encounter with Kyogen, and then a Kyogen actor interested in experimentation, led me to found the Noho Theatre Group in Kyoto in 1981. In fifteen years, Noho has produced twenty plays, including Shakespeare, Yeats, Beckett, and Woody Allen, in English and Japanese, with Noh and Kyogen actors and musicians, and Nihonbuyo (folk and Kabuki-derived dance) dancers. Peter Brook, in his experiments with *The Orghast at Persepolis, The Ik,* and *Conference of the Birds* and Eugenio Barba through the International School of Theatre Anthropology (ISTA) have of course similarly explored intercultural theatrical training and production universals, although I was unfamiliar with their work at the time.[2] Noho was a much more modest combination of ISTA and the African experiment, with a difference: experimenting with cross-cultural training and fusion productions, but doing so *in situ,* during a period of over fifteen years.

Outside Looking In

My first encounter with Kyogen was accidental. Knowing my interest in Japanese theatre, a friend invited me to the Sumiyoshi Shrine in Fukuoka for a summer Noh performance, where we knelt on tatami mats in the crowded, hot theatre. Feeling sorry for my obvious discomfort, my guide suggested that we go outside during the "intermission." As I stretched my hobbled legs I heard a resonant, rhythmic, comical voice coming from the stage. From outside the temple, peering through the wooden slats of a window, I saw my first Kyogen. It was lively, clear, and funny. We returned to the theatre, and I learned thereafter to take my "intermissions" during the dull parts of Noh rather than spurn my newfound love of Kyogen.

I settled in Kyoto, where I taught English, while feasting on the theatrical smorgasbord of religious rituals, community festivals, and classical theatre ranging from eighth century Bugaku court dance to Osaka's eighteenth-century plebeian Bunraku theatre and contemporary Butoh dance. I discovered that the Kabuki, which had originally attracted me here. was too flashy, non-literary, and melodramatic for my tastes. But I found myself captivated by the "total theatre" of Noh and commedia-like slapstick and earthiness of Kyogen.[3]

I wandered up to a seventh floor jazz club in downtown Kyoto, Lady Day, in March, 1980, drawn by a sign advertising "live music." There "master" (bar owner) Shigeki Suzuki, hearing of my background, introduced

---

2.   See Brandon, 1990 for an overview of twentieth century trends in intercultural influence.
3.   I had been well-prepared for Japan through interviews with the late Peter Arnott, author of the stimulating comparative overview *Theatres of Japan* and by Leonard Pronko's enthusiastic *Theatre East and West: Towards a Total Theatre.* Pronko suggests the similarities between Beckett and Noh that I would later explore.

me to Kyogen master Akira Shigeyama. My Japanese and his English were equally spotty, so we spoke to each other in a kind of pidgin, full of gestures, references to plays and films, and mixed language sentences. We had an instant rapport, stimulating me to attempt to communicate beyond small talk. At one point, I tried to explain the philosophical purpose of my sojourn in Japan with chopsticks:

Me: I want to see whether Western and Eastern theatre share the same origins [holding them together at the base] or are striving towards the same future [holding their tips together]

Akira: [nodding sagely, taking them from me, holding them parallel] But what if you find that they never meet?

We did not realize then that for the next fifteen years we would be exploring the vectors of our respective chopsticks.

On a fullmoon Sunday in May, Akira and I founded the Noho Theatre Group, with Laurence R. Kominz, then a student of Japanese theatre and literature under Donald Keene at Columbia University. Keene had been the first foreign student of Sennojo, Akira's father; Larry had trained with Sengoro, Akira's uncle for many years. We three intended to explore our mutual interests in each other's theatrical culture – and find out which way the chopsticks lay. We called our production group the Noho Theater Group. Noho's Japanese characters stand for the "method" or "laws" of Noh. In English, Noho means "Noh opened" to the possibilities of fusion with Western texts. The group's logo, created after the first production, featured both Noh's archetypal female masks, and the western comedy-tragedy masks.

The premiere production is pretentious program notes (mine) read in part:

By using the stylized techniques and rigid dramatic form of a totally alien tradition ... Western theatre can achieve a vitality and lyricism lost somewhere in its own history.

An organic, vital theatre will emerge: the bouncy, beautiful product of a faithful, happy marriage!

In 1996 Noho celebrated its fifteenth anniversary of a stable marriage. For better or for worse, its performers, method, and repertoire are much the same as a decade ago.

Noho debuted in September, 1981 and has since mounted twenty-five productions in collaboration with Noh and Kyogen actors and musicians, and through collaborations with over fifty artists from ten countries. Noho's core is comprised of Noh and Kyogen actors and musicians, with myself as director. Each production involves "guest artists," who in turn determine how close, and how far, from their respective traditions the performers will move.

Akira was born into the Shigeyama family, a family of Kyogen actors for twelve generations. Trained since infancy, he made his stage debut at age three in *Iroha*, "(Learning the ABC'S), soon followed with the role of the monkey in *Utsubozaru* (The Monkey Skin Quiver). Although he had dabbled in children's opera, and been involved in some of the experiments of his father, Sennojo, at the time Akira performed exclusively in Kyogen plays. His interest in Beckett was piqued by a *manzai* (Japanese vaudeville comedians) interpretation of *Waiting for Godot* a few years earlier. Akira enjoyed the bantering, clownishness of the actors, even as the darker resonances of the play were subliminally understood. My timing was fortuitous: soon after meeting Akira, I proposed a Beckett mime project.

Act Without Words I became our signature piece. Noho has presented it over a hundred times in numerous settings, ranging from university gymnasiums, proscenium theatres, outdoor amphitheaters, church courtyards, experimental basement clubs, and Noh theaters. I will describe in detail the rehearsal process, initial performances, audience responses, and subsequent developments of the piece. I hope that this focused account of one intercultural experiment will enable a broader perspective on creativity within traditional arts, training within Kyogen (and by extension Japanese and Asian theatre), and the process of translation and transformation inherent in intercultural productions. While descriptions of particular directing choices may seem somewhat detailed, I believe that by sorting through the play of small accommodations between Beckett's text and Kyogen dramaturgy we can see in microcosm the sorts of macro-tensions driving many intercultural projects and the training that underlies them.

Silent Challenge: *Act Without Words I*

Noho's first production was intended as a one-time only event, a true experiment. Akira would perform Samuel Beckett's *Act Without Words I*. I would direct. The same program included *Act Without Words II*, in which two men in sacks emerge to complete different daily routines before leapfrogging down a narrow plinth. Music, John Cage's 4'33" (performed on shakuhachi) and Fluxus musical pranks, rounded out the evening. The plays were performed for two nights in Kyoto at a small studio theater, "The Smoking Cat" (alias, Studio Varie), near Kyoto University.

Beckett's mime was written in French in 1956 as a companion piece to *Krapp's Last Tape*. It provided us with an appropriately physical and

Noho Theatre Group logo and performance advertisement

philosophical dynamic essential to Kyogen humor. A man is flung on stage by some mysterious force, teased and tortured by objects (the shade of a tree, scissors, a water pitcher, cubes, a rope) as he tries to survive in the desert. Unable to drink, to sit in the shade, or even to kill himself, the man ends up lying on the bare stage, all torments gone, passively watching the backs of his hands. Like Kyogen, there are few belly-laughs, not even snickers; the play is a series of 'ahhs,' ironic grins, and fatalistic grimaces at the futility of striving, and even of life itself. Critics cite influences ranging from the Greeks myth of Sisyphus to the Temptation of Saint Anthony, and psychological experiments on apes (Fletcher & Fletcher 1978: 113-14).

This play seems in retrospect to have been particularly well chosen to accommodate the needs of both the director and actor. It is short: ten minutes when done in the slapstick clown style, twenty-five minutes when interpreted in our more meditative version. There is no dialogue, which was an important consideration when Noho began, as Akira and I stumbled forward with our pidgin gropings. The story has the placeless, timeless abstraction of many Noh and Kyogen plays, and it was particularly suited to Kyogen's stylized comedy. In addition, the play is written in precisely stated stage directions: "The man is flung backwards on stage ... He falls, gets up immediately, dusts himself, turns aside, reflects ... (Beckett

1982:43).This repetition of forms reminded me of Japanese kata, the precise patterns that are the fundamental vocabulary of all traditional dance and theater. Akira, reading what amounted to a play consisting of stage directions, could easily imagine constructing his own performance. Soon after reading the script, in May, 1981, Akira agreed to perform it in late September. We began to work.

Translation, Transposition, Interpretation

In Beckett's play, wires and pulleys are employed to manipulate a tree branch, a carafe of water, and three cubes. My first decision was to translate the play into the conventions of Japanese theatre. The frontal, non-realistic nature of Japanese traditional theater, perhaps a residual convention of the religious rituals of its origins,make off-stage mechanically created illusions impossible. To take one example, in the Kabuki theater, the front draw-curtain is pulled open horizontally by hand, with a satisfying click-clacking of curtain rings; in Noh-Kyogen, the agemaku side-curtain is raised vertically by bamboo poles tied to the bottom corners. Depending on the entrance effect desired, it is whipped up or gently arched. In both cases, it is the formally-dressed *koken* (after looker) in Noh, or black-hooded *kurogo* (black child) for Bunraku or Kabuki, who acts as on-stage stage assistant. We thus replaced the pullies and wires of the text with a stage assistant, dressed in black, who manipulated the stage props. An American architect designed the tree, from a Japanese umbrella, and the bamboo pole to elevate the carafe of water. With the help of translation by Kominz, rehearsals began in various homes and rented studios. Since Akira performed infrequently in the summer and early fall, he could meet twice even three times a week.

The first rehearsals consisted primarily of selecting appropriate existing forms within the Kyogen repertoire. We sat down and read our respective English and Japanese scripts together, deciding on Kyogen equivalents for Beckett's physical movements and gestures. Akira would demonstrate what he thought was meant; I would observe and offer suggestions based on what 'read' clearly and powerfully to me, a neophyte with regard to Kyogen dramaturgy. Painstakingly, a basic movement vocabulary was developed during the first few practice sessions, then variants quickly followed in subsequent days. 'Flung on stage" was accomplished by a series of small turns, feet gracefully pivoting over each other as his arms flailed wildly, a pattern taken from scenes of the loser in a sumo bout (*Tôzumo* — Chinese Wrestling, and *Mizukakemukô*, – The Water-Throwing Son-in-Law). "Brushing himself off," patting three times for each sleeve – was taken from *Tsukimizato*, (The Moonviewing Blindman), a dark Kyogen comedy Akira's grandfather had turned into a bittersweet triumph forty years earlier.

Akira Shigeyama glances dismissively at the smallest cube, tea ceremony-style, in Beckett's *Act Without Words I*. Photo: Osamu Muranaka

The process of translating Beckett's stage directions to Kyogen kata was surprisingly easy, since a large number of the movements were readily found within the Kyogen repertoire: looking, renouncing, sitting, reflecting, carrying a heavy object. When gestures were not readily available within the repertoire, Akira would "invent" something: "Renounces" became exaggerated horizontal fanning in front of his face as his head shook from side to side; "looking" at the smallest cube was borrowed from the elegant ceremonious scrutiny of a tea bowl by a connoisseur: kneeling, both hands flat on the floor, head peering out between them, craning his neck.

My major role as director consisted of making sure the gesture selected was appropriate to the script. Akira was basing his gestures on Yasunari Takahashi's translation from English to Japanese and the I was editing Akira's inventions, three waves of renunciation rather than one. I was also responsible for making certain the gestures were not mechanically repeated kata, but followed the flow of the story as the Man grows wearier towards the end of the play, the falls were paced slower, to show them to be more painful, more acutely felt. This went against Akira's natural inclination to adhere to the slow build to a quick culmination (*jo-ha-kyu*, – introduction-development-climax) that is the basis of Noh-Kyogen music and movements. Although the nearly slow-motion finale seemed contrary to the normal Noh-Kyogen jo-ha-kyu acceleration of rhythms, such a

Akira grabs the carafe. Photo: Osamu Muranaka

deceleration was necessary to convey the full weight of the final attempted suicide, to let the play "breathe."

Although we were mostly attempting to translate Beckett's precise instructions into Kyogen or Kyogen-like gestures, we deliberately left a few decidedly un-Kyogen-like, even un-Japanese, actions, thus gaining a few laughs from the disparity between the kimono-clad Man and his occasionally very western posings. For example, the Man uses a length of rope and tries to snare the dangling carafe with a lasso: Akira threw the rope twice ineffectually, then finally tied a lasso and swung it with a cowboy's panache. Later the Man tries to fool the unseen malicious forces by pretending to bide his time while shuffling a cube along with his feet towards the tree. Akira sat on the cube, crossed his legs in a contemporary pose, and even pretended to whistle. As expected, Akira's clearly non-Kyogen actions drew the desired laughter at this anomalous behavior.

Akira starts to climb the rope. Photo: Osamu Muranaka

Stumbling Blocks into Springboards

Although most actions could easily be assimilated into Kyogen and Kyogen-like forms, we soon ran into some stumbling blocks with actions involving modern implements: climbing a rope, cutting fingernails. Although at the time worrisome obstacles, in retrospect the problems that we encountered in translating Beckett's mime to the stage elucidate differences between acting cultures, and highlighted Kyogen and Akira's improvisatory, bricoleur verve. Necessity to translate the untranslatable became the mother of intercultural invention.

When the Man discovers that the carafe is too high to reach, he climbs a rope that is lowered from the flies. Later the rope is released, and the Man plummets to the ground. Since the rope is dangled from a long bamboo pole held by the kurogo in our version, the Man could not actually

Akira considers what to do with a piece of rope. Photo: Osamu Muranaka

elevate himself, but used stylization to express "climbing." Although the
Kyogen repertoire contains actions such as to climbing a tree (*Kakiyamabushi*,
– The Persimmon Thief) and actually braiding rope (*Nawanai*, – Rope-
braiding), there is no climbing of ropes. After Akira demonstrated how a
mountain priest climbs a tree, we decided to transpose *The Persimmon Thief's*
mime from tree to rope. The Kyogen actor stands on a stool to "grasp"
branches with his hands. His fingers are held tightly together gracefully,
but with his fingers curling into a clamp at a 45 degree angle. While
declaiming the onomatopoeic sounds "Ei, ei, yattona," he appears to hoist
himself up, holding onto a branch while standing amidst the low branches
of the tree.

Akira cuts his fingernails. Photo: Osamu Muranaka

To climb Beckett's rope, Akira had to create a new kata employing Kyogen stylization and rhythms. We felt that actual contact with the rope would be too realistic, considering the graceful stylization of the rest of the play. Akira instead maintained the graceful finger alignment of the hands, holding the edge of his palm against the rope without actually grasping it. He then placed one hand over the other as he shinnied up the rope a notch. Once this bit of mime was created, we had to incorporate the new gestural vocabulary into the existing grammar of repetition, rhythm, and overall pacing. We worked out a sequence of two shinnies before his face glanced up once at the dangling carafe, a sort of vertical crawl stroke towards the tempting flask. The new kata now read clearly as a man straining to climb a rope toward the carafe, yet to me maintained its Kyogen essence: stylized realism that is graceful and rhythmic, beautiful to watch and easy to understand.

The problem of how to convey the scissors proved more intractable. The Man cuts his fingernails in the shade of the tree, represented by a parasol in Beckett's directions. When the tree branches suddenly disappear (the parasol is closed) the Man is blinded by the sudden light and drops the scissors. Later he cuts the dangling rope with the scissors in order to lasso the carafe. At the end of the play, he uses the scissors to attempt suicide.

The question of how to represent the scissors presented a number of related problems: safety, style, and beauty. Employing actual scissors seemed too realistic, modern, and dangerous. So Akira tried using a fan, that most flexible of Kyogen properties. In Kyogen, fans are regularly slipped from an *obi* belt to become a pipe, sword, or sake cup, before being tucked away. After a few trials, Akira came up with Kyogen "scissors." Placing the fan near his fingernails, Akira closed one rib with a sharp clack, then blew the "clipping" away. This perplexed me, since the fan did not resemble scissors. Akira explained that traditional Japanese scissors were V-shaped, and they were squeezed together to cut with the sharp inner edge. If we intended to perform only to Japanese audiences, such conventionalized scissors might work, but they would only confuse foreigners in the audience unfamiliar with this type of scissors.

A further problem arose: these same scissors are used to cut the rope later in the play. When the Man cuts the dangling rope, he would have to mime it as the *kurogo* snips it with his scissors. While not entirely absurd by Japanese conventions (*kurogo* assist costume changes for Kabuki dances by snipping threads on stage) this would seem to add a confusing additional chore to the stage assistant who already had to balance the dangling rope from a bamboo pole held firmly against his stomach. There seemed to be no happy compromise between Kyogen stylization and dramatic practicality. We opted for real scissors, but not the tiny tailor scissors of the original; we used comically exaggerated large black-and-silver shears. Akira cut his nails with the same two/one patter he had earlier employed in climbing the rope: snipping twice, blowing the cuttings off once, then moving to the next finger in a flowing, triple rhythm. Eventually Akira managed to incorporate this most unkyogen like of properties and actions into the overall contours of the play.

Blade to the Belly

Even on first reading, Akira readily understood the humor and pathos of the play's stage directions, with the sole and important exception of the "suicide scene." He could not understand the actions as written, and therefore could not make it clear to audiences. But perhaps because of this, the resultant accommodation to Japanese cultural conventions created a scene that was arguably the most successful aspect of the production.

After failing to find shelter in the shade, or water in the carafe, the Man "starts to trim his nails, stops, reflects, runs his finger along blade of scissors, goes and lays them on small cube, turns aside, opens his collar, frees his neck and fingers it" (Beckett 1983: 46). Even though it is unstated, the man clearly is contemplating cutting his throat to end life's continual torment. But when Akira read these stage directions, he was perplexed. "

Akira gropes for the already removed scissors to commit suicide.
Photo: Hosomi Yoshihiro

"'Isn't this Man supposed to be a common man?' 'Yes.' 'Then why is he killing himself like a samurai, and like a woman?.'" Traditionally only samurai would have the right to kill themselves, he explained, and they do so to protect their honor, not out of desperation or depression. I explained that I felt the Man, pathetic loser until now, might draw himself to noble heights for one last, desperate attempt at dignity.

But slitting one's throat, as the Man intends, Akira continued, is a method employed by a samurai's wife. She would not use the edge of the blade but he demonstrated she would thrust the blade of a dagger to pierce her throat. Why, Akira wanted to know, would this loser, if considering the noble escape of suicide, utilize a cowardly woman's way?

Well, then, I asked, how might a samurai kill himself? Akira demonstrated the kata, famous from Kabuki and television *chambara* (swordfight dramas), especially *Chushingura*, (The 47 Rônin). Wrapping the dagger in a clean cloth, Akira knelt, torso resting high on his heels, opened his practice cotton *yukata*, bared his stomach, then plunged the dagger in, pulling it across to the right. Meanwhile, he explained, a "second," sword drawn, would stand behind him, ready to lop off his head once the *seppuku* had been accomplished or should the samurai's hand waver at the last moment. The bloody deed was elegant, ceremonial, clear, and moving until Akira grinned as his hands simulated intestines tumbling out to the onomatopoeic sounds "guruguruguru." Later I discovered that Akira was demonstrating a scene from another family favorite, *Kamabara* (Suicide by Sickle), featuring a farmer's cowardly and clumsy attempts to do himself in.

We soon transposed Beckett's western suicide attempt to the Japanese mode. The decision to use ritual suicide created the theatrical equivalent of a paradigm shift, as other problematic props and actions fell naturally into place. A handkerchief was used to wrap the scissors – the only new property we added to Beckett's sparse staging. The middle cube became a ceremonial tray on which the Man prepared his implements. Rather than open his shirt at the collar to reveal his throat, the Man loosened his kimono to reveal his stomach. As in Beckett's original, just as the Man reached for the scissors, the box is pulled away (by the *kurogo*). The Man leans forward, fingers groping increasingly lower, the determination in his eyes giving way to panic, then dull pain as he sprawls forward in a humiliating belly-flop. As the Man bares his stomach, the *kurogo*, until then kneeling surreptitiously at the back of the stage, stands and moves to an angle behind the man, a 'second' to the suicide, before whisking away the box and scissors. For those familiar with Japanese suicide conventions, it was a wonderful parody; for those who were not, it foregrounded the black-garbed assistant as a figure representing Fate, or the Devil, according to some in the audience. When I showed a photograph of this scene to Beckett, he nodded approvingly, "So you're translating not just the language, but the culture?" (8 Aug. 1982).

Act Without Words I was performed again in Tokyo the following May, this time on a Noh stage, then at the Edinburgh Fringe Festival that summer. It became a staple of our foreign tours: Its simple props could be set up indoors or outdoors, and the wordless action could be followed easily. *Act Without Words I* has been performed over a hundred times in the fifteen years since its inception and remains in Noho's repertoire as a successful attempt at interculturalism.

Mellowing

Over the years, Akira has created an intense three-dimensionality to the piece, "making it his own" as much as any Kyogen role. More so, perhaps, since he was the part's originator and its only performer. Instead of having to follow his grandfather or father's model, as in orthodox Kyogen, Akira is free to embroider or minimize as he pleases, within the confines of the script. At a certain point, Akira no longer followed my direction. I could still choose the spotlight for his final staring at the backs of his hands, or remind him of occasionally missed reflections or reversed sequences. He would listen dutifully to my comments during technical run-throughs, nodding his head. But this signaled his understanding, not necessarily his agreement. Then he would ignore many of my comments as he moved to his own rhythms and sense of the particular day's audience. The timing varied according to the mood engendered by him and the audience's reactions, ranging from 25 to 30 minutes.

Meanwhile, Yasushi Maruishi, the Kyogen actor who replaced Kominz as the man in black after the first performances, fashioned a rich character from his role as *kurogo*. Maruishi thought the role more vital to the play's essence than the normal Kyogen stage assistant. Maruishi occasionally bristled when asked to set up props while on tour, as though he were a stage assistant rather than "stage assistant." He stressed to me the concentration and sense of timing needed to play his role:

> I'm not just a prop-mover helping him out. The success of the play depends on our mutual interaction. I've got to breathe with him, to feel his pace and mood so that I can react with the proper timing. If I move too quickly I will pull focus from him but if I don't move quickly at times, I'll keep him waiting before his next action, not a good thing. I'm supposed to be invisible, but it's not as easy as it looks!

Reactions at Home and Abroad

Kyoto audiences were a mixture of traditional and modern theatre goers.[4] Because reactions varied considerably, even in Japan, we actively sought to display our experimental hybrid fruits in cosmopolitan markets. *Act Without Words I* has been performed widely abroad, a staple of Noho's foreign tours to the Edinburgh Fringe (1982), studio, university, and museum theatres in the U.S. (1984, 1985, 1988, 1994), Hong Kong (1989), and the Avignon Theatre Festival (1994). Audience reactions are decidedly mixed. Some come away with a new understanding of Japanese theatre, and of Beckett. Others find that the fusion pieces lack the depth of the traditional plays on the same program. Young Japanese abroad, witnessing young foreign artists' interest, come away with a newfound respect for the musty traditions of Noh and Kyogen – a type of "U-turn" to their own tradition.

---

4. See Mari Tanaka Hori's summary of Beckett in Japan (1996). Hori notes "four different kinds of attempts at performing Beckett plays in Japan": authentic, radical adaptations by political avant-garde groups, traditional Japanese theatre interpretations, and arbitrary adaptations by others (1996:226).

Stage Assistant Maruisha offers Sennojo Shigeyama "scissors".
Photo: Osamu Muranaka

Tours abroad are exercises in improvisation: creating 'instant Noh stages' in small theatres, churches, and college auditoriums, in a few hours. We arrive in the afternoon of a performance, place meter-long bamboo fences down in the upstage right area to simulate a *hashigakkari*, focus specials for *Act Without Words I* – the most difficult of which call for a shadow in front of the umbrella-tree and simulated daytime outdoor light.

While most spectators praise its zen clarity and depth, some decry its slow pace, which replaces vaudeville slapstick with a meditative heaviness. And some, mostly non-Japanese, find the man in black distracting. One Japanese man, rather inebriated, lambasted me following a Smithsonian Institution performance in 1984: "Zeami succeeded in erasing all realistic elements from the stage, and for six hundred years Noh actors have been perfecting this bare stage potency. Now you come along, and put back all that clutter!" Mel Gussow accused it of "denaturing" Beckett's piece (*New York Times*, 12 Mar. 1986). A young master from a rival Kyogen family scoffed as I explained how we'd created "new Kyogen kata" for

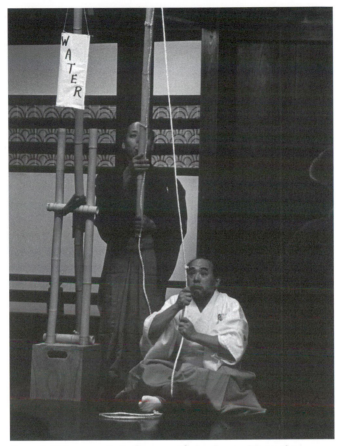

Sennojo Shigeyama tests the rope. Photo: Osamu Muranaka

Beckett's play: "You can't *create* kata! They are inherited patterns of perfected action and pacing. Maybe what you've invented will become a kata in a hundred or a thousand years, but right now it's just 'movement.'"(Kosuke Nomura, 19 Dec., 1985).

As for the actors, they find in Noho a high-profile venue for their non-Kyogen experiments, and an enjoyable escape abroad. Maruishi continues to encourage me, telling me that "step by step," gradually over time, is the only way that Noho can improve. Meanwhile, Akira, financially and promotionally very supportive, is artistically extremely laissez-faire. His attitude toward Noho may be clear from the introductory meeting for the Noho workshop in the summer of 1991. When a young American actor and teacher said that he felt "halfway in between" when trying to do something with his imperfect mastery of zen or yoga, Akira replied,

You may not have mastered Noh yet, but what you bring to it in your state of confusion is the interesting part. Besides, there is no real masterhood: once you've learned one thing really mastered it, and do it, three new problems present themselves. And once those three are solved, another ten crop up. So everyone, the world over is only halfway there.

His motto, he smiled, is, "There is no 'best.' Only 'better.'" Akira rarely gives advice except to say, "Interesting," or "Not interesting."

Timing, Time, Timelessness

Noho's *Act Without Words I* taught me many things about the importance of time in the development of significant intercultural experiments.

First, I realized how fortunate it was that I met Akira Shigeyama, the progressive son of a radical father, at the particular juncture of his life when he was seeking new methods of incorporating Kyogen into contemporary theater. I had known nothing of the Shigeyamas beforehand, and have since come to realize that Noho and the Traditional Theatre Training Workshops (TTT) that they assist in each year are not exotic appendages to their traditional activities, but seamless extensions of their family tradition of experimentation. Since World War II, they have sought to popularize Kyogen through schools tours, all-Kyogen programs, and torchlit Noh performances in castles and parks. They have experimented with using Kyogen techniques to interpret new works, including Aristophanes' *The Clouds*, Kabuki and Rakugo (storytelling) scripts, and folktales.[5] At thirty years old and just coming into his own as a professional in the popular Shigeyama family, Akira was "ripe" for experimenting outside the tradition. If Akira had not bumped into me, I am certain that he would have explored new ways to use Kyogen on his own, or with someone else.

Second, experiments exploiting similarities and differences among traditions require patience, breathing space, and repetition with different casts in various venues over time. I have, in subsequent years, directed other Noho productions involving larger casts, bilinguality, (Noh actors and musicians, dancing and singing.[6] But nothing approached in excellence *Act Without Words I*. As Noh and Kyogen grew more popular in the eighties, there was less rehearsal time available. The actors I worked with got busier as they grew older, demanding more paid performances in order to free up their schedules for rehearsals. Instead of the intense, long-term rehearsals

5. My recent dissertation details these activities (1997a).
6. See Salz, 1996 for an account of the intercultural frictions involved in directing *Ophelia*, based on Shakespeare's *Hamlet*.

of Noho's first years, we have had to make do with more modest plays, with the intercultural translations worked out the script in advance, so that rehearsals consist primarily of blocking. Script work and casting determine the outcome, and actors fall back on their orthodox forms rather than attempt risky experiments. Experiments have taken on the feeling of set moves of fixed pieces in a chess match rather than the delicious possibilities of cooking an eclectic stew.

Third, a "neutral territory" must be created for intercultural transplants to be nourished. Ironically, some of the most interesting Noho works of recent years have been done during the TTT summers with foreign actors and dancers in Kyoto. Since 1995, a Noho workshop has taken place in Portland, Oregon, under the auspices of Portland State University. There, removed from the pressures of the Japanese theater world, Kyogen and Noh actors have time to put more efforts into creating new and potent works. From the meager list of our successful productions (*Theater I* and *Rockabye* (by Beckett), *The Henpecked Husband* (based on a French morality play), *Ophelia* (an adaptation of Hamlet); Yeats' *At the Hawk's Well*) it seems clear that the essential factor is time: time to create, and then repeat the creations over time, preferably with changing casts and countries.

Finally, time and progress are not necessarily synonymous. I believe that our relative ignorance concerning each other's cultures allowed Akira and I to seek hard to clarify and refine, creating a theater piece of universal, timeless potency. My initial unfamiliarity with Kyogen, and Akira's of Beckett and western theater, actually contributed to the success of our first collaboration. We each relied on the other to explain the "tradition," and could thus observe each other's culture through a single, authoritative lens. As Noho continued, and I began taking Kyogen lessons from Sennojo (Akira's father and teacher), the "purity" of my Western sensibilities was tainted. I began ignoring the man-in-black; I didn't think the sliding walk of Kyogen was so odd; the slow unfolding of plot accelerating to a quick climax seemed natural to me. Akira likewise, through his continued performing of Beckett plays he has directed and acted in ten to date) and forays abroad (on seven tours with Noho, to Spain and Italy in 1988 "on sabbatical"), is no longer the pure Kyogen vessel of 1981.

For Noho to continue to create interesting interpretations of Western plays in a true intercultural manner requires a reversal of time, a return to the "beginner's mind" that was Noh theorist Zeami's lifelong motto, the innocence and eager experimentation of our first enchantment.

References

Arnott, P.D. (1969) *Theatres of Japan*. London: Macmillan.
Beckett, S. (1984) *The Collected Plays of Samuel Beckett*. NY: Grove.

Brandon, J. R. (1989) "A New World: Asian Theatre in the West Today," *The Drama Review* 33, no. 2 (T122) (Summer), 25-50.

Fletcher, B.S. and Fletcher, J. (1978) *A Student's Guide to the Plays of Samuel Beckett*. London: Faber and Faber.

Pronko, L.C. (1967) *Theatre East and West. Perspectives Toward a Total Theater*. Berkeley: University of California Press.

Salz, J. (1996) "Get Thee To a Noh Master: East Meets West Meets Hamlet." In *New Theatre Vistas*, ed. Judith Lee Oliva, pp. 149–164. Studies in Modern Drama Series, ed. Kimball King. New York: Garland Publishing.

(1997a) "Roles of Passage: Coming of Age as a Kyogen Actor" Ph.D. dissertation, New York University.

(1997b) 'Pidgin-creole Continuum and the Performance Entregarde.' In *Noh and Kyogen in the Contemporary World*. ed. J. R. Brandon, pp. 210-43. Honolulu: University of Hawaii Press.

Takahashi, Y. (1982) "The Theatre of Mind: Samuel Beckett and the Noh." *Encounter* 58 (April): 66-73.

Tanaka, M.H. (1996) "Special Features of Beckett Performances in Japan." In *Beckett On and On...* ed. L. Oppenheim and M. Buning, pp. 226-239. Cranbury, N.J., Associated University Presses.

PART III

SOME RECENT TRENDS

9

WORKSHOPS FOR THE WORLD: THE INTERNATIONAL WORKSHOP FESTIVAL

Clive Barker and Dick McCaw

One of the more remarkable features of theatre training over the last twenty-five years has been the growth of workshops. There is no single reason why this should be, although we can point to a number of factors which have contributed. There is no single pattern to the workshops although we can identify loose parameters. What holds together workshop and gives some sense of homogeneity is the drive to find some supportive, compatible and noncompetitive framework in which individuals can explore or extend the range of their theatre skills or means of expression. The group is important and initially very risky. A group of totally unrelated individuals sign to take part in a short period of intense work. Anyone who leads workshops knows that the first priority lies in establishing some manner of group cohesion and trust, which will enable the lowering of defences and the engendering of respect. In saying this, we could posit one point of origin and influence as the encounter groups of the 1960s, of which Essalen was the prime model. The alternative theatre movement of the 60s and 70s inherited and imbibed the sense and practice of breaking down barriers to freedom of expression, communication, and interaction. The best workshops of today still function as time out of time, islands separate from the mainstream of life. Those of us who regularly lead workshops experience a short period in which intense and revealing relationships are built up, which cannot be sustained. We are privileged to inhabit in this time the lives of other people, to know them and to let them go. It would not be too much to say that there is often a great deal of love experienced and exchanged.

Given these circumstances, it is not unreasonable for people to choose to work with workshop leaders who have experience or established credibility, through public recognition of their work, through publication, or simply by word of mouth. In its operations, the International Workshop Festival tries to maintain a pattern of activity in which credibility and trust is vested in the organisation not the individual leader, which widens the choice of available workshops and encourages would-be participants to be more adventurous. This carries with it the complementary responsibility for the organisation to find the participants who are suited to work with the leader. This responsibility is harder to discharge. We have little problem in guaranteeing that people who come to work with internationally famous directors such as the Russians Dodin, Sturua and Vasiliev, for example, will derive great pleasure and inspiration from their experience. We cannot in the same way guarantee that we can supply the participants who will delight and inspire them. Because of the nature of the workshop, throwing people together intimately for a short time, hiatus happens very rarely, if at all. But, it must always be a risk for the magi lured from the security and comfort of his or her native culture and a permanent company, in which all things work to protect the process of creating theatre from outside scrutiny and judgement, to drop defences and face an unknown group, with the added responsibility of making magic in public. Hence the paramount need to create group cohesion and trust.

An alternative way to establish trust between leaders and participants which has been developed, largely through the women's movement, is networking. Through the Magdalena Project, women from different countries have been brought together to take part in workshop sessions and this has led to a network of contacts being established which allows women involved in theatre in a variety of fields to move from contact to contact, workshop to workshop, and to publicise their activities. A similar, loose network centres on Eugenio Barba, the Odin Teatret and the International School of Theatre Anthropology. It would not be surprising to find there are others outside Europe of which we are not aware. In any case, it would be unusual for anyone regularly leading workshops not to set up their own network of contacts, through which to work.

The origins of these networks lie, as with Essalen, in wider networks created out of the concepts of the alternative society, culture and. consequently, theatre of the 60s and 70s. Women's networks, such as Magdalena, owe their existence to "conscience-isation" workshops of the Women's Movement, of which they have been both a functioning part and an offshoot. Whatever Gay and Lesbian networks exist have followed the same pattern of development. The pioneering work of The Living Theatre from the late 50s onwards – in breaking down the distinctions between audience and performers, the barriers between performance and life as it is lived – created important precedents for less formal interaction and communication. These precedents included an insistence that the theatre ought to seek a direct impact on and involvement with the lives of those who came to participate, and a wide range of experimentation to discover new theatre forms and techniques to achieve this. Peter Schumann, of the Bread and Puppet Theatre, has over thirty years experience of creating a way for theatre, painting, music, sculpture and language to exist together and address contemporary issues. As we write, he is leading a workshop on Newcastle-upon-Tyne, in England, to address the theme of the decline of the shipbuilding industry in Newcastle. Artists from all disciplines have been invited to work with local crafts people to explore the theatrical and construction techniques behind the creation of theatre and images of great beauty and power. At the same time, in the same city, Forced Entertainment, a younger performance group, whose recent work has blurred the lines between real cities and imaginary ones by exploring the city as a site for stories, dreams and photographic interventions, is asking participants to construct and document walks through a real city, collaging the evidence (photography, text and performance) in the top floor suite of a Newcastle night-club.

The formation of cooperative companies, following from the example set by The Living Theatre, has taken a number of different forms. Welfare State, a British group founded in 1968, has travelled mounting large-scale public spectacles and residencies in the manner of The Bread and Puppet Theatre and has also maintained a continual service to its local community in creating domestic rituals, such as naming ceremonies and memorial services, to allow wider entry into the magic and healing processes of theatre. In all of these, performers and participants meet and single to create the circumstances for change and growth, which is at the heart of the workshop experience. Theatre, which has for so long maintained a mystic isolation, opens its doors to create a more democratic alliance with it public out of a direct involvement with life in the real world.

The artists of the alternative theatre of the 60s and 70s, in search of new forms and content, embarked on a scrutiny of existing practices and a wide range of experimentation with new techniques. Not surprisingly, since many people inhabiting the alternative culture began to travel east in search of spiritual enlightenment, artists began to acquire techniques derived from many oriental theatres. So began a complex process of interaction between East and West, which is still reflected in an interest and demand for Indian, Chinese, and Japanese masters to reveal their secrets in workshops. Hand in hand with this search for oriental masters went a growing interest in a number of western theorists and teachers, whose work until quite recently has been restricted to a handful of devotees. Workshop opportunities now burgeon for those wishing to become acquainted with the physical techniques and methods of Feldenkrais, Alexander, and others, making these masters much more influential now than they were during their lifetimes. Although Laban's work has become a staple part of the teaching programme of most acting academies, there is, oddly, little opportunity to become involved in workshops. His student, Jean Newlove, runs workshops but appears to organise them out of her own contacts and has no connection with the main networks. One very interesting phenomenon is the Roy Hart Theatre, a group which began working on voice techniques derived from the theories of Alfred Wolfsohn. Following Hart's death in 1975 in a road accident, the group formed a mutual support system but, over the years, individuals have moved to develop their own versions of the techniques and to make these accessible through teaching programmes and also through workshops. The general pattern and length of workshops does not allow any prolonged development of technique (although people seek continuity through enrolling in consecutive workshops). The purpose of the workshop usually manifests itself through a revelation of the potentiality present in the participants, leaving them with the heartening memory of release and achievement but with the problem of finding their own way to sustain whatever development of abilities the workshop has revealed as possible.

The workshop provides opportunities for people to add some degree of personal involvement, to supplement interest and knowledge gained from reading ideas expressed in books or articles. The publication of Ross Kidd's assessment of his work in Botswana dealing with the problems arising in rural extension and agricultural development, which gave rise to the concept of Theatre for Social Development (in Kidd Byram) and Augusto Boal's publication of *Theatre of the Oppressed*, (1979) has led to a widespread international demonstration and dissemination of the ideas behind their work through their later leading of workshops. It would not be exaggerating to say that through these workshops the concept of what constitutes theatre and its range of social functions has been materially altered and the direction of the work of many practitioners has been diverted into other channels. During the period of Boal's exile from Brazil, the workshop became a necessary instrument through which to continue his work. The attempt to silence him in his own country only led to his ideas and practice being exported world-wide.

Lastly, one of the major features of the spread of workshops, particularly in England, has been the demand of funding agencies for some activity on the part of funded companies which demonstrates their commitment to education. One line of this began in the late 60s, when British theatre companies began to participate in educational activities. Leaving aside the independent form of Theatre in Education, where small companies were engaged continually in theatre work in schools, many theatre companies began to demystify their operations through performances for schools and young audiences, in the interest of building new audiences. A second line, developed where actors and directors would run workshop sessions for school around examination plays, particularly Shakespeare's. Crucial parts of the plays would be publicly rehearsed and alternative interpretations suggested as a basis for later discussion between students and actors. A somewhat puritanical attitude to giving public money to theatre companies by way of subsidy took up this aspect as a clear demonstration that the theatre was not simply a form of pleasure and could have some other more utilitarian justification. Clauses began to be inserted in subvention documents insisting upon some form of educational workshops in order to qualify for subsidy. Recent thinking has modified to recognise that there are some companies / individuals who can run workshops and some who cannot, or who are not committed to, or interested in doing so, and that large, badly run workshops do more harm than good in presenting theatre to young people and have little to offer of any educational value whatsoever.

The International Workshop Festival (IWF)

The IWF was the brain-child of Nigel Jamieson, then Mime Animateur for the Greater London Arts Association, who organised the first (London) International Workshop Festival in April 1988, drawing on contacts he had made during mime and dance festivals in previous years. In 1994, Nigel Jamieson left to work in Australia, although his advice and knowledge are still available on a consultative basis. From 1994, the Artistic Director has been Dick McCaw. At no point has the organisation had more than one other full-time member of staff and one part-time member. These have been supplemented by occasional help. At present the Administrator is Alex Cook, and Jenny Klein, the former administrator, works part-time on Marketing. The staff are backed by a board of directors chosen for their facility to offer advice within areas of their own specialisations. In the past the staff has been increased during the periods of the festivals by taking on local administrators, but this has proved inefficient, not because of a lack of quality in the people appointed, but because of liaison and the difficulty of training local staff to have a detailed and global overview in a very short space of time. In 1996 the festival was run on a hands-on basis, with the Artistic Director always present and assisted by Rachel Blech, who had until that point been the part-time member of the administrative team. Although this arrangement exposes the staff to the risk of burn-out through overloading, it is likely that it will be used in the future as it guarantees expertise on the spot should problems arise and it provides security and reassurement for the workshop leaders located far from home in regional areas of Britain faced with a working group of total strangers. Behind these arrangements lies the fact that the organisation is understaffed by at least one other full-time member, which present funding does not allow for. The company's incorporating memorandum gives its aims as follows. "The objects for which the Company is registered are to promote, maintain, improve, and advance education by the encouragement of the Arts, particularly by establishing master classes, seminars and other means of disseminating information regarding the Arts in collaboration with artists of international standing....." The first festivals were biennial, which was all that a small organisation with limited funding felt it was able to mount.

Nevertheless they were ambitious in the range of choices offered. From 1990 onwards the festivals spread out beyond London to Derry, Glasgow, and Nottingham, later to Edinburgh, Newcastle and, in the near future, they will be offered in Leeds and Belfast.

Nigel Jamieson defined the IWF's aims as being to organise a programme of high calibre workshops led by physical theatre artists, directors, and choreographers of international repute. The programme would offer performing arts practitioners the opportunity to broaden their artistic vocabulary and thereby augment a change of emphasis within British theatre and dance. It would also address the lack of training opportunities for practising professional performing artists and would hopefully bring a more international perspective to the performing arts in Britain.

To serve and extend these purposes the organisation has laid down a policy which has the following aims:

* to broaden the diversity and richness of the performing arts in Britain;
* to make the performing arts more reflective of and relevant to contemporary Britain and the rich diversity of cultures and communities it comprises;
* to challenge, inspire and enthuse performing artists in the midst of their careers;
* to provide facilities of time and space for artists to explore their craft;
* to provide a British focus for European training initiatives.
* to encourage a cross art-form perspective that will challenge Eurocentric ideas of compartmentalizing them and provide forums for artists working in different disciplines.

The Festivals

The restrictions of staffing, mentioned earlier, forces the IWF to concentrate events into a short space of time. But there are other advantages, The working year splits into five sections.

January	Writing applications and reports (of which more later)
February-April	Programming and contracting artists
May-June	Production and dispatch of the brochure. The IWF works entirely through mailing list, strategic placing of brochures (for example in the Edinburgh Festival Office) and word of mouth recommendation
July-August	Box office opens. Participant liaison
Sept-November	Managing the Festival
December	Writing reports and applications.

The crucial month is September, into which certain events have to be crammed because of the availability of premises. It is essential that as far as possible the workshops all take place in the same location (site-specific work, such as those cited earlier for Peter Schumann and Forced Entertainment, excepted). A festival of workshops is an entirely different event to a series of workshops or season, precisely because of the concentration of activity in one place at one time. It is imporant to bear in mind that the clientele are professional artists and teachers working in the field of the performing arts and that the festival offers a vital opportunity for them to meet together for the exchange of ideas, techniques, and enthusiasms. The existence of a number of workshops in the same building with a cafe allows participants and workshop leaders to meet, discuss, and interact. Each day begins with a voluntary warm-up for all participants and ends with a voluntary cool-down. Evenings are given over to talks and discussions in which participants have the chance to meet other workshop leaders, to hear them talk about their work, and to question them. A festival of workshops is an event far greater then the sum of its parts; it provides a much-needed space where professionals from Britain and abroad can refresh themselves, meet other artists working in similar and related fields, and have the time to reflect on, and nourish their creative lives. The entire operation is geared to creating the ambience and the environment in which the richest possible artists' exchange can occur.

Workshops in London are spread over two weeks in two sets. Individual workshops last either one week or take place over a weekend. The 1996 festival in London contained seven weekend and nine week-long workshops. The regional festivals were naturally lighter. A complete listing is at the end of this essay. Three of the planned London workshops had to be cancelled in 1996 due to a funding crisis when expected subsidies were removed just as the programme was due to be finalised. Week-long workshops are spread over twenty-five hours. Weekend sessions ten. Participants vary in number, but twenty is usually the maximum. The number is decided by two factors, how many the leader specifies and how many apply. Each workshop leader has an assistant to attend to their needs. These are usually young artists who are admitted into the workshop free in exchange for their work. Fees paid to workshop leaders are in three grades, depending on three categories within which the leaders might fall. In 1996 these bands were £100 for workshops led by British teachers who have not yet established a wide reputation, £125 for teachers and artists who have a solid profile in Britain as important teachers and workshop leaders, many of whom return regularly to take part in the festival. The £150 band is for artists who we are always being asked to book but who are in constant demand world-wide and are difficult to pin down. It is important that the pricing is kept to as low a figure as possible to enable artists, who cannot be expected to have large amounts of surplus cash lying around, to participate. It is also important that as large a part of the fees as possible is paid to the leaders for their services. The IWF works on narrow margins to maintain excellent relations with both sets of artists.

Funding – A Lifetime Full of Applications

The IWF receives funding from the London Arts Board (LAB) and the Arts Council of England (ACE) on a three year franchise basis. The Regional Arts Boards and local government in the festival regional areas also contribute. Other government agencies, such as the British Council, give smaller grants to assist with bringing in some teachers and there has been some help from foreign government agencies assisting with fares and subsistence to allow their artists to travel to Britain. The Baring and Gulbenkian Foundations have given (generously) in recent years, as has the Esmee Fairburn Trust, which supports all the video and monograph documentation. Grants have been made from the Lottery funds to equip the office to a high enough standard to deal with maintaining and updating a data bank of training resources in Europe. The basic principle is that all work outside London should be self-supporting, leaving the major grants to finance the London festival and the administration. Up to now there has never been a year in which the major grants covered the core costs of the organisation and each year has meant walking a financial tightrope with minimal staff. The strain exerted on staff in the latter quarter of the year, running the festival and trying to balance the budget at one and the same time, has been considerable and dangerous. The ACE funding is complicated by being split between three departments, Drama, Dance, and Training, all of whom are and probably will continue to be constrained by standstill budgets and cuts.

At one point in the Spring of 1996, it looked likely that the festival would have to be cancelled in its entirety when the policies of the Dance and Training departments in the ACE changed. Other priorities were set, quite legitimately, and the IWF found its subvention severely cut. This was compounded in the same week by *reforms* in local government which effectively removed the budget of the Nottinghamshire County Education Committee and £15,000 from the IWF's funding. Because of the vagaries of the funding system, the IWF has always had to plan festivals before funding was fully committed. A system of personal contacts has engendered trust among artists that even though there is no contract the IWF will fulfill its offers. In 1996 it was decided to go ahead with the festival when it was realised that the crisis affected the whole organisation and not the workshops alone. Since most workshops covered their costs (and some even produced a surplus in earnings) there was little economy which could be made by cutting workshops, when what was most at risk was the central administration. To cancel the workshops would not have saved the IWF but simply have hastened its end. Some saving was made by cancelling three workshops which entailed heavy travel costs and asking other artists to find their own accommodation in London. The trust built up over a long time is compromised when this happens and it would be further endangered if something of that order were to happen again. As it was, the 1996 festival scraped home with a very small surplus.

1997 saw the end of the Baring and Fairbairn grants and also the end of the three-year cycle of franchise funding from both the LAB and the ACE. Other areas of lottery funding were opening up, in a heavily competitive field, and the LAB and ACE grants were open for renegotiation. Because of these pressures, more time is spent in the office filling out applications for funding than is spent carrying out the work itself for large periods of the year. It has become axiomatic and a mark of survival so far that the staff have developed a great expertise in filling out applications and negotiating with agencies. Without these talents the organisation could not survive.

Diversity of the Workshops and Their Achievements

The IWF inherited certain needs and imperatives from the past, some reaching back into the early days of the Alternative Theatre of the 70s, before the stagnation of the Thatcher period set in. Its formation also came at a time when there was an emergence of new ideas (although the change of ideas and direction in the late 80s and early 90s has not as yet found an analyst and chronicler. What was clear at that time was the growing interest in new mime and the formation of companies, such as DV8 and Theatre de Complicité, working towards new hybrid forms under the generic title of Physical Theatre. The major impetus came from within the dance world, where a number of choreographer led companies emerged aiming to develop a new dance vocabulary that was capable of tackling current issues. The broadening of the artistic vocabulary in both dramatic theatre and dance created a need for some form of interactive workshops which would address questions of skills and techniques to further the development. This was Nigel Jamieson's original intention and it continues to inform the IWF's expanded programme. Around the same time that Jamieson was formulating his idea the established success of the London International Festival of Theatre in bringing new and usually exciting companies from abroad finally began to make the impact on the London theatre scene that it deserved. Many of the directors or leaders of those companies, such as Anatoli Vasiliev and Flora Lauten, have subsequently led workshops for IWF. During this period several organisations which assisted technical development and the internationalisation of these new trends were formed.

Among these, Physical State International was important for answering both needs. At the present time only one other organisation, the Centre for Performance Research, based now in the University of Aberystwyth on the Welsh coast, has not succumbed to the financial pressures of the early 90s, although the Magdalena Project, based in Wales in Cardiff, also mounts workshops as part of its networking activities among women in the performing arts.

It would be invidious to try to cover the whole range of workshops offered by the IWF but particular events can be singled out. Some workshop leaders have become regulars, returning to work sometimes with those who have taken these earlier workshops or with new groups of participants. Henry Smith, Jos Houben, Mladen Materic, Enrique Pardo, Dominique Dupuy all now have established reputations and a network of students in Britain, International celebrated and innovative artists such as Andre Serban, Lucinda Childs and Zygmunt Molik have worked alongside British artists. Keith Johnstone has been brought back from Calgary in Canada in what is hoped to be a reintroduction of his ideas and experience into Britain, from where they have been too long absent. The last ACE apppraisal singled out the opportunities the workshops have given to Lloyd Newson of DV8 and Yvonne Brewster of Talawa Arts for research and development. The formation of the IWF came at a point in the development of Black theatre and dance in Britain during which both moved on to a different level of self-confidence and achievement. Supporting this has been a part of the programme and a major event in this area is planned. The troubled area of Northern Ireland has always been a special concern. The marginalisation of this area politically, economically, and culturally has led us to mount a series of workshops which both celebrate the vocal traditions which are so rich in the province and help forge contacts with the rest of the world. These have been called *Finding a Voice* which expresses both lines of attack. Peter Schumann's workshops promoting care and concern in places of strife led to the formation of two companies working in Northern Ireland. Two of the world's experts in working creatively with the oppressed in repressive political situations, Barney Simon of the Market Theatre in Johannesburg and Augusto Boal, have both been to Derry, a learning situation on all sides. Many of the IWF's workshops are unsuitable for people with special needs. although every effort is made to accommodate them. Jos Houben in one workshop, which involved a participant with wasted legs, gave a startling demonstration of how the skill developed in performance could be transferred and used to great effect in the field of special needs. The main achievement in this area has been in Derry, where Wolfgang Stange has held two workshops with participants with learning difficulties. As examples of creative and pedagogical practice these could not be equalled and they provided a whole new set of insights into ways of enabling the marginalised to work through to expression.

The two workshops given in London and Glasgow by Jacques Lecoq had the effect of quadrupling the British intake to his school. In Nottingham, which has probably the richest ethnic mix of any regional city in Britain, and which has pursued a policy of racial integration through respect at the highest level instead of the lowest, artists from many parts of the world have spent time working in schools before coming together for a weekend of workshops. Children in Nottingham have been given the chance of meeting and Working with Australian Aborigine, Lakota Sioux, Manipuri and Phillipino artists along with individual artists such as the two leading figures in African dance, Koffi Koko and Germaine Acogny. Carlotta Ikeda the Butoh practitioner, Alan Bolt from Nicaragua, David Freeman of Opera Factory, and the London School of Carpoeira.

The level of teaching in British acting schools has always been high, but never higher that it is at the present moment. One aspect of training which has changed rapidly in recent years has been the development of an international attitude both in the contacts made, teachers (brought in as well as home grown), and the use of techniques derived from other performing disciplines and traditions. It would be unrealistic to attribute this solely to the IWF, which acts as one agency among several fostering this breaking down of the age-old isolation of the British theatre. Given the present state of the British theatre that these young actors will have to find work in, it may be that we are training actors for a theatre which does not exist. Perhaps they will change it through the pressure they exert. In any event, the IWF serves the cause in providing opportunities for the teachers to hone their skills and widen them. Teachers are similarly offered a chance to work in situations where they can experiment and test their work. Patsy Rodenburg, Head of Voice at the Guildhall School and for the Royal National Theatre, whose work has a consistent line through it of freeing the voice as a first stage in liberating the individual in many forms of expression, will this year be working with dancers, the performers who, in many more ways than one, have been denied a voice.

When the IWF grant from the ACE Dance Department was cut in 1996, the situation was not simple. Faced with a substantial cut in its own budget, the Dance Department decided to prioritise the Regional Dance Agencies which have responsibility for stimulating dance in their areas. The IWF has consistently worked closely with the Dance Agencies and has encouraged them to mount their own local workshops as a grassroots follow-up to the festivals. A victim of its own success, perhaps.

All of the IWF workshops end in some form of documentation, either written or visual. Peter Hulton, the head of the Arts Documentation

Unit, is a member of the IWF board of directors and is closely involved in documenting many of the workshops in monograph and video formats. These exist as a record of what was done during the workshop, a research resource for future consultation, as an aide memoire for those who took part, and are available through the Arts Documentation Unit for general sale to interested parties and institutions.

The workshops of the IWF are supported by an extensive research and development exercise. As a result of this, the IWF now has a massive international network of contacts and maintains a data bank of information on institutions and individuals who offer a wide range of training facilities. This is a major resource for consultation. A directory of professional training organisers, titled *INTO EUROPE,* was published from the data in November 1994. This directory contained 108 entries and rapidly sold out the 400 copies printed. A second edition, expanded to more than 250 entries, is to be published shortly by ACE.

Ultimately, however, the achievements of the IWF lie with the participants who enthusiastically work so hard and in many cases come back for more.

Future Policy

The IWF's original intention of mounting a biennial festival of workshops has been impossible to maintain. One reason lies in the difficulty of persuading potential funders to support the organisation during the fallow years. Funding always follows projects and not administration. Funders like to see some physical manifestation for their money. In the years between the full festivals it has proved advisable, and worthwhile, to run smaller sets of workshops, both in London and with our regional partners. As the organisation has grown to maturity, the complexity of these events has expanded to rival that of the full festivals The turning point in this was the mounting in the Autumn of 1991 and the Spring of 1992 of a project called *Soviet Visions.* Five leading Russian directors carried out workshop projects in Britain over a five-month period. Mark Zakharov explored new approaches to playing comedy through what he calls his inner laboratory method. Robert Sturua, director of the Rustavelli company, worked on *Hamlet.* Genrietta Yanovskaya, director of the Moscow Theatre for Young Spectators, posed the question: why Chekhov called his tragic plays 'comedies'. Anatoli Vasiliev, whose productions of *Cerceau* and *Six Characters in Search of an Author* had enjoyed great success in the London International Festival of Theatre, began work with five directors, five designers and fifteen actors, in the Royal National Theatre Studio. Lev Dodin, director of the Leningrad Maly Theatre, brought three of his collaborators (movement, voice and acting) and fifteen of his actors to work with twenty five actors,

Brochure advertising "The Way of the Warrior" for the International Workshop Festival, London and Düsseldorf, April 1998

drawn from Britain and Europe, for a month-long workshop in the Border town of Melrose.

Propelled by the fact that 1997 saw the end of the three-year cycle of franchise funding, a draft programme was developed outlining the workshop's intentions up to the year 2001, under the title of *A Body of Knowledge*. Following the artistic policy which has always been interdisciplinary and intercultural, the programme looks at how different disciplines, traditions, and schools approach fundamental aspects of performance. These approaches reveal the manifold possibilities of the body in motion and *new* approaches to familiar physical tasks. Each festival centres on one aspect of performance.

The future tone and direction of this programming has already begun to some extent, shaped by a one-off project in the fallow year of 1995, *The Performer's Energy*. The idea behind this workshop was to explore the links between the performing and martial arts disciplines in its training methods. Through a series of workshops, led by Oriental, African, Brazilian, and British masters, the source(s) of the performers' bodily and vocal energies were examined and worked on. A series of talks, demonstrations, and finally performances in the London South Bank Centre opened out the work to public scrutiny and understanding. Around 1,500 people attended the public events.

Encouraged by the projects' success, an extension was planned for Spring 1998. *The Way of the Warrior*. The relationship between the martial and performing arts remained the central concern of the project. More broadly, there were explorations of the links between medicine and religion – both integral to the development and nature of the martial arts forms. Discussions took place with possible funding partners for the programme to be presented in London, at the South Bank, and later in Düsseldorf, Berlin, and New York. With this, the IWF entered the public and international arenas.

Following the 1995 *Performer's Energy* Workshop, the 1996 festival took as its theme *Movement*.

In 1997 there was a two-pronged festival. In London, a series of interdisciplinary workshops explored the links between *Voice/Dance/Movement*. These saw a joint workshop between the voice specialist Patsy Rodenburg and Antonia Franceschi, a former soloist with Balanchine's New York City Ballet. Another equally intriguing workshop combined Jonathon Lunn of the London Contemporary Dance Theatre and Anthony Minghella, director of the Oscar-laden *The English Patient*, which explored the relationship between spoken text and dance. Meanwhile, *With the Whole Voice* in Glasgow and Belfast brought together singers from the Maghreb in Algeria, the Sakhan region of Siberia, Southern Italy, and Georgia with those from the Gaelic communities of the Western Isles of Scotland and Donegal.

Later in 1998, the full festival, *A Common Pulse*, centred on rhythm, through two major projects. The first follows the rhythms of the Yoruba people from West Africa over the Atlantic Ocean to the Caribbean and South America. The second was an exploration of rhythm from an Eastern European perspective.

1999 centred on *Person/Figura-Character and Performance.* Where do characters come from? Our memory, observation, inspiration, demons? What transforms a piece of wood into a live character on stage? Does the actor play the mask, or is she or he played by it? These questions about the relation between character and performance are at the heart of theatre, dance, puppetry, and mask. From Siberian shamans to Butoh dancers, invited teachers explored and expounded radically contrasted and opposing accounts of character all in pursuit of a 'truth' and a 'reality' of performance.

The year 2000 aims to pull the previous themes together under the title *Passages and Dialogues.* The festival will revisit, develop, and explore some of the *passages* of ideas from culture to culture, country to country, as well as the exchanges that have taken place between teachers over the previous five years. Related to this there is to be a series of workshops focussing on dialogue, which will be the culmination of a three year project with Anatoli Vasiliev.

The final festival in the series in 2001, if we are all still here, will be *The Sense of Space,* a collection of workshops which will explore, amongst other things, the theatricalisation of space, scenography, the stage and the village circle in traditional dance, body space, and returning to the opening theme: the actor's presence in space.

All of this, of course, depends on the one great skill necessary to pull it off. To pay acceptable fees to the masters who lead the classes and to keep entry fees down to the point where as many participants as possible are able to afford to take part, money must be found. Seventy-five percent of the budget is dependent upon outside funding sources, public and private. In the end, all art and learning depends on the skill with which you can fill in application forms.

References

Boal, Augusto (1979) *Theater of the Oppressed.* New York: Urizen Books
Kidd, R. and M. Byram (1977). "Popular Theatre and Development: a Botswana Case Study," *Convergence* 10, 2:20–30.

1996 International Workshop Festival

LONDON
Weekends

Rosemary Butcher	UK	Contemporary Dance
Ken Campbell	UK	*The Importance of Comedy*
Edward Clark	US/UK	Yoga Theatre
McDermott & Dartnell	UK	*Body, Play, Emotion*
Mladen Materic	UK	*Organic Sequences*
Rick Zoltowski	UK	*Bodying Forth*

Weeks

Clive Barker	UK	Theatre Games
Dominique Dupuy	France	*The Poetics of Movement*
Claire Heggen	France	*The Actor and the Object*
Keith Johnstone	Canada	*Impro*
Garet Newell	US/UK	Feldenkrais
Enrique Pardo	Peru/France	*Sound Moves*
J P Perreault	Quebec, France	Dance/Theatre
Henry Smith	US	*Movement, Power, Presence*

EDINBURGH

Jos Houben	Belgium	Feldenkrais and Mask
Slava Polunin	Russia	Clowning

GLASGOW

Gennadi Bogdanov	Russia	Meyerhold's Biomechanics
Mandala Theatre	Poland	An Actors' Workshop
Anatoly Vasiliev	Russia	Adapting Dostoevsky

NEWCASTLE *A Sense of Place*

Peter Schumann	US	Processional Theatre
Tina Etchells	UK	*Tracing the City*
& Hugo Glendinning		
Maria Abramovic	Former Yugoslavia	*Cleaning the House*

DERRY *Finding A Voice*

Helen Chadwick	UK	Voice
Ellen Lauren	US	The Suzuki Method
Wolfgang Stange	Germany	Dance
Andrew Dawson	UK	Feldenkrais
Julian Crouch	UK	Mask/Puppet Making

NOTTINGHAM *Stamping Ground*

Shiro Daimon	Japan	Kabuki
Carlotta Ikeda	Japan	Butoh
Koffi Koko	Benin	African Dance
Elsa Woliaston	France	African Dance

10

SITI – A SITE OF STILLNESS AND SURPRISE: ANN BOGARTS'S VIEWPOINTS TRAINING MEETS TADASHI SUZUKI'S METHOD OF ACTOR TRAINING

Eelka Lampe

"If you really go for the stop [at the end of each individual stomp], you'll be a wreck afterwards. [But that's what you need to do.] The goal is stillness, true stillness. It's a bigger problem, a better problem. The goal is living inside of stillness on stage. If you are still, you can move an audience."

(Steven Webber, Suzuki Training "maintenance session" Saturday, October 5 1996).

"Meet your fellow players with fresh eyes, there is still a lot you can learn about each other as performers and people." "Allow yourself to be surprised [...] The desire to do anything comes from something outside your body [...] Do you know where everyone is in space?"

(Barney O'Hanlon, Intermediate Viewpoints Training, Tuesday, October 8 1996)

Since 1992, Anne Bogart's Viewpoints Training and Tadashi Suzuki's Method of Actor Training have joined forces, opposing forces, it seems, to create something new. The emerging results in this work in progress are extraordinary. The actual site of the creative merger are the actors' bodies of Anne Bogart's SITI (Saratoga International Theater Institute) Company founded in 1992 by her and Suzuki in order to promote an international exchange between theatre artists, especially on the level of training.[1]

What started out as a grand international vision reacting against the status quo in the American commercial and regional theatres, soon became an exploration of what can happen when the Suzuki and Bogart training approaches are practiced together. The twelve company members of SITI have been training in both systems for years. Some of those who are

---

1. For a detailed account on the beginnings of SITI and background information on both directors, see Lampe, 1992; 1993; and 1995.

teaching the workshops have studied and worked with either director for more than a decade. The performers are in the middle of exploring in rehearsals with Anne Bogart during their ongoing workshop teaching what it means to clash vertical and horizontal energies (to borrow Grotowski's terms) to enhance the "watchability" of the actor. Productions like Bogart's *The Medium, Small Lives, Big Dreams,* and *Going, Going, Gone* have startled audiences in the United States and Europe because of their bold vision of performing the human body in space and time. This theatre is highly physical, precisely choreographed, and infused with a heightened energy that is light years away from psychological realism.

The following piece is the tale of two directors with a vision and a group of performers who have made it their own, thereby transcending the original cause into something brilliant and almost intangible. This article is an attempt to communicate about the craft and the experience of these two distinct training forms and how they are in the process of being linked by their foremost practitioners. The writing is based on my background knowledge of over a decade of closely following Bogart's work, my research on the Suzuki method since 1992 through SITI, and recent updated fieldwork in SITI's New York City workshop program.

Suzuki Training

> The way in which the feet are used is the basis of a stage performance. Even the movements of the arms and hands can only augment the feeling inherent in the body positions established by the feet. There are many cases in which the position of the feet determines even the strength and nuance of the actor's voice. An actor can still perform without arms and hands, but to perform without feet would be inconceivable.
>
> (Suzuki, 1986:6)

Saturday, October 5 1996, Maintenance Session (10:00 a.m. – 12:00 p.m.)

9:45 – In a rented dance studio at Fareta on Broadway in Greenwich Village, New York, a group of performers casually warm up for the session, mostly doing stretching exercises focus on opening the groin muscles. Some chat with each other during and in-between what look like very individualized routines. A few engage in aerobic bits, like running vigorously in place. This group is a mix of students who have trained with SITI during the spring or summer or in their current six week session. The Saturday training is meant to be as the name suggests, an opportunity to keep up or refresh the discipline.

(a)

(b)

Suzuki method: basic exercise #1. Photos: Eelka Lampe.

(c)

(d)

Suzuki method: basic exercise #1

10:00 – Steven Webber calls everybody to the floor to begin. He introduces me as a longterm researcher of Bogart's and Suzuki's work. He asks whether anybody objects to being photographed. Nobody minds.

"Basic 1," he announces. The 11 participants (later 13) assume their positions in three loose rows standing behind each other in one half of the rectangular studio facing Steven and myself. Three other visitors sit on the floor all the way in the back of the space, unintroduced.

Basic 1
Beginning position: standing straight, two heels touching, toes out on a 45 degree angle.

Steven shouts "One." Performers bend their knees slightly sliding forward on their right foot.

Steven shouts, "Two" Left foot joins right foot, again touching at the heel, into a slight plié.

"Three," pelvis lowers as far as possible into a "squatting" plié.

"Four," body rises back up to beginning position.

They repeat this sequence over and over again, responding to Steven's calling out numbers with various timings. Occasionally, Steven smacks a Shinai to the ground in unpredictable patterns. The Shinai, a bamboo stick with nylon string attached to either end which was originally a weapon in the Japanese fighting technique of Kendo, makes a whipping sound that functions as a signal to the performers to freeze their current position and to recite out loud and in unison a monologue (Menelaus' first monologue from the *Trojan Women*). When Steven calls out, "on ten," rather than freezing, they speak while slowly coming up from the squatting plié back to a standing position. Another addition to the routine is to ask the students, again on a count of ten starting from the squatting plié, to move slowly and in a controlled manner to a position of lying on their backs and then to come back up gradually, before resuming the Basic 1 routine. Even during this procedure, whenever Steven beats the Shinai into the ground they start reciting the text. The connection between physical control, breath control, therefore control over speaking is the ultimate goal of training.

Basic 2 is next.
Beginning position: standing, feet together, parallel, with knees slightly bent.

"One," lift right leg up as far as possible with knee bent towards the body and foot flexed towards the body.

"Two," stomp foot down straight.

"Three," slide same foot forward.

"Four," go up on toes.

"Five," come down again.

Next, "one," lift other foot and repeat sequence.

(a)

(b)

Suzuki method: basic exercise #2. Photos: Eelka Lampe

I ask that the actors strike the floor with all the energy possible; the energy that is not properly absorbed will rise upwards and cause the upper part of their bodies to tremble. In order to minimize such a transfer, the actor must learn to control and contain that energy in the pelvic region. Focusing on this part of the body, he must learn to gauge continuously the relationship between the upper and lower parts of his body, all the while continuing on with the stamping motion.

(Suzuki, 1986:9)

Steven tells participants that they have to move their focus and stop their focus consciously. In other words, the mind has to be with the movement of the pelvic region or more precisely the "center" (a point about an inch and a half below the navel that functions as the gathering center for the energy of the pelvic region) at all times.

Next, Steven announces "**Stomping**." Leon Ingulsrud, a senior Suzuki student and SITI company member, has arrived and now joins the group. He also indirectly leads the subsequent exercise. Steven puts on music which is distinctly percussive and to my ears has a very "foreign" quality to it. Ironically, it is distorted American Big Band music slowed down or sped up electronically by a Japanese sound engineer who collaborated with Suzuki on *Trojan Women* many years ago.

The performers stomp to the beat in unison while slowly walking in irregular individual circular patterns. This stomp is different from the one in Basic Exercise #2 in that actors only lift the knee until the thigh is approximately parallel to the ground.

In Suzuki's words:

The gesture of stamping on the ground, whether performed by Europeans or Japanese, gives the actor a sense of the strength inherent in his own body. It is a gesture that can lead to the creation of a fictional space, perhaps even a ritual space, in which the actor's body can achieve a transformation from the personal to the universal.

(1986:12)

The stomping continues for a few minutes until Steven stops the music abruptly which causes the performers to fall down on the spot. In retrospect, I realize that what looked like arbitrary circular patterns were, in fact, designed to bring the performers to the back of the room. So that when they fall down, we see one pile of bodies in the rear of the room.

Steven puts on meditative Shakuhachi music, Japanese bamboo flute, to which everyone rises very slowly as if awakening to a new world. Everybody has his or her individual vision, hinted at in the imaginary focus of their eyes. And once "resurrected," everybody walks forward slowly in a distinctly chosen upper body position, mostly reflected in the positions of their arms. When the Shakuhachi music stops, they all freeze in their positions.

Steven remarks, "You have to get to the 'edge of the stage' when the music stops. You were all caught up in executing the vision and then had to rush forward towards the end." This comment makes clear how crucial the performer's awareness of time and space is in the Suzuki training. Absolutely nothing the body does and the mind does in relationship to the body and its position in space is arbitrary.

Steven then asks the group to divide themselves into two. The performers now take turns watching each other work. This is a common practice in all the Suzuki training sessions I have observed. The idea is that the students learn not just by doing but also by observing the process others are going through, especially learning from their mistakes.

Basic 3 is called.
Beginning Position: heels touching, 45 degree angle, knees slightly bent.
"One," lift leg to the fullest with knee bent in the diagonal and flexed ankle towards leg.
"Two" stomp while stepping forward.
Repeat lifting the other leg, and so on.

After the exercise, Steven points out how important it is to release the groin area after the lift, which is "like wrapping the leg around," to achieve stillness. The sharp contrast between quick focused and often accelerated movement and complete full stops is a trade mark of all the Suzuki exercises. The philosophy behind this basic principle of training is that Suzuki believes energized stillness can attract and channel the attention of an audience and in fact move them internally. I see a connection here to the martial arts practice of Tai Chi Chuan where big outside movement usually implies small inside movement and, in reverse, small outside movement means big inside movement (i.e., apparent stillness might conceal a very active alive center).

Basic 4 prepares the performers for creating snippets of fiction.
Beginning position: standing straight, feet at a comfortable width from each other, facing front.
"One," on the beat of the Shinai, the participants turn their entire bodies towards the back, using the right foot as the axis for turning, and assume a

Suzuki method: basic exercise #3. Photo: Eelka Lampe

wide-legged squatting position. The upper body is relaxed with the head and arms hanging forward and sideways respectively.

"Two," on the beat of the Shinai, they turn back to the beginning position.

A significant aspect of this exercise is to train the students' responses to the unpredictable beat of the Shinai. "Basic 4" highlights the success of their response especially because they have to go from utter relaxation back to focused attention.

After this preparation, Steven takes them without interruption into the **"Standing Statues"** exercise. The group takes individual fictive upper-body positions amplified by their arms with every other beat; amplifications, the neutral relaxation position is now to the front instead of towards the back. Again, the spacing between the beats is deliberately irregular. Occasionally, Steven calls out "speak," and they repeat the Menelaus monologue.

The corresponding routine of **"Sitting Statues,"** training the same principles but emphasizing the strengthening of the pelvis and center, then concludes the first hour of the session.

"Take 5 [minutes]. Stay focused." Some use it as a bathroom break, others simply relax and stretch. Very little talking occurs.

The second hour resumes with **"Walking."**

Led by Leon to ongoing percussive music (again distorted Big Band music) the performers walk single-file, imitating whatever type of walk he assumes. At the end of the space they break their stances and walk back to the beginning of the line where Leon starts a new step once he sees the last ones finishing the previous one. The ten different walking steps can be briefly characterized as follows:[2]

1. basic stomp (as in Stomping and Shakuhachi)
2. triangular step, making toes meet
3. walking on the outside of the feet
4. flicking the feet to the outside with the "attack" coming from the hip
5. walking on toes
6. stomping sideways
7. stomping sideways, crossing feet
8. sideways in plié step
9. fast shuffle walk
10. toe shuffle in crouched position arms stretched out as if presenting a gift.

Steven once more stresses how crucial it is to fully go for the stop, for "true stillness" at the end of each step. If fully realized, this proposition is excruciatingly exhausting. "If you really go for the stop [at the end of each individual stomp], you'll be a wreck afterwards. [But that's what you need to do.] The goal is stillness, true stillness. It's a bigger problem, a *better* problem. The goal is living inside of stillness on stage. If you are still, you can move an audience."

The following exercise, "**Slow Ten Take a Ten**," promotes working together as an ensemble. This is in contrast to most of the other exercises, with the exception of "Stomping and Shakuhachi," which even though they have moments of working together in unison mostly stress the training of the individual performer's physical instrument in its relation to space and time. "Slow Ten" evokes a theatricality that is group created.

The performers face each other standing in two rows at either end of the "space" (still only half of the actual studio). They stand in a way that will allow them to pass each other midway without bumping into one another. To traditional Japanese Gagaku music (empirial court music, high flute and deep drums) the performers move slowly towards each other.

---

2. Compare with Tadashi Suzuki's references to specific walking steps in his chapter "The Grammar of the Feet" in *The Way of Acting* (1986). Suzuki is looking for an actor's expressivity through his or her feet. Comparing modern theatre to the traditional Noh and Kabuki he concludes, "one reason the modern theatre is so tedious to watch, it seems to me, is because it has no feet" (1986:7).

Start of Viewpoints training: running through open space. Photo: Eelka Lampe.

With their knees slightly bent, they step silently and controlled, heel first, one foot in front of the other, consciously moving along an imaginary line drawn through their body centers. Each one assumes a fictive gesture with the focus far out in the distance. At an imaginary line, and apparently coinciding with a particular section in the music, they turn simultaneously to move back to where they came from. when the music stops, they stop, now facing outwards at their beginning position.

In the beginners class I visited earlier, senior Suzuki teacher and company member Kelly Maurer pointed out, "when you turn, Suzuki would say, 'don't just turn your center but turn the whole room.' It takes a lot of energy" (Oct 1, 1996). Steven told the beginners to concentrate on the feet on the floor. "The relationship of the feet to the floor is constantly changing. [...] It looks smooth but what happens internally is rather aggressive. Control the rate of speed of your feet in the air. Turn at the same speed as walking."

To the more advanced students of this maintenance session, Steven says, "moving the center across the floor in a concentrated speed that's what moves the foot forward." They do it again to different music, Philip Glass. It is a recent and I would say natural and necessary development that SITI is experimenting with its own music. "There is a line of energy through the entire exercise. When you finish, it is still going. You are still but the room is still moving through you."

Steven refers to the Japanese performing principle of "jo ha kyu" (see Zeami on Noh, 1984). He says, "it is a Japanese term about story: beginning, middle and end." But then he quickly revises his own simplified introduction, "it is about order, then breaking, shattering – something is happening, and finally not ending but acceleration into something new. 'Kyu' with the turn, carry that back across the floor. [...] it is much more about *how* you are moving your energy. You can see someone do 'Slow Ten' and they are not doing the form right but they are doing it right!"

The ensemble aspect of this exercise is that ideally they should all move in sync with their own line and subsequently all turn at the same time and with the same speed.

The emphasis of moving the feet straight through the center line, or having the center causing the foot to move in that way, reminded me of a basic principle in Kalaripayatt, the martial arts form that has informed Indian Kathakali.

The last item of the day is "**Marching**." Again led by Leon to different percussive music, they do two types of stomping. The first round with knee up, stomp, slide forward while holding an imaginary spear above the shoulder parallel to the floor. The second one is a silent stomp while forming a circle with the thumb and index finger at eye level in the center line.

During an informal chat with the performers afterwards, several said that they come to the maintenance session when they can, which in most cases means if their rehearsal schedule allows. One person acknowledged that it is a "challenge to create an ensemble even though we might not know everyone, but the common vocabulary makes it possible." This comment reveals a distinctive feature of SITI's work: in contrast to other performer training workshops which might be more individualized (you go to a modern dance class or a voice class and get from it whatever you want individually), SITI's training philosophy is infused by Anne Bogart's belief that effective theatre grows out of ensemble work and that learning to work with an ensemble has to begin during training.

When I asked some performers, how the Suzuki training has affected their performing, I received several answers. For example, "my sense of time changed," "it applies to everything, that is, I have more control over my body; it gives me a sense of rigor. Also, this is the closest we can come to actual performing, because we are not always in shows all the time." "It made me see myself from the outside, like the audience would."

What connects these comments is a sense that the training gives the performers a heightened awareness of their own bodies and the space and time they are moving through. This is certainly a goal Suzuki would confirm. He wants actors to have an elevated sense of their being and surroundings, which ultimately implies to be able "to read" the energy of the audience. Practicing these kinds of skills on a concrete physiological level during training, relates Suzuki to Bogart's desire to treat training and workshop as close as possible to real performance experiences.

For SITI the training has become part of the identity of the company, according to Leon Ingulsrud "more of a life style than an education." Although this practice and conviction seems to resemble the philosophy of the SCOT (Suzuki Company of Toga) company, there is a distinct difference. In Japan, the training remains tied to specific productions whereas in the U.S. it informs people's work individually: be it a SITI company member, or a student who trains in their workshops and takes what she learns into her own professional life.

Looking back at the history of the Suzuki Method of Actor Training, one finds a pragmatic origin. I was told that two SCOT actors, Mr. Toyokawa and Mr. Fukao, developed all the exercises which comprise the current training in the late 1960s and early 1970s for a specific production. Mr. Suzuki saw the exercises, used them, and gave them a theoretical framework. The individual actors moved on, not having a particular interest in the training per se.

The production that was pivotal for most exercises was *Trojan Women*, the first of Suzuki's works to remain in the company's repertoire for a number of years. The training was developed to teach new members how to play the chorus. The music for "Stomping" and "Walking" has its origins in the production, as does the frequently used text which is Menelaus' first monologue from the play. Suzuki himself apparently prefers more recently to use the passage of "Tomorrow, tomorrow ..." from *Macbeth*. SITI has been using additional texts as well. For example, from *Romeo and Juliet*. Chekhov, or even more modern plays.

Will Bond told me that SITI members are in conversation with members of the SCOT company. "There is more hard drill in Japan, they have been training the traditional way. We over here are breaking the exercises down more. And the Japanese have become quite interested, 'what are you saying about this exercise?' they ask." (October 9)

Bond acknowledges that what they are doing in SITI is not the same as what Mr. Suzuki is doing, but that they "are mindful of an organic development of the Suzuki training." SITI teachers also teach their students via imitation. Bond explained that they start out with the four Basics, "Basic 1" etc., then introduce the "Basic Stomp and Shakuhachi," followed by the beginning of the walks, one or two a day. Their six weeks workshops offer classes from Tuesday through Friday, 10:00–11:45 Basic Suzuki or Intermediate Viewpoints; 12:00–1:45 Basic Viewpoints or Intermediate Suzuki.

The movement vocabulary is introduced before students are asked to speak, but the teachers emphasize the connection to speaking right away. There is a suggestion among company members now to introduce speaking earlier because they feel it might get shortchanged otherwise. Leon explains, "western techniques that have been focusing on the center of the body are mostly dance oriented, therefore not utilizing the cultivation of this specific physicality toward verbal expression. On the other hand, many specific western voice trainings emphasize the importance of relaxation above all else. Suzuki training is striving for a balance between tension and relaxation to make the voice come directly from whatever physical state the body happens to be in."

An issue which is brought up often with Mr. Suzuki and that is somewhat controversial is, how Japanese this training form is. SITI member Leon, who has served as Mr. Suzuki's translator for many years and who studied Noh in the U.S. in the past, explained he agreed with Mr. Suzuki that "Japanese influence is coincidental" because there are such clear elements of Kathakali, modern dance, and ballet present in the form next to some walking styles which resemble Noh or Kyogen walking. But Leon feels that a clear connection to Noh can be found in the fact that the Suzuki training, like Noh, is "talking straightforwardly about the intangible form of energy" a performer works with. "There is a similar concern in Noh and Kyogen to create a physical state and then maintain it. In Noh, however, the performer locks the center in, whereas Suzuki is looking for an expression that can flow through the center" (October 5).

Intermediate Viewpoints

Tuesday, October 8 1996 (10:00 a.m. – 11:45 a.m.)

On the 7th floor of 47 Great Jones Street, one of La Mama's rehearsal spaces in New York, a group of seven women and two men are warming up: stretching and loosening joints. I recognize four familiar faces from the Saturday Maintenance Session.

Barney O'Hanlon, whom I met originally during his first production with Anne Bogart ten years ago, is teaching the session. After he introduces me, he simply asks the students to start walking while he is putting on some modern classical music. They do so, crisscrossing each others' paths in unpredictable patterns. Barney joins the exercise but keeps talking. "Meet your fellow players with fresh eyes. There is still a lot you can learn about each other, " Barney reminds the members of the group who are now working in the last week of their six weeks workshop.

Barney keeps giving them instructions while they are moving: "Increase the tempo. [They will be running eventually.] Find empty holes between people. Arms nice and easy at your side. Breathe low. If it is good [what's happening], it's not necessarily in the center [of the space]. Look for large holes between people. And walk again. When you get close to someone let it turn you. Allow yourself to be surprised, keep yourself off balance. Now do a combination of two, walk through spaces and turn on contact. The desire to stop comes from an impulse outside of you, to go, also. If you see someone stop, take their place. Now altogether: through spaces, "turn off stops and replace people."

This beginning segment of the session, while introducing the two viewpoints of **tempo** and **topology** (floor patterns invisibly "painted" by the performers' feet), most of all trains performers' **kinesthetic responses**. These kinesthetic responses are the key viewpoint-element of Bogart's Viewpoints which she adapted and expanded over the years from Mary Overlie's "6 Viewpoints" improvisation technique for postmodern dancers.[3] While Overlie's categories were designed to help dancers create material efficiently through structured improvisation, Bogart's goals were aimed at actors. She wanted actors to develop such physical awareness that at any given moment on stage they would be creating a physical tapestry in support of or often in creative tension with the literary part of the performance.

Barney continued the session by building on the foundation he had set. "Let that go and walk. Pick someone and follow that person, then let them go. Add everything else [i.e., through spaces, turn off stops, replace people] to 'following.'" And he repeats: "The desire to do anything comes from outside your body."

This reminder is a crucial difference between Bogart's approach and Suzuki's; in the former, everything originates from inside the performer's mind and body. The reason why these two approaches work so well together is that they truly complement one another. The different focus on the internal or the external experience is not so much confronting the performer with a contradiction as it is presenting a creative paradox: ideally any performer should work with the highest internal and external awareness simultaneously.

Barney goes on: "add tempo changes. Be aware of your spatial relationships, be aware of what you are creating in space at all times. " This short comment implies four additional viewpoints: **spatial relationship, shape, gesture** and **repetition**. Because this is an intermediate class in the final week of a lengthy workshop, Barney does not need to break them down. The performers know that at this point they can consciously play with adding distinct body shapes, gestures, and work off other players by repeating gestures or shapes that they have been creating.

---

3. For a more detailed discussion of Overlie's technique and the history of Bogart's Viewpoints see Lampe, 1994.

Barney encourages them: "Moments of collision are moments of great potential as an actor. Let the architecture play a part, too. How can you work with people that are not next to you. Do you know where everyone is in the space? " Here we hear of another viewpoint, **architecture**, which is about incorporating the physical shape of the space into movement choices. Furthermore, Barney challenges the students to take kinesthetic awareness to the level of **kinesthetic response.**

While everybody is still moving, Barney changes the general warming up and Viewpoints review training to the main subject of this particular session. "We are going to play with focus today. Where is the focus at any moment? The focus of the audience? Use your third eye. Your center is connected to the center of other players. Experience what's going on." The attention to the audience, in this case only Barney and myself, and to the center is clearly informed by the Suzuki training.

Barney changes the music and asks the students to pick a text of their choice for the next section. Although each performer is working with a different text, the actors are asked to speak together and finish at the same time. While still working physically with the Viewpoints, they recite their texts over and over gradually becoming quieter until they eventually fall silent.

The incorporation of text as part of the "Viewpoints" is a relatively new development that coincided with the early collaboration with Suzuki. It certainly was reinforced by the integration of movement and text in the Suzuki training, but, according to several company members, it would have solidified nevertheless on its own. Similarly, the use of music during the Viewpoint training became a staple after sound designer Darron West joined the company and lent his ideas about soundscape as part of a performance "tapestry" to the training. Again, it happened to be a fitting correlation to the Suzuki approach.

It seems that the integration of text is the least matured element in the Viewpoints' training. Understandably so, if one remembers that Bogart has been developing the physical components of Viewpoints since 1975 and only began experimenting with language in them in the early 90s.

Barney, who is probably the most advanced advocate and teacher of speaking as an active part of the Viewpoints training, refers to speaking as "a gesture in space." He feels that "the impulse to speaking can come from a physical event" and the training emphasizes that one becomes available to react on that level. Barney thinks that the Viewpoints can help "wake up language." He acknowledges that the "language viewpoints" are so far experimental, but he is trying "to develop actual exercises to get there." His viewpoints for language are: tempo, pitch, dynamic, kinesthetic, architecture, shape, repetition, and gesture.

As much as Barney is in favor of the Viewpoints approach to speaking, he also fears it could become nothing more than an aural soundscape. For him it is important, especially when it comes to an actual production, "to be in the moment with words " so that there is some genuine communication. "Saying it one way and then saying it again in a different situation differently."

As a teacher, Barney is a product not only of his physical training but also his musical education. He studied violin from age seven to eighteen, and is a trained singer. Therefore, he also likes to refer to the verbal viewpoints as a musical score where the different voices are interwoven like the strings and basses in a symphony. Interestingly enough, he does see a difference between the idea of an aural soundscape, which he opposes, and the concept of a musical score for speaking. His goal is "to teach yourself to hear on a new level which is not the daily life level" (October 31 1996).

When the speaking dies down, Barney comments, "Yes, let it die, keep working physically. Even if you are working on a physical structure, how can you keep it alive inside? " The challenge of infusing external movement with internal life, once again echoes the major principle of Suzuki training. For years, before Bogart encountered Suzuki's work, she had always been seeking this kind of aliveness in her actors. But at that time she did not ask for it or teach it during her Viewpoints training. Only when it came to staging did she ask the actors to breathe life into their characters while they were executing a precisely set choreography. This caused problems for some actors who were not used to working in this manner.

Barney gives more advice to the students, "If text comes up, go through it as a group, with crescendo and decrescendo, for example. I will call out some-one's name. That person will become primary focus, the rest is ensemble. The chorus doesn't have to be upstage to support! Next time I call someone as primary focus, they should speak. Take kinesthetic response off language, too. Try and create the obstacle physically in your body (a Suzuki influence). I'm not calling names anymore, try to get a sense of where the focus is on your own."

As a final section before the break, Barney announces, "You know the music. When it comes on, you know what to do." He puts on some disco-type music and they all break into a dance which looks choreographed. I later ask Barney about the purpose of this exercise. He explains that it is an ultimate goal for him to create such "in tune" ensemble work that even during the formal staging of a play there would be room for sudden spontaneous choreography in unison.

When Barney calls for a break at 11 am, it is the first time since 10 am that they stop moving. "Good work," Barney compliments them. In yet another reflection on the Suzuki training, he talks about the connections between the voice and physical state of the body. He also discusses the difficulty of focus, "You don't need to move away from where you are. When I call your name, it is precisely because I probably saw something right there in that moment."

During the second half of the workshop, Barney explores the Viewpoints for staging. This process is a very slowed down Viewpoints exercise in which every choice made by each actor is examined, repeated, and fine-tuned, before it becomes part of the group's ensemble choreography.

The session concludes with a brief talk about the experience of staging in this way. One performer remarks that it is hard to repeat a certain sequence so many times and still keep it fresh and interesting for oneself and therefore for an audience. Barney responds with a quote from Anne Bogart, "You have to kill something before you can bring it back to life."

The Link

As a company SITI is unique in the United States because its members can largely survive by working solely for and through SITI. SITI members venture out to colleges and festivals all around the country and the world (Ireland, England, Denmark, Russia, Turkey, Australia, Columbia) to teach the two methods in conjunction. They earn their salaries through workshop teaching and touring. In addition, their development and fundraising efforts have been successful over the past few years. In may 1997, SITI will perform at the Miller Theater at Columbia University with three different productions from the repertory.

Asked about the connection between the Suzuki and Viewpoints training for them as a company, various members agreed that it is constantly evolving. Leon Ingulsrud commented that "Suzuki and Bogart come together in the plays, in the productions. Both have a shared set of standards and then there is freedom for the actors within that constriction" (Oct 5 1996). Barney O'Hanlon made some very specific points regarding process, "the company rehearses with Viewpoints but maintains them with the Suzuki training (how to stay alive inside)" (Oct 31 1996).

Tellingly, Barney explains at the same time how Viewpoints has become "more of a discipline" than simply a rehearsal technique, which it served as when Bogart was teaching at NYU's Experimental Theatre Wing in the 1970s and 1980s.

Barney mentioned how the company is interested in connecting Viewpoints and the Suzuki Method more. He and Kelly Maurer were teaching a workshop in Tennessee and rather than teaching the two different approaches side by side in separate classes, they taught classes together, switching from one approach to the other within the same class. Barney was excited about this recent successful experiment. He noted that

"Viewpoints is very free and Suzuki is very formal: Viewpoints can bring to the Suzuki body aliveness and fullness and Suzuki training can bring to Viewpoints an incredible understanding of the body in space, a 360 degree awareness."

In my opinion, both methods focus on a heightened mental and physical aliveness on stage and on an increased awareness of one's environment. The difference between the two methods lies in the fact that the Suzuki approach aims for these goals from the inside out and the Viewpoints training cultivates it from the outside in. Another way of addressing the issue is to refer to the Suzuki training as primarily a solo exercise to cultivate one's self, or, more precisely, one's feet and center as foundation and expressive tools from which vocal work naturally arises; and to see the Viewpoints training as primarily a group exercise to cultivate one's relationship to others as well as one's kinesthetic and visual/aural awareness. Because of their similar goals but opposite approaches, the two methods are truly complementary. What started out as a bold experiment in 1992, has become a very promising artistic venture in inspiring performers around the world.

References

Bond, W. (1996) Phone interview with the author, October 9.

Ingulsrud, L. and Webber, S. (1996) Interview with the author, October 5.

Lampe, E. (1992) "From the Battle to the Gift. The Directing of Anne Bogart." *The Drama Review*. 36 (1), 14-47.

(1993) "Collaboration and Cultural Clashing: Anne Bogart and Tadashi Suzuki's Saratoga International Theater Institute." *The Drama Review*. 37 (1), 147-156.

(1994) *Disruptions in Representation: The Directing Practices of Anne Bogart*. Ann Arbor: UMI.

(1995) "The Paradox of the Circle: Anne Bogart's Creative Encounter with East Asian Performance Traditions," in *Anne Bogart – Viewpoints*, edited by J. Smith and M. Dixon, pp 151-162. New Hampshire: Smith & Kraus.

O'Hanlon, B. (1996) Phone interview with the author, October 31.

Suzuki, T. (1986) *The Way of Acting*, translated by J. T. Rimer. New York: Theatre Communications Group.

Zeami (1984) *On the Art of the Noh Drama*, translated by J. T. Rimer and Y. Masakazu. Princeton: Princeton University Press.

11

ENTERING THE POLITICAL DISCUSSION BY ARTISTIC MEANS: ELIA MASTERCLASS ON ACTING 1994

Jacqueline Martin

The European League of Institutes of the Arts, ELIA, was founded in 1990 and is an independent network of approximately 300 Arts Education Institutes, with members in 36 countries, covering all the disciplines of the Arts: Dance, Design, Theatre, Fine Art, Music, Film and Architecture.

ELIA holds conferences every year as well as seminars/ masterclasses on relevant themes. These conferences are highly regarded and well-attended by approximately 400 deans, teachers and students from the Arts Institutes in the European Union.

The general aims of ELIA are to:

- promote international cooperation between students and teachers of academic institutes of arts throughout Europe
- collect and provide information among European schools of art with a view to establishing and/or improving exchange programmes and joint projects
- advise national, international and supranational institutions concerned with international co-operation in the field of education in the arts and to act as an interest representation
- defend and encourage the specific needs of education in the arts and of art production such as singularity, imagination and creativity
- provide support for and promote the contribution made by academic institutions and colleges of art and design, performing arts and music to the development and unfolding of culture
- help maintain or establish adequate social and political conditions for a free development of education in the arts and of art production
- uphold and defend the diversity of cultures and stimulate communication between European and non-European cultures viewed as partners in a global society

A major conference was organised by ELIA in Berlin in 1994 entitled '*taken at the flood – art in our times*' whose two main themes were concerned with teaching art/being an artist, and posed the question if it were possible to enter the political discussion by artistic means.[1] In an endeavour to address these issues ELIA organized a masterclass in theatre to serve as a catalyst at the Berlin Conference with a group of twelve selected drama students from seven countries and twenty-five teachers who had the opportunity of working with six masters representing the different disciplines of theatre and coming from different traditions of actor training.

The text chosen for the students to work on was *MEDEAMATERIAL* by the German playwright, Heiner Müller, who was regarded as the successor to Brecht in the 1950's as many of his early plays were written in the Epic mode and are fine examples of Agitprop theatre. In more recent times Müller considered Brecht's 'theatre of enlightenment' an obsolete tool for the treatment of the complex reality of our age and was convinced that a new dramaturgy, a new concept of theatre, a new strategy of performance had to be created, although he still believed that theatre/performance was a means to influence audiences.

Müller constructed the play from newly-written material and fragments of earlier writings. It contains three short sections. The first part, 'Waterfront Wasteland' evokes East Berlin suburbia with its lakes, commuter trains, housing developments etc., a polluted landscape swarming with people, whose minds (according to Müller) are just as polluted. The second part 'medea material' stays close to the traditional *Medea* story, though it has become mostly a monologue of the betrayed aging woman and mother, framed by two brief dialogue scenes of which the last consists of two lines only. The final section, 'Landscape with Argonauts', reads like and probably is based on a dream, the dream of a man's (the author's?) voyage across oceans and landscapes in their terminal state of pollution by technologies, art and war, ending with the extermination of the voyager who turns into a landscape, the landscape of his death. An end which evokes the image of an ultimate holocaust.

This masterclass on theatre was entitled *Towards a Multidisciplinary Approach to Acting*[2] and it was closely aligned to the themes of the Berlin conference – particularly the question of whether it is possible for artists to enter the political arena by artistic means. Its specific aims and objectives were:

---

1. See *ELIA Conference in Berlin, 28 September – 2 October, 1994, 'taken at the flood – art in our times'* (ELIA Secretariat, Amsterdam).
2. A full documentation of this masterclass is available: *The 1994 ELIA Masterclass on Theatre, 'Towards a Multidisciplinary Approach to Acting'*, ELIA Secretariat, PO Box 15079, 1001 MB Amsterdam, The Netherlands.

- to investigate new methods of integration between voice, movement and acting
- to investigate how students in theatre coming from different European cultures with many different traditions of actor training work together, and the role of language in this connection
- to investigate how a common theme that is current in many different European societies (Medea being a stranger in the country she lives in) can be visualised with a diverse group of students and teachers
- to try to rediscover Theatrical Reality and encourage the students to look for alternatives to Naturalism as an acting style
- to explore the possibility of 'entering the political discussion by artistic means'
- to investigate how the pedagogical traditions of the (former) Eastern bloc could merge with the traditions of the West and offer the students a new and challenging dialectic
- to merge the Brechtian and Stanislavskian approaches to acting
- to investigate the whole question of 'domination/submission' by relating to the feminist stance in these different countries
- to encourage the students to see themselves as Europeans with a common European heritage and to give them the ambition to be actively involved in the development of Europe

In order to combat Naturalism's strategy of simply' doubling reality' and in an attempt to find this Theatrical Reality, it was hoped that the chosen text, Heiner Müller's *MEDEAMATERIAL*, would provide the nucleus through which to explore a multidisciplinary approach to acting and at the same time address the important political issues outlined above.

The Students

The students taking part were Tommi Korpela (Finland), Kulli Koik and Peeter Raudsepp (Estonia), Catherine Green, Matthew Dunster and Kate Roberts (United Kingdom), Miriam Kohler and Benjamin Kiss (Germany), Daniela Nane (Romania), Christo Mitzkov (Bulgaria), Fenneke Wekker and Rogier in 't Hout (The Netherlands).

The Masters

The six masters who were invited to contribute to the Masterclass came from different traditions of actor training roughly representing Brechtian and Stanislavskian approaches were:

Cicely Berry who is the former Director of Voice of the Royal Shakespeare Company where she has worked since 1969. She has written three books on voice, the latest, *The Actor and the Text* is widely used in the theatre and deals with how modern acting approaches can relate to heightened language. She has worked on Shakespeare in a number of foreign countries, has directed a number of Shakespeare productions, and was awarded the OBE in 1992.

Hildegard Buchwald-Wegeleben who was in charge of movement education at the Schauspielschule des Deutschen Theaters, which was founded by Max Reinhardt. In addition to her work in movement training for actors she was movement teacher at the Berliner Ensemble from 1961 until 1981. She has also had considerable experience offering intensive courses in movement for teachers and students on a national and international level. She worked with her accompanist of many years, **Joachim Keller**.

Kristin Linklater who is a master teacher of voice and has specialized in Shakespeare. Her books, *Freeing the Natural Voice* and *Freeing Shakespeare's Voice* are leading texts in the actor training field. She has conducted workshops for the Royal Shakespeare Company and Peter Brook's *International Centre for Theatre Research* in Paris. She has coached at the Stratford Festival in Canada, the Gutherie Theatre in Minneapolis, the Lincoln Center Repertory Company, the Negro Ensemble Company, the Open Theatre with Joseph Chaikin, and on many Broadway productions.

Angelika Waller who has been a teacher at the Hochschule für Schauspielkunst 'Ernst Busch', for many years and since 1992 she has been a Professor in the acting department. She was invited by Brecht's wife, Helene Weigel, to join the Berliner Ensemble in 1966 where she has enjoyed a long career as an actress. She has also numerous film and television productions to her credit.

Uwe Lohse who has been teacher of music since 1976 at the Theaterhochschule 'Hans Otto' in Leipzig. From 1976 to 1985 he was musical director of the Theatre Orchestra at the Städtischen Theatern Karl-Marx-Stadt, then director and musical director of a small theatre in Friedrichstadtpalast, Berlin. In 1992 he became a Professor at the Hochschule für Schauspielkunst 'Ernst Busch' in Berlin. He has composed theatre music for a number of productions.

Jacqueline Martin who has a wide range of experience in both the practice and theory of voice in the theatre as well as having directed a number of plays and operas in Australia and Sweden. She is author of *Voice in Modern Theatre* and co-author together with Willmar Sauter of *Understanding Theatre:*

Performance Analysis in Theory and Practice.[3] She conducted the ELIA Masterclass on Voice in 1993 and is currently researching the art of rhetoric as a possible medium for the actor of today to recapture audiences.

The Structure for the Masterclass on Theatre *Towards a Multidisciplinary Approach to Acting* is outlined below.

Stage 1 - Preparatory Workshop Amsterdam (25 June – 1 July, 1994)

The first stage of the Masterclass was held over six days in Amsterdam during the International School Festival. The students worked on the following areas with the Masters:

Voice/Text – Kristin Linklater; Singing/Music – Uwe Lohse; Acting/ Directing – Angelika Waller. Jacqueline Martin co-ordinated and summarized, assisted by Taco de Neef and Wytze Visser who also served as a translator. Due to previous commitments, neither Hildegard Buchwald-Wegeleben nor Cicely Berry could participate in this stage of the work.

Kristin Linklater worked mainly on the 'Voice in the Body,' encouraging the students to express thought and feeling over a wide range and to respond physically to their imaginative impulses. In addition, she encouraged them to explore their language and national differences, playing such games as 'International Kindergarten,' where the students improvised and played with the experience of feeling different sounds in their mouths, and finding a way of communicating with each other across the language barriers.

Uwe Lohse composed music for the first part of the text, 'Waterfront Wasteland', and worked with the student's audio responsiveness, physical response to rhythm and motivating sound by thought. He worked on the mise-en-scène of this section together with Angelika Waller, where the students were directed to speak the text as if reading a foreign language for the first time. Again the emphasis was placed on the theme of *Medea* – that of being a stranger in a foreign country.

Angelika Waller concentrated on the second part of the text, 'medea material,' which she divided amongst four Medeas and four Jasons, two nurses and two children. She encouraged the students to find a strong physical gestus (a physical attitude) and not to play with sentimentality.

---

3. Martin, J. and Sauter, W. (1995) *Understanding Theatre: Performance Analysis in Theory and Practice*, Stockholm, Almquist and Wiksell International.

Working along Brechtian lines, she pointed out various 'turning points' in the text – such as exile, slave, and children. She outlined the main theme as 'being a foreigner trying to find a way out of the situation' and drew many parallels with the power struggle in Europe. During this stage of the work, each of the students was invited to share with the group how the power struggle, which is exemplified in the Medea/Jason situation, could be related to power struggles in their own countries.

Jacqueline Martin talked about Heiner Müller and drew comparisons with Euripides' *Medea* as well as Müller's previous *Medeaplay* (1974) and the Theatre of Images. She assisted the students to discover the major themes of the play and to see the relevance of the play to contemporary society. She made the students aware of how the language was 'harshly' erotic and how to look for the verbal images which establish the mood of the piece as well as to cope with the structure of the writing (no punctuation and some words and phrases in capitals).

A presentation of the Work in Progress was made at the end of the week, followed by a planning meeting with Cicely Berry. Over the vacation, the students were given work to prepare on 'Landscape with Argonauts' for Kristin Linklater, who requested that they should start a journal into which they should write down their reactions to the play each time they read it; to include any items from their national newspapers which might seem relevant to this section; to write a short poem starting with any of the following lines from this final section of the play:

> 'How dangerous they are, the actors
> I and I-no-more
> The theatre of my death
> Do you remember do you no I don't
> Word-mud is a no-man's body
> The rest is poetry'

Cicely Berry, who was to concentrate on the connections with language in Berlin, requested that the students prepare short excerpts from Shakespeare's *Hamlet* and from *Preludes* by T.S. Eliot. She planned to enter the post-modern language in Müller's text through an inter-textual exploration of other verse forms. In order to assist the students, she arranged for a cassette recording of these pieces to be sent to each of the non-English speaking students.

[N.B. It is worth pointing out that the co-ordinator and ELIA organisors were so perturbed by the 'product-orientated' way in which the acting classes were conducted during the preliminary stage in Amsterdam that they drafted a letter to all masters over the vacation reminding them of the pedagogical goals of the project.]

Stage 2 - ELIA Masterclass on Theatre Towards a Multidisciplinary Approach to Acting, Berlin (18–27 September, 1994)

During this time, the students continued working with the masters while twenty-five teachers also had the opportunity of working with the masters as well as observing some classes. A summary of the individual masters' approaches follows.

Kristin Linklater's pedagogical approach to the text is an anti-intellectual one. She stresses the importance of the marriage between the text and the performer, encouraging the students to get the language out of their heads and into their bodies. She believes that the more a person feels freely and thinks clearly the better he/she will be communicating in dialogue. The freeing of emotion frees the eloquence.

To achieve this, she worked on the students' imaginative and physical responses to color through sound and words. Emphasising the importance of synergy, or 'the connections' between the images and sounds in the word. Linklater devised many exercises to elicit this, such as playing with imaginary balls of different weights and sizes, power games and making statues to express emotion.

The link to 'Landscape with Argonauts' was very gradual, progressing from phrase to phrase, where individual, personalized responses to the text were even 'massaged' out by Linklater where she felt this was necessary for the students to allow the images to work on their emotions. This entailed Linklater physically massaging tension areas in the students, as they lay prone on the floor, in order to help them release these responses more fully.

She encouraged the students to personalize the emotion, particularly in relation to the poetry which they had written themselves. The students recited/read in their own languages and then made a summary of the content in English for the group. Much of this material was very strong and very moving, and it was ultimately woven into Müller's text. Naturally this affected the playing style, which did not achieve a 'Theatrical Reality' in the way that Angelika Waller was seeking in the students, based on the Brechtian '*gestus*' but rather a heightened reality which was based upon their own personal contributions. Parts of their own languages were retained and contributed to making a very strong European statement about the political issues being explored.

Hildegard Buchwald-Wegeleben has a great respect for individuality in acting. Her approach to movement training, unlike Linklater's, is through the head and not the body. She believes there should always be a reason to move – a motive – and that body consciousness is much more important for an actor than body movement. She outlined the importance of diametrical opposition in movement, and helped the students discover the force of gravity as well as the principles of contrasts and oppositions embodied in the counter-balance point dividing the torso from the lower legs.

In getting the actors to experience this, Buchwald-Wegeleben worked on a number of different exercises guided by the overriding principle that the most important aspect of this work is a love of acting: in an art, as she sees it, that is about reaching out to the public and conveying something to others, not about individual experience. Her work never particularly concerned itself with the texts, but through her classes she made her contribution to helping the students see the difference between the two styles – Naturalism and Theatrical Reality the former meaning as in everyday life and the latter meaning 'framed' as in real life, where it can be observed.

Cicely Berry is very interested in language and being able to articulate in languages of all types. She does not believe that actors should think about single words as much as they should consider the whole structure of the language and learn to develop a feeling for the flow of verbal delivery: 'language can be treated as music – rhythm, tempo and dynamics, and really using the vowels and consonants, but most important for actors is a feeling of physical language because language is movement.' She believes that the physical/emotional energy should come into the speaking, that words and language should surprise, provoke, and exhilarate. As with Buchwald-Wegeleben she also believes that a good actor is always thinking in opposites.

In her work with the student actors Berry used a wide variety of texts from Shakespeare as well as modern works. To incorporate the physical aspect into the language, Berry uses a lot of movement, such as walking, jostling, changing direction at punctuation marks, running around the room, kicking objects, pushing etc. whilst speaking the text.

Linklater and Berry worked together on 'Landscape with Argonauts,' starting with the text after a basic action of going on a journey was established. The individual poems which the students had written were incorporated into this text. The shape for this piece of work was left until very late in the masterclass as both masters believed that their classwork was of more pedagogical importance than a showing. They directed the students to explore the political arena in a very personalized way and the results were very moving. Their section of *MEDEAMATERIAL,* was the final one, and a good example of young artists drawing heavily upon their own experiences to make personalized, political statements about the power struggles in their own countries. They also managed to intersperse their personal poems with Müller's text and thereby his text took on more contemporary relevance.

Uwe Lohse believes that an actor should not be trained to be an opera singer or a musical star, but that he has to develop special musical skills for his own profession. In achieving this one must always have an intention – an attitude to the text – a note should never just be sung. His own preference for disharmonic singing, which was the form of the 'Waterfront Wasteland,' informs his approach, because it represents the individual in a group. As a result it became essential for the actors to determine why they sing together – to determine their motivations.

To achieve his aims, Lohse devised a number of exercises to help the students find a way of using their voices and movement at the same time – both with and without the piano – which eventually fed into the mise-en-scène for 'Waterfront Wasteland.' In working on this scene together with Waller, the students were urged to summarize their feelings into one sentence and sing with that attitude. Because of his background, Lohse was not interested in emotionality, and in terms of achieving Theatrical Reality his work came close to that of Kurt Weill and the *songspiel* tradition. However, for many of the students it was a very difficult task and outside their frame of reference.

Angelika Waller had problems to overcome in the rehearsals at this stage as she had directed the students towards a result in Amsterdam rather than focusing on the process of acting. She wanted the students to see the difference between Realism (describing what you can do) and Naturalism (playing a fictive situation on stage). This difference was the foundation of her Brechtian pedagogical approach, as she directed the students not just to show temperament, but to play situation and to keep their *gestus*. She illustrated where this difference lay with a video made in Amsterdam during their work-in-progress.

Towards this end, she provided each of the students with a long ex-army coat which she explained was a handicap, not a costume. She encouraged the students to recount their personal experiences of war and domination in their own countries and to relate this to the 'medea material.' She insisted on attitudes, making the 'turning points' clear and playing without sentimentality. (According to the Brechtian aesthetic, the turning points are where a character faces a dilemma and must make an ethical choice about how to proceed.)

At this stage, some of the students wanted to explore other roles and to experiment more, but Waller kept going back to what they had done – insisting that it was too 'surface-like,' 'too sentimental' and too much like theatre. Her concept of using four Medeas and four Jasons and sharing the dialogue and action between them all simultaneously demanded enormous concentration and precision in physical / vocal attitudes. Added to that, her insistence on using song, in the 'Waterfront Wasteland' section, in the same manner, i.e., with a big physical *gestus*, was almost an impossibility for the students who had no frame of reference for this style of singing / performance.

Stage 3 - Results of the ELIA Masterclass on Theatre

The results of the Masterclass work-in-progress were presented for an audience consisting of members of the ELIA Conference *Taken at the Flood – Art in our Times* and the participating teachers. This was followed by a number of seminars dealing with methods of working in the Masterclass and a panel discussion, where comments and observations were invited from the audience. It was interesting that two of the masters, Waller and Linklater, refused to give a practical demonstration of their work methods – the former because she felt it should be revealed in the students' acting, and the latter because she was determined to signal that the voice work was equally as important as the acting. Many participants were disappointed as a result.

Evaluation

Taking into consideration the feed-back from individual interviews with the students, letters, comments from the masters, and the conclusions of the participating teachers, it was generally felt that in spite of their familiarity with working in a multidisciplinary way, the students were all challenged in one way or another. Surprisingly, many of the students had difficulties in opening themselves to new experiences, as if they were afraid that they would learn something contrary to what they believed was 'the right way.' Some masters also had difficulties in extending their familiar approaches, and complained about the restrictive nature of the format. This caused a lack of trust and co-operation on their part and, worst of all, a refusal to communicate!

Naturally the language and cultural differences were many at the outset of this project, and in spite of some frustrations related to obvious differences in levels of ability, the end result was a group of young artists who had developed tolerance and understanding towards each other and a willingness to work together.

Working on *MEDEAMATERIAL* was not easy because it is abstract and, whilst the theme is extremely challenging, its language is difficult, particularly for students who do not share a common language. Nevertheless, it raised many important political issues for discussion. The final outcome was a committed exercise, and although the first two sections were 'directed' more than developed, the last was a completely personal statement by the students.

The method of work in the first two sections really succeeded in exploring Theatrical Reality, even though the process of attaining it seemed pedagogically unsound, because the students were pushed so hard towards a product. However, in their classwork with the movement master, Buchwald-Wegeleben, the students were extended in this area because she is such an excellent pedagogue and obviously had the students' improvement as her goal.

Throughout the Masterclass the students were encouraged to discuss the political situation in their countries and in Europe as a whole. They were all very committed to making an artistic contribution through the *MEDEAMATERIAL* exercise to the new 'Europe' as representatives of their own countries within the European Union.

For some of the masters it was more difficult to bridge the gap between East/West traditions than it was for the students. An explanation for this is not easy to grasp. In spite of some complaints from the acting master, Waller, that the students had to cope with 'feeling' in the morning and 'thinking' in the afternoon, the students did not appear to experience problems in merging the Brechtian and Stanislavskian approaches.

Through her invaluable way of working on language and text, Berry gave the students many 'keys' to opening the poetic language of Müller's difficult text. The major theme of *MEDEAMATERIAL* was discussed intellectually and related to the students' particular problems in their own countries. The fact that there were four Medeas and four Jasons provided ample opportunity for very careful and exact work on attitudes and relationships. It was not an easy process because the abstraction and physical demands caused some problems for less-experienced actors.

The teachers were critical that whereas the goals and objectives were positive and important, they were carried out too exclusively in the student's project and not dealt with sufficiently for the teachers. The relationship between the two parts of the project was the most critical one, but the teachers were literally excluded from the work-in-progress both in Amsterdam and in Berlin, except for two brief occasions in Berlin. Most of the teachers had been under the impression that the project would allow observation of the students' work-in-progress with the masters on a daily basis and that they would be able to work with the leaders on the problems the students were experiencing, but neither of these took place.

Although the teachers believed that the basic concept of the project was excellent and that further encounters of this sort should be developed, they felt unanimously that too much emphasis was placed on the need for a result in the form of a performance, thus placing unnecessary pressure on the students. This they felt defeated the experimental purpose of the project as a whole. They were also aware of the problems of co-ordination and communication between the masters. The fact that Waller could not/ would not discuss her work methods was a bitter disappointment for them all.

In conclusion, the topic 'multidisciplinarity' stimulated the participating teachers to want to pursue this further. They submitted a concrete suggestion regarding a follow-up project for a future ELIA masterclass – a multinational, multilingual, multidisciplinary performance of a common text.

When asked what conclusions about multidisciplinary acting they could draw after the masterclass, most of the students said they had come to realize how important it is for an actor to be able to use different forms in the theatre and the importance of voice, movement, and singing skills. Collectively they could see that multidisciplinarity opens the doors wide for communication.

On the question of the political role of the artist in the theatre today, and what they have learned from their colleagues, the students' observations are presented below:

Catherine Green: 'It was wonderful to find out that so many young actors around the world learn similar things (and you can learn by each other's differences). The 'Landscape with Argonauts' piece helped me to realise that actors, no matter where they are from, can create a piece of theatre together that says something important about the world they live in, and that the choice to make political art need not mean that this art will not contain humour. Quite the contrary, although weighty in its subject matter, the piece seemed to entertain and grasp our audience and made a difference to what they felt. I am in my final year at Drama School in London, and it all seems to be so commercial – selling yourself to agents, etc. But in Berlin I took part in theatre that was worth putting on, and I remember that a lot lately, as I try to hold on to the reason why I wanted to become an actor.'

Daniela Nane: 'The artist's role is both in the theatre and beyond.'

Tommi Korpela: 'I was happy to find out how different we still are in what makes us rich in life and art.'

Matthew Dunster: 'I have learned that it will take more than a union of governments to alleviate all our preconceptions and prejudices. We celebrated our cultural differences and shared problems that were caused by individuals.'

Fenneke Wekker: 'I felt that there is a real new European generation. I had the feeling that the students were much more willing to learn from other cultures and languages than were the adult masters.'

As a new paradigm for the teaching of theatre today, this approach brought together teachers, artists-to-be, and experienced masters with different, dare I say opposing, ideologies and cultural backgrounds to create a platform for discussion on the political and social responsibility of artists in our time specifically connected to arts education. This sort of 'opening up,' of sharing approaches to working with theatre education, is a crucial issue in our changing world where tolerance and understanding 'the other' should be fostered at every turn.

The more we question the importance of 'process' over 'product' and the relevance of the 'aesthetic' in theatre education today, the more chance we have to challenge the values perpetuated by the popular media today. In this way we can contribute to improving the content of what is loosely termed performance in contemporary society.

All things considered and bearing in mind the problems which might be encountered, perhaps the time is right for exploring the ELIA masterclass model in theatre education today.

12

ALBA EMOTING: A REVOLUTION IN EMOTION FOR THE ACTOR

Roxane Rix

Introducing Alba Emoting

The student inhales deeply through the nose into her abdomen, then releases breath through her mouth in short bursts, trying to maintain relaxation in her limbs as she attempts to empty completely of air; the coach places a hand low on her belly, urging her to pull the breath more deeply into her body. She does, and is startled and confused when she suddenly begins to sob. Not only is she certain that this is not the intended effect, but she doesn't know why she is crying: she is experiencing no memories or images, only an acute physical sensation of deep despair. The coach encourages her to allow the release of feeling; she weeps for nearly half an hour.

Days later, after much practice, the student accurately reproduces the three elements of the pattern (breathing, facial expression, and posture) and finds herself just as suddenly joyful: not from a feeling of success, but because the pattern has finally induced the genuine emotion to which it organically belongs. She feels the effector patterns resonate with the myriad tiny individuations that make her joy her own: joy that she can now call up at will.

This is Alba Emoting™, a scientifically devised system for generating emotional states through precise physical patterning, without the use of memories or images, that is slowly penetrating American actor training. Known for years among groups of theatre practitioners in Europe and South America (where the system was initially developed), Alba training has reached perhaps a hundred actors and teachers in the US to date (1996); several hundreds of others have been exposed to the technique in presentations and workshops at national and regional theatre conferences since 1991.

The system (or technique, or method—for the purpose of this discussion, I am using the terms interchangeably) is already generating strong passions, both positive and negative. So far, the negative impressions are largely and most strongly held by those who have little or no direct exposure to Alba, some of whom find the *idea* of generating emotion entirely through physiological stimulation overly mechanistic or even soulless; to others, this same idea is the essential attraction of the technique. Few, if any, who actually learn the Alba technique retain such negative impressions, even if they begin with them.

A Survey of Emotion Research

Controversy has, of course, always accompanied theories of emotion, beginning with its definition: What is an emotion? A brief overview of major theories, and the conflicts among them, may serve to provide both a context for the perceived tension between Alba and other more commonly employed techniques, and a foundation for understanding the method itself.

René Descartes is generally credited with bridging ancient and modern theories of emotion with his 1649 treatise, *Les passions de l'ame* (Gardiner, 1970:7), the first published theory to focus on physiology as the basis of "passions" (though, as Gardiner notes, the idea of bodily states as central to emotion is at least as old as Hippocrates). Descartes' dualistic view of body and soul – the body as a machine which experiences emotions as a result of agitation of the soul discharging 11 "spirits" through glands, nerves, and blood vessels (Gardiner, 1970:7) – has strongly influenced all emotion theory since, creating what is often referred to as the "mind-body problem" (Candland, 1977:22).

Indeed, debate in regard to the question "What is an emotion?" has, for more than a century, raged over this so-called mind-body split: is emotion a physiological event or a cognitive one? "The first view maintains that bodily reactions ... control and determine what we feel. The second view posits that bodily reactions are secondary effects ... indicators of emotions" (Grings & Dawson, 1978:3). Late 19th century American psychologist William James promoted the idea that "the bodily changes" which accompany emotion and "our feeling of the same changes as they occur *is* the emotion ... Moods, affectations, and passions.. are in very truth constituted by, and made up of, those bodily changes which we ordinarily call their expression or consequence" (James, 1962:11-12).[1] For James, arousal state precedes cognition (the subjective recognition of feeling): "I see a bear, I tremble, I am afraid" (Candland, 1977:22). And without somatic

---

1. Parallel independent research by Danish physiologist Carl Lange posited similar ideas; hence, this view became known as the "James-Lange Theory."

and visceral changes there is no emotion, but mere thought: "We might see a bear, and judge it best to run, but we could not actually feel afraid" (Buck, 1984:47). The opposite view ("I see a bear, I am afraid, I tremble") was most ardently proposed by W.B. Cannon in the 1920s, though Alan I. Leshner 1977:87) notes that the casting of the theories as mutually exclusive is probably erroneous. Cannon believed that physiological arousal follows, rather than leads, cognition of an emotional state; that neural stimulation centered in the thalamus in turn stimulates "areas of the brain in which the experiential qualities of emotion are added to mere sensations" leading to visceral arousal via the release of various hormones (Leshner 1977:87-91). Both points of view include a stimulus, and neither denies roles to body or mind in experience of emotion; but each defines "emotion" as the second event (after stimulus) in the causal/temporal sequence. Cannon's theory has long been the more accepted of the two; with advances in scientific technology, however, the most recent research has, in fact proven James correct. Daniel Goleman cites studies by neuroscientist Joseph LeDoux which prove that sensory information travels first to the brain's emotional center, which begins a physical response before a second signal reaches the neocortex (the "thinking brain"), which then interprets the information and refines the reaction (Goleman, 1995:15,17).[2] If I see a bear, I do, indeed, tremble before I realize that I am afraid.

If we define the whole of emotional experience as a phenomenon involving all three aspects—stimulus, cognition, and physiological arousal—the actor's challenge immediately becomes clear: there is no stimulus in the fictive world of the play beyond that provided by fellow actors (which may in the best of circumstances, be considerable, but cannot be depended upon moment to moment); in Stanislavski's words, "There is no such thing as actuality on the stage" (Stanislavski, 1989:54). The attempt to fill the gap left by lack of genuine stimuli has been central to Western actor training (certainly, in the U.S.) since Stanislavski and the birth of realism brought to the fore the idea of truth on stage. Most techniques – emotion memory (with or without physicalization of reexperience), "magic if," belief in circumstances, substitution, use of images, objects, and so on – attack the problem through cognition: the actor uses the mind to create stimulus for emotion. Actors trained in American "Method" techniques rely on this self-induced stimulus to create a genuine expressive response, with more or less success depending on talent, physical development, and strength of

---

2. As cited by Goleman, "sensory signals from eye or ear travel first in the brain to the thalamus, and then – across a single synapse – to the amygdala; a second signal from the thalamus is routed to the neocortex – the thinking brain. This branching allows the amygdala to begin to respond before the neocortex, which mulls information through several levels of brain circuits before it fully perceives and finally initiates its more finely tailored responses" (1995:17).

imagination; even actors trained specifically to discover from reexperienced feeling "simple, expressive actions with an inner content" (Stanislavski 1989a:49) nonetheless begin with a cognitive base Alba Emoting is revolutionary because it approaches the "stimulus gap" from the other point of the triad: physiological arousal through purely physical means. While many actors, at times, consciously use breath, posture and relative states of tension and relaxation to enhance and sustain emotional states, Alba Emoting is the first method to identify specific, universal patterns in these reproducible aspects of emotional expression, and systematize them into a technique to produce and express emotion at will. This use of direct physiological arousal in a sense turns nature on its head. In taking on the physical characteristics of an emotion, the body begins to *feel* that emotion: the limbic system, sympathetic and parasympathetic nervous systems begin to respond as if there were a stimulus creating the response (at risk of stretching the point: I tremble, I feel afraid – but there is no bear at all). Subjective involvement may be consciously modulated, "allowing [actors] to experience as much of the feeling component as they desire" (Bloch, 1993). That it is the body, not the mind, which *expresses* emotion cannot be denied, even by the most ardent proponents of cognitive techniques; what seems discomfiting to some is the idea that, aside from consciousness of technical muscle movement in time, virtually effortless), the mind may be left out entirely. While some Danish and Chilean actors who have worked with Alba Emoting for a number of years would, like James, identify "emotion" wholly as physiological arousal, agreement with this point of view is neither necessary in order for Alba Emoting to function for an actor nor particularly germane to discussion of its value. An Alba-trained actor still must commit to circumstances, characters, actions etc., but will enjoy greater flexibility and availability of expression. He or she is also free to continue to use psychological techniques in addition to the method—but, in my experience, is not likely to want to.

Development of the Alba Emoting System

Alba Emoting is based in physiological reality: what the body actually does during the experience of emotion. Dr. Susana Bloch, a neuroscientist and primary creator of the technique, drew its basic principles from experiments that she and a colleague, Guy Santibañez-H, conducted at the University of Chile in Santiago in the early 1970's (Bloch & Lemeignan, 1992). Santibañez had recorded changes in the respiratory movements of patients with anxiety neuroses while they spoke about conflictive events; when he then instructed them to recite the events again while maintaining even, relaxed breathing, the patients reported less stress and anxiety. Expanding data collection to include other physiological parameters such as heart rate, arterial pressure, and muscle tonus, Bloch and Santibañez confirmed the initial results with both normal subjects under hypnosis, and with trained actors using emotion memory; more significant, the data also suggested a high degree of universal physiological response to emotion. They identified six emotions – joy, sadness, anger, fear, erotic love, and tenderness – as "basic" "because they correspond to universal invariants of behavior – in a Darwinian sense – and are present in the animals and in the human infants" (Bloch & Lemeignan, 1992) and proposed that all other emotions are, in fact, blends of these.[3] Wondering if the physiological experience of emotion could be aroused physically, without a real or imagined stimulus, they focused on the aspects of emotional expression that could be reproduced at will, and created prototypes of changes in respiration, posture, and facial expression, which they called "emotional effector patterns." The pair also created a seventh pattern, based on Santibañez's first observations, to return the body to emotional neutrality through relaxed alignment, slow, deep breathing, and release of facial tension, which they termed the "step out." Naive subjects taught to reproduce emotional effector patterns were, in fact, found to experience the corresponding emotions; they were also able to neutralize the biochemical arousal using the step out pattern, (Bloch & Lemeignan, 1992). Later, Bloch, Santibañez, and Pedro Orthous found a high correlation between data recorded from subjects using the patterns (originally termed the BOS Method) and those of subjects reliving actual emotional experiences; the only significant difference was the trained subjects' greater ability to leave the emotional experience through the step out (Bloch, Orthous & Santibañez, 1987).[4]

Further development of the system was temporarily halted by the Pinochet revolution. Bloch left Chile, and, from her post at the University of Pierre and Marie Curie in Paris, resumed experiments "as an avocation" with actors from the Teater Klanen of Denmark. (It was during this period that the technique was renamed Alba Emoting, after a production of Lorca's *House of Bernarda Alba* [Bloch, 1994]. Aside from a few articles available, in scientific journals, the still-experimental technique was unknown to U.S. actors and educators until Bloch's 1991 presentation at the annual conference of the Association for Theatre In Higher Education. She offered workshops at ATHE conferences over the next several years, finally making plans to

---

3.   While some theorists include disgust as a basic emotion, Bloch views it more as a reflex. It should also be noted that, though anger is often termed a "secondary" emotion – a reaction to another feeling, such as fear or hurt – "basic emotion, as defined by Bloch and Santibañez, describes the internal experience of emotion *per se* rather than its stimulus.

4.   Detailed presentation of scientific data from experimental applications of emotional effector patterns with actors may also be found in Bloch, Lemeignan & Aguilera (1991), Lemeignan, Aguilera & Bloch (1992), and Santibañez & Bloch (1986).

begin formal training sessions, satisfied that the method was "now refined and ready for a wider diffusion as an alternative technique for the work of actors" (Bloch, 1993).

Alba Training

In Cachagua, Chile, in October of 1993, Bloch offered the first training seminar in Alba Emoting open to actors and teachers worldwide.

Limited to ten people, the two-week session attracted a polyglot group of participants from Europe and South America, as well as four from the U.S. Nancy Loitz of Illinois Wesleyan University, Michael Johnson-Chase from the University of Wisconsin-Milwaukee, Stephen Book, a private acting teacher from Los Angeles, and myself. None of we Americans knew one another, nor had previous experience with the technique beyond ATHE workshops (if that). Though my own limited experiment with the breathing patterns had proven to me their power to evoke emotion (Rix, 1993), I remained to be convinced about the system as a whole. Novices compared to our classmates (several of whom were Danes and Chileans who had worked with the technique during its development), the doubts and questions we brought would, over the course of the session, come in turns to the fore. (And, certainly, we "Yanks" were distinguished by our impatience to understand and learn, and our willingness to struggle *loudly* when we didn't!)

"For the first 3 or 4 days I was appalled. Most of us looked embarrassingly wooden, contrived, and like very bad actors when we did the patterns. We became argumentative and cross with each other. At one juncture it seemed as though the whole training was going to fall apart. ... Finally, as we became more skilled, it became apparent that there is a critical difference between doing the patterns poorly and doing them well .... the details of any given pattern are complex and take some time to learn." Michael Johnson-Chase (1994), in this comment describes not only our experience in Chile but one aspect of Alba Emoting in which skeptics sometimes mistakenly find validation: in the first phase of learning, the Alba technique looks and feels phony, often to the point of absurdity. The apparent result (which is not a result at all, but a first step) appears a grotesque stereotype of emotion. While occasionally a new student will experience genuine emotion on the first try, it is far more common to feel ridiculous – and/or irritated and frustrated at the difficulty of precise technical reproduction – and even the rare student who genuinely contacts emotion the first time will not likely be able to reproduce it reliably. This first phase, which Bloch terms "robotic," is entirely technical: for each emotion, the student repeats, to its maximum intensity, a precise respiratory pattern (which includes not only rate and depth, but force, placement in the body, and, for some patterns, slight holds), creates a specific facial mask, and modulates posture along the dual axes of tension/relaxation and approach/avoidance.[5] Having attended several of Bloch's workshops (and had what I thought were some successful experiences), I was astonished to discover in Chile how much more precision and subtlety is required than had ever been apparent; for the first few days the experience was, indeed, often awkward and frustrating. I was also surprised by the occurrence of anomalous reactions during the robotic phase, such as when the pattern for joy left me sobbing. (I have since seen this occur with my own acting students relatively often – usually crying, but sometimes laughter – and come to value it as a strength of the technique, a non-psychoanalytic "flushing out" of old tensions necessary for some to gain emotional freedom.)

The sessions rarely ran more than two hours, and were usually twice a day; during a session, we would never work a pattern steadily for more than three or four minutes, and work on the patterns was interspersed with exercises to increase subtle control of breath, tension, and muscle isolation. Step-outs were called frequently; as precise as any of effector patterns, the step-out procedure was particularly emphasized at first, as it is the "safety net" for the body's return to neutral after intentional biochemical flooding. (The step-out works equally well for actors who have generated emotion through more traditional cognitive means. It can also neutralize the effects of "genuine" emotions in life, once they are no longer being generated by internal or external stimuli; since however, it is usually healthier, psychologically, not to attempt escape from genuine feelings, Bloch strongly discourages this application.)

Within a few days, most of us had begun to master at least one of the patterns, and, by turns, experienced the second phase of the learning process: induction. This is the "magic moment" when the individual's genuine emotion emerges (often quite suddenly and intensely) from the practiced pattern, and the variations of emotional expression which make each person unique mingle and merge with the prototype. As well as bolstering confidence in the technique, this experience answered a common question with which most of us had been struggling: what about individual difference? In fact, it appeared, aside from possible physical abnormalities (which probably cannot be corrected) or psychoemotional distortions (which both can and should be corrected by actors!), individual variations in emotional expression are minute; what, for some, initially appear to be conflicts between the patterns and genuine experience ("I don't do that

---

5.   For a specific description of each emotional effector pattern, readers are referred, especially, to Bloch & Lemeignan (1992), and Bloch, Orthous & Santibañez (1987). [A reprint of the 1987 article may also be found in *Acting (Re)Considered: Theories and Practices*, London: Routledge, 1994. Philip B Zarilli, ed.]

when I cry") are almost always the result of entanglement: the individual's habituated mixed emotional response. (I discovered, for example, that, in life, being afraid makes me angry, and anger makes me sad; though I had never noticed this before, once I saw it, it was perfectly clear.) I have come to use the analogy of a hand. If you and I each have normally formed hands, our hands will look essentially the same: even though your fingers may be longer, mine wider, your skin smoother, etc., both are recognizably hands (certainly, we won't mistake the other's hand for a foot!). The effector patterns are like the basic structure of the hand; our individuations, the myriad subtle features that distinguish your hand from mine. Once an actor has broken through entanglements to the expression of pure emotion he or she can then mix emotions at *will*, according to character interpretation rather than habituation (e.g., characters I play no longer automatically become angry from fear – though I am still, of course, free to make that choice).

The powerful experience of induction erased old doubts but, for some, replaced them with new ones: generating an emotional state physiologically does, indeed, feel strange at first, and some wondered whether they really *wanted* to work in this way. Whether or not memories or images accompanied induction (and they may or may not), the experience of emotion not stimulated by thought or perception was rather eerie; many confessed pervasive feelings of emptiness. Fortunately, this, too, was short-lived. Once accustomed to the feeling of "contentless emotion," in fact, it became *fun* to be able to summon an emotional state at will and step out of it with equal command.

In this last stage, which I would describe as "integration," the actor gains control of the intensity of the experience; the removal (or, at least, weakening) of emotional blocks, and increased technical proficiency, allow the feelings to flow easily rather than to burst through unexpectedly (the most unsettling aspect of the induction phase). While none of us attained equal proficiency with every pattern – each struggled with at least one or two patterns, depending, again, on our personal blocks and temperaments – the understanding of how the patterns work in the body, which comes only with experience, allowed us to progress more quickly, and with less fear of the intensity of induction. And, though the emergence of genuine feeling is an important part of the process, even before induction on the remaining patterns, the physical *appearance* of the emotions was becoming increasingly natural. I also observed, in myself and my classmates, a remarkable increase in relaxation, freedom of expression, and overall sense of well-being, both in and out of class: posture had become more naturally open and aligned, vocal tensions faded, and, most startling to me, lines had dropped out of our faces. The elusive, and much sought-after, quality called "presence" had strengthened dramatically in us all.

During the final few days of the session, we began rudimentary application of pattern work to text—not attempting the mixing of emotions that might usually be appropriate for a given character or circumstance, but simply experimenting with applying pure emotional effector patterns while moving and speaking our chosen text. For those of us who had begun as novices, this was extremely difficult, and we often lost the pattern, the text, or both; but we also felt, and observed in one another, moments of great clarity and power. The more experienced students, of course, were much more successful. Their work was clear, vibrant, and affecting, appearing neither mechanistic nor self-indulgent.

I learned a great deal more about the Alba training process both through my own advanced training and later, especially, through offering beginning training to my graduate students, in a special course I designed for the purpose. Though much of my approach to the course was modeled on my own first training, I also examined closely the frustrations and struggles that had seemed unique to we Americans, in an attempt to find ways to address them. Part of my approach was to add a broader cognitive base – in essence to educate my students and myself in the psychology, biology, and sociology of emotion – as well as to draw on an understanding of acting pedagogy and actor process that Bloch, as a neuroscientist (albeit one with great personal sensitivity and dramatic flair), is still, herself, developing.

Like Bloch, I began each session with lengthy warmups: individual stretching and relaxation followed by free movement, strengthening and awareness exercises (I found Grotowski exercises to be particularly helpful), then attention to basic technical skills required for accurate pattern reproduction (particularly tension/relaxation isolations and abdominal breathing); the selection of exercises and time spent on various skills was determined by the specific pattern work planned for the day. The patterns (which were never identified by name, so as to discourage trying for a result) were built piece by piece, usually beginning with breath; while all three elements of a given pattern would usually be introduced in one session, attempts to put them together were kept brief, as extraneous tensions would almost certainly arise quickly at first. Physical positions were varied constantly (e.g., standing, sitting, lying on the floor) both so as not to create an unintentional association with a particular position and because there seems to be a good deal of individual variation as to which "gross" position of the body is most likely to help someone toward the first induction. Anomalous reactions were much more frequent than they had been among my peers in Chile (all of whom had considerably more actor training than my students); at some time in nearly every session one or two students would start to sob, at which point the other class members would follow a protocol established in the first session – a step out followed by a sustained tenderness pattern – while I turned my full attention to the person experiencing upheaval. The protocol was modeled on Bloch, but more formalized, both because I did not have, as she had, an experienced assistant to continue working with the students, and because my students were initially more prone to become fearful at these sudden outbursts. This reaction faded quickly after the first time or two; the class came to embrace, and even celebrate, these incidents as breakthroughs in growth.

The paradox of approaching emotion through physical patterning is that it is at once safer than psychological techniques, in that it does not ask the actor to mine personal experiences, and at the same time potentially more volatile, because it goes directly to the core of physiological experience. I placed great and constant emphasis on discipline, safety, and self-care; students always had permission to step out at will if an experience became too intense or frightening for them – and also had to agree to step out on my command whether they felt like it or not; both the students and I needed the security of my unquestioned responsibility and authority to guide them either toward release, or to step out of the experience. Release is a necessary step in the process, whether "intended" through the pattern or not; but, sometimes, there arises a sort of "body fear" of strong feeling of which the students themselves are not necessarily aware. When the latter takes hold, it can be impossible to release in the moment, and tends, instead, to escalate into hysteria. My teaching to date suggests that this fear is often a product of past experiences connected to a particular emotion. For most, the fear dissolves through a gradual, gentle approach to whatever pattern is producing it; I strongly suspect, however, that this applies only to past experiences which have been psychologically resolved, i.e., in which the reaction stems from buried body memory rather than a failure to have adequately worked through the life experience.[6] Resolution of feelings from life experiences is, of course, necessary for any actor in order to achieve full emotional expressiveness; the only difference in working with Alba Emoting is that the directness of the technique renders awareness and confrontation of such feelings unavoidable.

The initial experience of learning Alba Emoting seems, for most, to fall roughly into four parts: the first quarter generates awareness, enthusiasm, and some instant breakthroughs; the second, frustration, confusion, and fatigue; the third, induction, which involves both (for lack of a better word) epiphany, and, for many, a transition through unsettling feelings of emptiness; and the fourth, satisfaction and a feeling of well-being. Experience suggests to me that the initial basic training, for Americans, at least, largely involves "clearing the channels": flushing out

---

6. Indeed, according to LeDoux, the body may have emotion memories which were never fully recorded by the conscious mind at all. (Goleman, 1995:18)

old tensions and returning the body, in a very real sense, to its pre-socialized ability to recognize and express emotion purely and directly. I have perceived the same effects in my students as I observed in Chile: lines dropping out of people's faces, eyes becoming brighter and clearer, etc. Long before developing technical expertise, such basic skills as concentration, awareness, centering, and psychophysical integration also show visible improvement. It is also important to note, however, that the flushing process can induce temporary physical eruptions in some people: one of my students passed through headaches, tremors, and hives, and another developed, for a period of about six hours, a fever of 104 degrees (a doctor confirmed that he wasn't ill, and the fever disappeared as suddenly and inexplicably as it had arisen). What these two students had in common was, I believe, significant: both began the work unusually bound up with muscle tension, in comparison with their peers, and each demonstrated an extraordinary ability and will to break through those tensions in a short amount of time. It is also notable that, once assured that these manifestations could be a reaction to the work, neither was particularly frightened or upset, but more or less took them in stride. While such reactions are rare – and I suspect that subconscious resistances protect those unready for this level of upheaval from progressing in the work quickly enough to produce them—they do underscore the tremendous need for care and respect in approaching this type of work.[7]

Alba Emoting in Performance

Application of the work in performance is, of course, the final question. "If some actors in a play were using Alba," a student asked me, "and some weren't, would I be able to tell which were which?" The answer is, "Only if they were doing it poorly!" Like any other basic technique, Alba Emoting done properly is invisible – one might only notice, that some actors are

---

7. Until 1997, the availability of training in Alba Emoting was kept limited by Dr. Bloch in order to develop a corps of advanced students and teachers; but the number of actors and teachers familiar with the system is poised for more rapid growth, as, for the first time, beginning training sessions have become available on a regular basis. At this writing, Alba Emoting has been incorporated in Chile (which Bloch has established as the world center for Alba Emoting) and, in the U.S., trademark registration and incorporation as Alba Emoting North America are underway. Certification standards have been set (six levels, self-use competency to Master Teacher) in order to maintain the integrity of the work and insure quality of instruction; certificates awarded will be registered with AENA. AENA plans to offer annual intensive training sessions in the U.S. with Dr. Bloch, open to participants worldwide, groups and institutions may now also arrange on-site sessions with any of three instructors in Europe, South America, and the U.S. (the author among them) certified to offer Alba Emoting training independent of an established acting curriculum. This number is expected to grow significantly within the next few years as current teachers and apprentice teachers reach greater levels of mastery.

more vibrant and expressive than others. Alba only "shows" in the early, awkward attempts to apply it—just as the actor still focusing on iambic pentameter is not likely to render a believable Hamlet. In practice, I discourage my students from beginning with direct application in performance after just one course of training, but, rather, to work as they had before, and simply allow the awareness and clarity of expression developed through the work to emerge on its own. Characters (just as people in life) most often experience mixed emotions: jealousy, for example, might involve fear in the breath, angry eyes, and the muscle tonus of erotic love; conscious application of Alba Emoting to create this believably requires a sophisticated skill level. Even with tentative mastery, however, an actor may apply emotional effector patterns effectively in selected moments he or she finds particularly emotionally challenging, to sustain an emotional reaction (e.g., laughing), and, certainly, to develop the desired psychoemotional state in preparation for entering the dramatic action. Conscious application with text through every moment of a performance takes considerable technical skill, and is not necessarily the goal: while it can be done, this becomes largely a matter of the actor's individual inclination. I would compare it to scoring for actions: when first learning that skill, I require student actors to identify an action verb for every moment they are on stage; in practice, I know that, eventually, most will employ such specific scoring only for the moments which they find especially difficult – because playing actions will have become so ingrained that it will happen without conscious decision. Once the body has learned to express emotion freely, expression can come on its own through actions and concentration on given circumstances; however, even an actor who chooses to apply the work only to this extent is inescapably aware of any tensions that warp the intended effect. The Alba Emoting system is still in development, and much is yet to be discovered about the potentialities of direct application in performance. I anticipate that, like the work of Stanislavski, refinement and the deepening of understanding of the technique will continue over many years, through many practitioners. But it is here to stay, if only because, like the Stanislavski system, it is based in organic truth. And truth, as is often said, will out.

Why Alba Emoting?

One of the greatest gifts derived from training emotional expression through physiological response is that the actor no longer has to be concerned whether or not the desired clarity and intensity of expression will be available: the body no longer needs to be urged toward expression by the mind, which is then free to immerse in the fictive moment. The actor is also no longer bound by his or her own habituated expression of emotion (though, certainly, this may still psychologically influence interpretive choices): a significant—and, until now, seemingly not addressable – weakness of approaches such as emotion memory is that they inherently rely on the individual's socialized reactions (again, before I learned Alba Emoting, any character I played would always be angry while fearful). And, though the technique takes many years to master fully, even the most rudimentary level of skill enhances emotional expression, awareness, and presence on stage. Actors trained in Alba certainly can, and do, work seamlessly with those who don't have this training; the greatest difference, according to my more experienced Chilean classmates, is that Alba speeds the process of finding the emotional truth in a given moment. Most important, the actor has a device, through the step out, to neutralize biochemical arousal after the performance, and can freely decide whether or not to invite the character home for the night!

Because Alba Emoting is so new to American actors, I have constantly solicited the reactions of my students through formal surveys. Though early in their training, their responses to the method have been strong. Their comments speak eloquently about the system; I close with just a few:

> – I have better acting skills than I have ever had before... I have better control of my body, my emotions, and my breath.

> – I am convinced this is an awesome, freeing acting tool ... All my basic acting skills have been sharpened. ... Focusing on my body, face, and breathing instead of only my memories has polished my acting a great deal. This is an incredible fact knowing that I still struggle with five out of six patterns and I can already see growth in my work!!
> – It seems to me that making choices and deciding how to play is going to be [a much] shorter process. I've always thought that acting was predominantly an emotional experience – now I believe it can start in the physical and choices are so much clearer!

> – I find Alba Emoting safe, and a practical tool. [Safer] than potentially dangerous-to-the-psyche emotional memory. ... Practical in that the reaction can be *quick*.

> – [Alba offers] an 'in' to scene work – a non-cerebral immediate doorway, [a way to] jump from one emotion to another quickly and effectively, something *new* that could really impact me as an actor.

–   A tangible, workable method with almost immediate results... I wish I could go back and re-do some of the parts I played – there's so much more I can do.

–   More is at my disposal emotionally and physically ... My awareness ... has grown significantly.

–   For me, [Alba] is the ideal connection between the physical and emotional that any actor needs. It aligns your entire being.

–   This has improved my empathy ... communication [of emotion] and self-awareness. ... I understand myself better, and what makes us human.

References

Bloch, S. (1993) Alba Emoting: A Psychophysiological Technique to Help Actors Create and Control Real Emotions. *Theatre Topics*. 131–138. (1994) Personal interview.

Bloch, S. & Lemeignan, M. (1992) Precise respiratory-posturo-facial patterns are related to specific basic emotions. *Bewegen & Hulpverlening*. 1, 31–38.

Bloch, S. & Lemeignan, M & Aguilera-T, N. (1991) Specific respiratory patterns distinguish among human basic emotions. *International Journal of Psychophysiology*. 11, 141–154.

Bloch, S., Orthous, P. & Santibañez-H, G. (1987) Effector patterns of basic emotions: a psychophysiological method for training actors. *Journal of Biological Structures*. 10, 1–19.

Buck, R. (1984) *The Communication of Emotion*. New York and London: The Guilford Press.

Gardiner, H.M., Metcalf, R.C. & Beebe-Center, J.G. (1970) *Feeling and Emotion*, Westport CT: Greenwood Press.

Goleman, D. (1995) *Emotional Intelligence*. New York, Toronto, London, Sydney and Auckland: Bantam Books.

Grings, W.W. & Dawson, M.E. (1978) *Emotions and Bodily Responses*. New York, San Francisco and London: Academic Press.

James, W. (1962) William James on Emotion. In *Emotion: Bodily Change*, edited by D.K. Candland, pp. 11–16. Princeton NJ, Toronto and London: D. Van Nostrand Company Incorporated. [Excerpted from (1890) *Principles of Psychology*. Volume II. New York: Holt and Company].

Johnson-Chase, M. (1994) Notes on proposed questions: panel on ALBA Emoting, conference of American Theatre in Higher Education. Unpublished abstract.

Lemeignan, M., Aguilera-T, N. & Bloch, S. (1992) Emotional Effector Patterns: Recognition of Expressions. *European Bulletin of Cognitive Psychology*. 12, 173–188.

Leshner, A.I. (1977) Hormones and Emotions. In Candland, D.K., Fell, J.P., Keen, E., Leshner, A.I., Plutchik, R., & Tarpy, M. (1977) *Emotion*. pp. 86–148. Monterey CA: Brooks/Cole Publishing Company.

Rix, R. (1993) Alba Emoting: A Preliminary Experiment with Emotional Effector Patterns. *Theatre Topics*. 139–145.

(1998) Learning Alba Emoting. *Theatre Topics*. 8:1, 55–72.

Stanislavski, C. (1989) *An Actor Prepares*, translated by E.R. Hapgood. New York: Routledge [first copyright 1936, USSR: Theatre Arts, Incorporated]

Stanislavski, G. (1989a) *Creating A Character*, translated by E.R. Hapgood. New York: Routledge [first copyright 1949, USSR: Theatre Arts, Incorporated].

Santibañez-H, G. & Bloch, S. (1986) A Qualitative Analysis of Emotional Effector Patterns and Their Feedback. *The Pavlovian Journal of Biological Science*. 21:3, 108–116.

NOTES ON CONTRIBUTORS

Dr. Kazimierz Braun is a director, writer, and scholar. Formerly he was the Artistic Director and General Manager of the Teatr Wspólczesny (Contemporary Theatre) in Wroclaw as well as a Professor at Wroclaw University and Wroclaw School of Drama in Poland. Currently he is Professor of directing and theatre history in the Department of Theatre and Dance at the State University of New York at Buffalo in the United States. He has authored several books on theatre, his most recent being *A History of Polish Theatre, 1939–1989, Spheres of Captivity and Freedom* (Greenwood Press, 1996).

Clive Barker is best known for his book *Theatre Games: A New Approach to Actor Training* (Methuen, London, 1977) which sets out the basis of the work which has kept him occupied world-wide ever since. He is recently retired from university theatre teaching after thirty years and is joint editor of *New Theatre Quarterly*. He has chaired the board of directors of the International Workshop Festival since 1994 and has led workshops in the festival.

I Nyoman Catra is one of Bali's leading performers and is on the faculty of the National Institute of the Arts (STSI) in Denpasar, Bali. He has received fellowships from the Fulbright Foundation and the Asian Cultural Council.

Steve Earnest is currently an Assistant Professor of Theatre at the University of West Georgia. Previously he has published in *On Stage Studies, The O'Neill Review,* and *Western Stages,* among others. He holds a Ph.D. in theatre from the University of Colorado – Boulder.

Ron Jenkins is Professor of Theatre at Wesleyan University and author of *Subversive Laughter* (The Free Press, 1994). His fieldwork in Bali was sponsored by the Asian Cultural Council.

Eelka Lampe is an independent scholar living in New York City. She has been following the work of Anne Bogart for some ten years and the Saratoga International Theater Institute (SITI) since its formation in 1992.

Dick McCaw was a founding member and administrator of the Actors Touring Company and The Medieval Players. He has lectured internationally on the Medieval theatre and is working on Bakhtin and Popular Theatre. He was administrator of the International Workshop Festival in its early years and has been artistic director since 1994.

Jacqueline Martin is currently Senior Lecturer and Coordinator of the Open Program of Arts at the Queensland University of Technology (QUT) following eighteen years in Sweden where she is Associate Professor of Theatre Studies at the University of Stockholm. She is author of *Voice and Modern Theatre* (1991) and co-author of *Understanding Theatre: Performance Analysis in Theory and Practice* (1995).

Barry O'Connor is an actor and teacher in the Drama Department at the University of Newcastle in Australia. His research interests include acting, Restoration Theatre, and Drama in Education. With his colleague Mark Gauntlett, he is the co-author of *Drama Studies*, published by Addison, Wesley, Longman (1995).

Janne Risum is an Associate Professor at the Institut for Dramaturgi at Aarhus University in Denmark. She is an active participant in the International School of Theatre Anthropology and has published widely in the fields of acting, theatre history, and women in theatre.

Roxane Rix has been a director and teacher of acting for more than ten years. She is has an MFA in Directing from the University of Minnesota and a Certificate in Acting from the Sonia Moore Studio; her Level 4 Certification in Alba Emoting is currently the highest in the United States. She is a founding member and President-elect of Alba Emoting North America.

Jonah Salz co-founded the Noho Theatre Group in 1981 and is the director of Traditional Theatre Training for the same group. He teaches comparative theatre at Ryukoku University in Japan and writes on intercultural theatre as well as actor training.

Ian Watson teaches at Rutgers University – Newark where he heads the Theatre Arts Program. He is especially interested in interculturalism in the theatre. His publications include *Towards a Third Theatre: Eugenio Barba and the Odin Teatret* as well as articles in *New Theatre Quarterly*, *The Drama Review*, *Modern Drama*, *Teatro e storia*, *Gestos*, and the *Latin American Theatre Review*. He is at present editing a collection of essays on interculturalism in the work of Eugenio Barba.

Lisa Wolford is the author of *Grotowski's Objective Drama Research* (University Press of Mississippi, 1996) and co-editor, with Richard Schechner, of *The Grotowski Sourcebook* (Routledge, 1997). Her writings have appeared in *The Drama Review, New Theatre Quarterly, Canadian Theatre Review,* and *Slavic and Eastern European Performance*. She is Assistant Professor of Theatre at Bowling Green State University in Ohio.

INDEX

Other titles in the Contemporary Theatre Studies series:

Other titles in the Contemporary Theatre Studies series: